About the author

I spent most of my working life as a professional dance instructor, designing and producing theatrical shows for children. When a severe back injury resulting from a car crash forced me into early retirement, I started looking for new ways to be creative and find a new outlet in life to express myself. Writing filled this void and allowed me to clarify, accept and eventually script what has happened to me over the years, which makes for a compelling and, at times, difficult read.

For a very long time I tried to come to terms with what I have been through and how it has affected both me and my family. Having finished this book, I am now able to look back and reflect on my life in a way I never thought possible. The sheer number and variety of traumas I have experienced is almost incomprehensible and the horrors of some of the situations are a lot to take on-board. These have shaped me into the woman I am today.

Within the book you will experience my life in its rawest form, including a suicide, a ruined career, a lengthy lawsuit, a terrible marriage, an abusive husband, terrified children, a debilitating illness, broken families, dreams shattered, hope, fear, and impossible choices.

Only when you are at your lowest, when you feel that life has taken too much from you, do you look deep inside yourself and make a choice. This story is my choice.

This is a work of creative non-fiction. The events are portrayed to the best of the author's memory. While all the stories in this book are true, some names and identifying details have been changed to protect the privacy of the people involved.

LIFE BEHIND THE MASK

JESSICA STORM

LIFE BEHIND THE MASK

Vanguard Press

VANGUARD

PAPERBACK © Copyright

2023

Jessica Storm

The right of Jessica Storm to be identified as author of
this work has been asserted by her in accordance with the
Copyright, Designs and Patents Act 1988.

All Rights Reserved

No reproduction, copy or transmission of this publication
may be made without written permission.
No paragraph of this publication may be reproduced,
copied or transmitted save with the written permission of the
publisher, or in accordance with the provisions
of the Copyright Act 1956 (as amended).

Any person who commits any unauthorised act in relation to
this publication may be liable to criminal
prosecution and civil claims for damages.

A CIP catalogue record for this title is
available from the British Library.

ISBN 978 1 80016 396 6

*Vanguard Press is an imprint of
Pegasus Elliot MacKenzie Publishers Ltd.*
www.pegasuspublishers.com

First Published in 2023

**Vanguard Press
Sheraton House Castle Park
Cambridge England**

Printed & Bound in Great Britain

Dedication

I dedicate this book to my amazing parents, who gave me life and SAVED that life; even though it meant sustaining injuries to themselves, which were to last a lifetime.
A true display of pure unconditional love.
Without them I would not be here to tell my tale.

To my three wonderful sons, the reason FOR my life, the reason I keep fighting, even when the odds are stacked against me and the reason I will always go on living and fighting.
They are my reason to be, my purpose… My Life.

My beautiful grand-daughter Victoria, for believing in me and my abilities and keeping me young in heart and mind.

My beautiful and youngest grand-daughter Rose, for giving me precious love, joy and focus.

I love and thank you all for bringing such riches into my life.

Acknowledgements

I thank the following people, without whom I would not be here, writing my story.

My dear sons, who I must mention again, because of their unflinching love and support, throughout my life. I admire them greatly, for being the incredible men they have become, in spite of what they endured whilst growing up.

My dear friend Julie, who stayed by my side through thick and thin. She picked me up every time I fell and encouraged me to fight on.

My dear friend Elizabeth, who I met later in my life. From that first meeting she has been a constant support to me and shown understanding and kindness beyond belief.

My family and friends, whose support and encouragement have given me the strength to want to continue living.

The incredible doctors who physically repaired my body and the counsellors who have helped me maintain my sanity through everything.

Finally, that 'UNSEEN FORCE', whatever and wherever it may be, that came to my aid time and time again.

Chapter 1

It is 27th April 2008, and my mind starts to wander as I am sitting in the waiting room of Sarah, my counsellor, staring at the neutrally painted wall. My thoughts turn back to three days ago, when I celebrated my fifty-fifth birthday. I enjoyed a wonderful, celebratory meal with my much-loved family. During this time, I could step out from the 'Mask' that I hide behind, which has now become a major part of me. For a short time, my expressions were genuine and came naturally without forethought or fear of repercussion. I focused on the feeling of utter joy as I blew out my candles, my three sons looking on, smiling.

On a daily basis, I put a tremendous amount of energy into acting as though everything in my life was marvellous, hoping no one would guess the truth. I try to put on a brave face and smile, but the smile is just a part of the "Mask" which disguises the reality of my life. Life, which is totally different to the façade I outwardly present. Many unshed tears hide behind the false expressions I convey. During my birthday celebrations, I could, for a short time, almost forget the painful memories which continue to haunt me daily.

"Mrs Storm, Sarah is ready for you."

As the receptionist uttered the words, I came back down to earth with a jolt. The birthday candles faded into obscurity, and I am back sitting in the office of Sarah, with whom I have been meeting regularly for the past few months.

After thirty-two long years, the moment has eventually arrived when I must confront my horrifying demons, face my traumatic past and hopefully lay it to rest. This process, I hope, might bring me some peace, and enable me to move on with my life.

During the latter part of 2007, the horrendous nightmares I had been experiencing intermittently for so long clawed their way back into my mind, to torment me yet again. Nightmares about the terrible and extremely frightening events which have occurred throughout my life. Every night, I was waking in the small hours, screaming and shaking, sweat pouring off me, terrified of the horrific pictures whirling around inside my head. I would drift back into a restless sleep, only to wake screaming again. This situation, in turn, led to panic attacks and flashbacks during the daytime. Eventually, I was trapped in a continuous cycle and living hell. It was like having a horror movie playing in my head, over and over again, without any way of switching it off.

In desperation, I consulted my doctor, who referred me for an emergency appointment at a local mental health clinic.

I was in a dreadful state when I arrived for my first session with Sarah — nervous, unsure and somewhat afraid. I didn't know what to expect. I spent most of the time crying uncontrollably as, at her request, I related a brief outline of the past traumas in my life. Horrific events that hadn't been adequately addressed but buried away.

Sarah was very pleasant and kind, and as she listened to me she showed genuine interest and concern.

When I had finished speaking, I sank into my chair like a deflated balloon. I was exhausted, drained of all energy. Tears were streaming down my face. I was shaking involuntarily and felt like I had just run a marathon.

After taking me through some short relaxation techniques, Sarah handed me a much-appreciated cup of coffee.

"Drink that, Jessica, and try to relax. For you to have experienced such dreadful things and be sitting here today, speaking to me about them, is quite incredible. Many people would have crumbled a long time ago. You are here and ready to seek help. That shows that although you don't realise it, you are emotionally an incredibly strong person. In answer to your question, you most certainly are not mad! However, you need help to ease this enormous burden you are carrying."

I physically relaxed further into my chair. Hearing that Sarah could help me to get out of this living hell instantly brought some comfort. To be told by an expert that I wasn't going mad was an immense relief!

"You are suffering from a condition known as post-traumatic stress disorder."

I looked at Sarah with a vague expression, not understanding the diagnosis. She continued with her explanation.

"Imagine a jam jar, Jessica, in which you have put all the problems, difficulties, fears and traumas that you have experienced. Instead of facing and dealing with these issues, you just replaced the lid on the jar and tried to forget them. This is because you put all of your energy into dealing with other people's problems and therefore ignoring your own. Eventually, the jam jar was filled to overflowing, and the lid was forced off. This has allowed the hidden contents to flow out, giving you no choice but to face them."

What Sarah said made sense to me, and I strangely felt a sense of relief, and hope, in the confirmation that I did indeed have a problem but was most certainly not going mad!

"Jessica, confronting and dealing with thirty years of torment is a huge mountain to climb. But that doesn't mean that with commitment and patience it isn't assailable. It most certainly is. However, it will be a tough, painful and distressing climb."

I let Sarah's words sink in for a moment. If I chose not to attempt this climb, I would always be haunted by the past; the nightmares wouldn't stop, and the horror and torment would continue to haunt me. Now was the time to face my past, however difficult and distressing the task was going to be.

Thus, I began the worst journey of my life, with Sarah by my side. Starting from childhood and working through my adult life, I relived every painful, terrifying and traumatic experience. Not only the facts, but also experiencing again the emotions I felt at the time. By the end of each session, I was a complete physical and emotional wreck. However, Sarah always offered comfort and helped me compose myself before sending me on my way.

I would then, until my next session, do the homework that Sarah had set me. This involved listening to a tape recording of myself speaking during our recent session, thus reliving the experience yet again. I had to listen to the recording again and again, monitoring the level of stress it caused me. The aim was to continue doing this until the degree of stress and discomfort was significantly reduced.

To begin with, as I started to listen to my voice in the privacy of my home, I would break down uncontrollably, sometimes letting out wild screams of anguish, pain, fear and distress. Following Sarah's advice, I would frequently punch a cushion, venting my suppressed anger and emotion, as I relived over and over the terrible event I was combating.

As I again sat in Sarah's office, waiting for her to join me, it dawned on me that my foot was involuntarily tapping on the floor, something I always did when I was nervous. I was wringing my hands together in my lap, sweat trickling between my fingers as I did so. My heart was pounding against my chest wall, and my breathing was heavy. I was nervous and frightened at what I was about to confront.

Today we were continuing to work through the terrible events which had occurred during the year preceding the death of John, my first husband. These events were the result of his terrifying schizophrenic behaviour, and today I had to speak to Sarah and relive the horrendous day of the 'Pigeon Massacre'.

John kept and raced pigeons; some of these birds were incredibly beautiful, and he loved them passionately.

My father, being very skilled with his hands, had built John a loft to house his pigeons at the far end of our large garden; it was quite a magnificent achievement. The main wooden, oblong-shaped loft contained nesting boxes for the birds, work surfaces and food storage boxes. The primary structure was raised up on a deck that ran all the way around the loft. Steps led up to this area, and it was here that John, and sometimes I, would sit. On Saturday afternoons after a race, he would shake tins of seed to encourage his birds to come home. I can still remember the feeling of excitement and relief John felt when each bird landed safely; he loved his racing pigeons, and they were a great source of pleasure for him.

As Sarah entered her office, she immediately saw how distressed I was. I asked her for some water and tried to do the deep breathing exercises she had shown me.

"I understand how difficult this is, Jessica, and it's up to you if you feel able to continue today. However, it may sound harsh, but you will still have to face the event next time."

Sarah was right. If I was to finish the journey I had started, I couldn't leave the path on the way. After composing myself, I took an enormous deep breath and began to tell Sarah the story of the event I was here to relive.

On the Sunday morning in question, my father was watching cartoons on television with my then three-year-old son, Christopher. Meanwhile, my mother and I were in the kitchen making coffee, while John had disappeared down the garden to clean out the pigeon loft.

I was spooning coffee into cups and chatting happily to my mother when, suddenly, the door leading to the back garden swung open forcibly and John fell into the kitchen. My mother and I both gasped in horror at what beheld us and were temporarily rendered speechless. Then, from somewhere deep inside me, a voice clawed its way out. "My God, John, what on earth have you done?"

"It wasn't me," he screamed at me, "it was you; you've killed my pigeons, you wicked bitch!"

"What are you talking about?" I asked as calmly as I could, not wanting to agitate John further.

"They're dead, all dead, and you don't care!"

As I beheld John's dishevelled appearance, I immediately realised what he had done. Oh, dear God, his behaviour was going from bad to worse and still he refused to accept professional help.

The front of John's shirt and trousers were smothered in blood, as were his hands and forearms. Blood was smeared across his face, where he had tried to wipe away his still-flowing tears, and hanging loosely in his right hand, blood dripping slowly from it onto the kitchen floor, was an axe!

John was by now sobbing and crying violently. His shoulders were heaving up and down in response to his convulsing breaths.

My heart seemed to be beating furiously in time with John's breathing; while my mother stood rooted to the spot, her eyes wide open in shock at what was before her.

"Mum, go and fetch dad, please, and you stay with Christopher! Mum, move!"

My mother jerked back to reality and seconds later my father had joined John and me. As a fleeting look of horror swept across his face, he took control of the situation.

"Come on now, John," my father whispered, gently taking the axe from John and laying it in the kitchen sink. He then led John to sit on the steps outside the kitchen door. "What's been going on here, then?" my father asked John. "Jessica, go and fetch a brandy, please, and bring it to John."

I did as I was asked and then watched my father place his arm around John's shoulders and speak to him quietly. He had to be calmed down; otherwise, there was no knowing what he might do next.

As they spoke, John was adamant that I had killed his birds, which, of course, I most certainly had not. This always seemed to be the pattern of his behaviour. For some unknown reason, John always blamed me for what he did. My father eventually managed to persuade John that I couldn't have been responsible, as I hadn't left the house all morning. John's response to this was that I did it while he was asleep in the middle of the night! Finally, he reluctantly accepted my father's patient persuasion, that it must have been an outside intruder. We, of course, knew the real truth — John had slaughtered the birds himself.

"Come on now, John," beckoned my father, "let us go and sort this mess out."

As they made their way down to the loft, my dad called to me to fetch disposable gloves and black sacks. This I did, and when I arrived at the loft, my father cried suddenly, "No, Jessica, don't look, stay there!"

"Aaargh!" I screamed out loud, as Sarah paused the tape recorder and took my hand.

"It's okay, Jessica, deep breaths now, breath through the emotion as you let it come out."

I was rocking back and forth, trembling and crying. "I can't do it, I can't look at it, I can't, I can't!" I cried.

Sarah was so patient and relaxed that slowly, gradually, I became calm again. My body stilled, my crying stopped, and my breathing became steady, and I knew that I had to continue. If I didn't do this today, I would have to do it next session. I nodded to Sarah, and as her finger pressed the record button once again, I steeled myself to return to the gruesome scene I had briefly left moments before.

My father's instruction came too late. I was already at the open door of the loft, frozen to the spot as my eyes swept over the carnage laid out before me. The entire walls inside the loft were covered in blood and feathers, discarded as the terrified birds had flown around in panic, desperately trying to escape their attacker. The straw in the nesting boxes was matted with blood, and on every surface and all over the floor lay dead birds in pools of their own blood, their dismembered heads lying beside them. In an inexplicable moment of uncontrollable frenzy, John had decapitated every single bird.

"Jessica you're shaking," said my father. "This is no place for you; go back inside the house... Jessica, go!"

I walked in a daze back down the garden and into the kitchen and then, as I saw the bloody axe still lying in the sink, I was forced back to reality. I was violently sick. Robotically, I ran water over the axe to remove the tell-tale blood, but the dreadful scene that I had just witnessed would not leave my head.

I was so frightened, terrified to the core as to what John was capable of. When and how was this going to end? If only I could have seen at that moment what the future held and how this nightmare reached its conclusion.

I had repeatedly tried to get John to seek help for what was happening, but he refused, insisting that there was nothing wrong with him. At that time, professional help could not be forced upon him without his consent. I didn't know what to do; my parents and I were becoming more and more desperate and found it harder and harder to cope with his schizophrenic behaviour.

I was leaning against the sink, staring into space, wondering what to do, when my father and John returned. As was the usual pattern following one of John's strange incidents, he remembered nothing about what had occurred.

"Your dad and I have done a brilliant job cleaning the loft today," he said, brightly. "But I can't find my birds at the moment. I expect they'll be back soon. Can we have some coffee now, please?"

As I waited for the kettle to boil, I hugged my father. "Thank you," I whispered.

As he and John went to change their clothes — John completely unaware that those they were wearing were blood-stained — I poured water into their cups of coffee.

Tears of sadness and despair flowed silently down my face and dropped into the cup before me into oblivion.

As I sat sobbing uncontrollably, my body wracked with emotional pain, I felt Sarah's comforting arm around my shoulders.

"Well done, Jessica, you have just climbed an enormous hurdle today. You should be very proud of yourself. It's okay, just let all those tears and emotions come out."

As I made my way home later, I felt a sense of achievement at having got through the day's session successfully. I knew that my homework this week was going to be tough, but I was determined I was going to do it. I just couldn't give up now.

Chapter 2

As I lay in bed that evening, trying unsuccessfully to sleep, my thoughts drifted back to the day's session with Sarah. The ghastly memories of the events we had discussed kept playing through my mind. Inevitably, I drifted into a restless sleep, settling into the nightmare that continually haunted my nights.

"STOP IT, DADDY. STOP IT! DON'T SHOOT MY MUMMY!" My son's screams pounded upon my ears like a thunderbolt, while falling deafly upon his father's.

"Dear God help me!" I pleaded, as complete and utter terror embedded itself into the deepest depths of my being. My heart beat so fiercely, I thought it was going to burst through my chest. I was shaking uncontrollably, and sweat was running down my back and soaking my hands, making it harder to maintain my grip on the barrel of the gun. I tried in desperation to push it away from me. As the searing pain of overworked muscles crept up my arms, I felt my strength draining away. Exhaustion crept in, determined to beat me. My breathing quickened, and I realised I couldn't hold him off much longer. My eyes focused wide, in sheer panic, on the barrel of the shotgun, inches from my face.

I sit sharply up in bed, disorientated, panting with fear, shaking uncontrollably as again sweat trickles slowly down my back, as if trying to make the terror last longer. Is this living nightmare ever going to leave me?

Slowly, I become accustomed to my surroundings. I begin the nightly regime I have adopted to try and calm myself. My breathing becomes deeper and slower, I feel my body start to relax and allow my mind to drift off and indulge in more beautiful thoughts.

My early life was very different to the traumatic life that I have lived from the age of twenty-three. At the tender age of three, I discovered the wonderful world of dance, when my parents enrolled me in classes at the Gillian Devine School of Dance.

The vivid memory of that first lesson remains with me. As I stood in the dance studio, I felt very proud, wearing my tunic with the initials G D embroidered on the front, in red. My heart was beating with excitement. My toes inside my pink ballet shoes were tingling with the desire to start moving. I was going to learn to be a dancer!

The studio was a large, square room, with a wooden floor and glass mirrors on the wall to the right. The far wall contained two large windows, which looked out onto Miss Devine's garden. The left and rear walls had many pictures of famous dancers on them. Margot Fonteyn, Alicia Markova and Nadia Nerina, to name a few; who all in time became my heroines. In the left corner of the rear wall stood a piano, at which sat a chubby lady with a big smile on her face!

I must confess to being somewhat in awe of Miss Devine. She was a very tall, eccentric lady (I realised as I grew older), dressed in a black leotard and a long, black, floaty skirt, and her hair was knotted tightly on the back of her head. She had a rather long face, with a pointed nose, and wore bright red lipstick.

As Miss Devine moved, her skirt billowed around her, mirroring a carousel. When she spoke, she gestured in a very exaggerated way, throwing her arms and hands wide. I remember thinking, even at such a young age, that she had beautiful hands, with long, expressive fingers.

As she danced, it seemed to me that her hands were going to reach out forever; a skill I later learned myself.

Following Miss Devine's instructions, we began to move around the room, and I was totally lost. Lost to a world of sheer pleasure and joy, the joy and freedom of movement. This was the beginning of the passion and love of dance and the theatre that remains with me still.

We skipped and walked around the studio, trying to keep our backs straight and our heads erect. We learnt how to point our toes and to make beautiful shapes with our arms. We would then try to jump very high, while pointing our toes in the air and bending our knees when we landed.

Miss Devine would continually be calling instructions to us — "Heads erect, girls, pointed toes, smile!" At the same time, she would be flinging her arms about and immersing herself in the task in hand — trying to teach us to dance!

I vividly recall an extremely unusual spectator who used to watch our classes. Whatever the weather, one of the large windows in the dance studio always remained open. As soon as the music started to play, Miss Devine's horse, which lived in her garden — I said she was eccentric — would appear at every class and push his head through the window!

I remember the class coming to an abrupt halt the first time we experienced this. We all froze in amazement, mouths open, and then dissolved into fits of laughter. To see this brown head, belonging to a horse, his mane swinging from side to side as he showed his teeth, almost in a smile, was completely unbelievable!

But it happened at every class. Without fail, 'Petrushka' — apparently named after a puppet in a Russian ballet story who comes to life — would appear at the window. I'm sure I recall on more than one occasion his head nodding in time with the music!

Miss Devine was a very knowledgeable teacher, and I remember with fondness the time I spent at her school. She was very strict and made us work very hard, but was very kind, and my dance classes with her were the highlight of my week.

I thoroughly enjoyed the tap classes, learning how to shuffle and tap our feet on the floor to the lovely bright music that accompanied our classes. The happy lady who sat at the piano in the corner played this.

However, the ballet classes were my real delight. Making beautiful shapes with our bodies, learning to straighten our legs and pointing our toes until they felt as if they were going on forever. Jumping and spinning in time to the beautiful music. The music seemed to become a part of me, and I felt as if I was flying!

I knew from a very early age that this was to be my life.

However, when I was about eight years old, a terrible thing happened, and I thought my world was about to end.

The Devine School of Dance closed, and I was distraught. I sobbed and sobbed in total despair. How could I possibly survive without dance?

As luck would have it, though, fate smiled kindly upon me. A dance teacher was appointed at my junior day school, and my parents allowed me to join her classes. I soon realised that this was an entirely different set-up, and one that was to shape my life forever.

Chapter 3

Very soon after I started dance classes at my day school, my dance teacher approached my parents to ask if I could attend classes at her school of dance. Students were accepted by ability into her school, and apparently, I showed potential, and hence her request for me to further my training with her. So it was that I enrolled at the Janine Venning School of Dance.

Apprehensively, I arrived for my first lesson, not quite sure what to expect. My total lack of inhibition at age three was not so strong five years later. However, my nerves soon faded away, as I became totally immersed in my new surroundings and experiences, lost again in the joy of dance. I realised straight away that the standard was very high, and all the students in the class were extremely talented. I did not let this deter me; if anything, it made me work even harder to achieve their level of proficiency.

Janine Venning presented an entirely different persona to that of Miss Devine. She was very trim and elegant and usually wore dresses that nipped in her slim waist and then flared out around her. Her hair was always immaculate, resting on her shoulders and curling over. I recall she brought a basket to class in which she carried a small King Charles spaniel. I wondered whether all dance teachers were eccentric, or just ardent animal lovers!

I soon felt at home in my new dance school and began to make progress. The classes were hard work, and Miss Venning was quite a taskmaster.

"Posture, posture, posture. Straighten that back, Jessica; you are not a squid!"

She used to come up with unusual ways to tell us we were doing something wrong and that it had to be changed.

"Point your toes, you are not a penguin!" was something I regularly heard from Miss Venning.

I adored every minute I was in her company, as she imparted her incredible knowledge and gradually moulded me into the dancer I aimed to be. I began taking examinations and achieving superb results, and also participated in local dance competitions.

One such competition I recall very vividly. I was about nine years old and very new to the competition circuit at that time. Miss Venning entered me into a category where contestants, through dance and mime, had to convey the role of a chosen character. I played Bernadette of Lourdes, a young French peasant girl. While out walking with her sister and a friend one day, she saw a vision of the Virgin Mary; the first of many such visions she was to encounter during her lifetime. It was a beautiful and very sincere dance that Miss Venning had choreographed for me, and although nervous to begin with at taking part in the competition, I soon relaxed and thoroughly enjoyed the experience. To my amazement, I won first place, gaining a mark of 90%, apparently the highest awarded in the competition, and my photo was in the local newspaper the following day!

What a wonderful experience that was, and it became the first of many such experiences which occurred during my dance training.

Throughout my childhood, dance was to become my life, what I lived for, and it is with great affection and love that I remember the many sacrifices my parents made to enable me to nurture this love.

By the age of eleven, the decision had to be made as to which senior day school I was to move on to. I was so certain that I wanted to be a professional dancer that I told my parents I wanted to go to a full-time vocational school. There I would receive the training and learn the skills, not only in dance but also acting and singing, covering all aspects of musical theatre, to help me achieve my ambition.

However, when they approached Miss Venning to seek her advice as to how to go about this, much to their amazement her response was not what they had expected. She was against pursuing the idea, suggesting we perhaps consider it at a later date; maybe when I was sixteen. At the risk of sounding conceited and in spite of Miss Venning being a superb teacher, my mother and father felt that she wanted to keep her very talented students, as with all the outstanding talent she had in her school, no one, it seemed, went on to professional training.

Of course, we understood that the students' excellent examination results and competition successes were good for her school, but I felt it very unfair that she wouldn't help and encourage me to move forward. I couldn't accept Miss Venning's decision, and as always, my parents were right behind me, and therefore we applied to various vocational schools ourselves and secured some auditions for me.

The auditions were quite nerve-wracking, but at the same time exciting. To be inside these wonderful schools and perform in front of their highly respected teachers was in itself an enjoyable experience. During the auditions, the candidates were expected to take classes in various dance forms, to sing and recite poetry. I recall with much gratitude my Music and English teachers at school helping me prepare my songs and poems. The audition process proved very successful, and I was offered places at some of the leading vocational schools in the country. I was elated; my dream was now within reach.

My parents couldn't in any way afford to pay the exorbitant fees that had to be paid to attend any of these schools, so they applied for a local education authority grant, which was the usual process for anyone needing assistance in paying these fees. That was when my world came crashing down. The response from our local authority was that no money was currently available for vocational education.

This was an enormous blow, but my mother and father weren't giving up that easily. They went to the local education office and asked to speak to someone to discuss this decision, and when they were told that the decision wasn't negotiable, they proceeded to stage a sit-in! Armed with Thermos flask and sandwiches, they sat in the reception area all day and eventually, by late afternoon, realising that my parents weren't going to be fobbed off, they were granted an interview. Sadly, it was to no avail; the decision stood, no funds available.

Not prepared to give up, my parents' next move was to approach my grandfather, my mother's father, who was quite wealthy, and ask him if he would help. His reply was heart-breaking, and, I felt, was quite cruel. He said that if I wanted to pursue a "proper career" such as medicine or law, he would be more than happy to finance me, but not to go into a career in the theatre; in his view this was utterly immoral and not to be supported.

This was the end of the line; there was nowhere else to go, and I had to accept the devastating decision that I could not go on to vocational school and pursue my dream of becoming a dancer.

I was completely heartbroken, and for weeks I buried my head under my blankets at night and cried myself to sleep. However, I gradually came to terms with the situation, and when I stopped wallowing in my misery, I began to realise and appreciate just how hard my parents had tried to give me what I wanted.

I continued dancing with Janine Venning and, albeit reluctantly, attended the local grammar school. Over time I made a crucial and life-changing decision. if I couldn't dance myself, then I would teach others to do so. I knew I couldn't walk away from the dance world completely, and if I could help others to achieve their ambition, then that's what I would do with my life.

I would become the best teacher of dance I could be, and hence my training took on a slightly different course.

Chapter 4

My memories of my childhood are in the main very happy ones. However, like most of us, I'm sure, there are lurking in the subconscious a few not so good ones. I remember a time when my parents seemed to be arguing a lot. I would lie in bed listening to them shouting at each other and praying for them to stop. I don't know why I felt scared, because my siblings didn't seem perturbed and just slept on, but I definitely experienced feelings of fear. It appears these arguments were provoked because my father was very jealous — one of his few faults — and if my mother so much as spoke to another man, my father would fly off the handle. I only mention this because I wonder whether my parents' arguments may have been the beginning of the fear of anger that I carried with me into adulthood. Fortunately, in time my parents seemed to resolve their issues, and they continued to live and love together until my father's death in 1988.

In spite of this negative memory, when I recall my childhood, I experience a warm glow when remembering the many wonderful memories that stay with me, and I would like to share a few of my favourite ones with you.

Because money was very tight in our household, when it came to Christmas and birthdays, my skilful father would make presents for us. I recall a toy garage he made for my two brothers, complete with a little shop and petrol pumps. He crafted a beautiful, white-painted dolls' cot for my sister, accompanied by a white lace canopy, cover and pillows. For me, my wonderfully talented father built an amazing dolls' house, in which he had decorated each room with different wallpaper and made tiny pieces of furniture. There were beds, table and chairs, a settee and much more.

In my teens he made me a lovely kidney-shaped dressing table with lilac, flowery fabric draped around it and a large mirror on the top. I felt very grown-up to receive such a lovely present.

Our most treasured toy was a farm, complete with farmhouse, stables, barns, fences and even a duck pond! This beautiful creation is still being used today. My three sons have derived great pleasure playing with the farm over the years, and it is now being enjoyed and cared for by my young grand-daughter.

Things like sweets and fizzy drinks were a luxury to be enjoyed on occasion. On Friday evenings, if my father's wages allowed, he would come home from work with a bag of mixed sweets. My brothers, sister and I would sit on the floor by his feet, and he would count the sweets into four equal piles, one for each of us, consisting of blackjacks and fruit salad chews, pink shrimps, jelly snakes and a penny chocolate bar. If any were left over, my mother would be given those.

As children, we engaged in simple games and pleasures, such as playing tennis in the middle of the street, roller-skating up and down the pavement, or sitting on the kerb edge, playing marbles. Activities which would be frowned on today, of course, due to health and safety and children being subjected to germs, but it never seemed to do us any harm.

During school holidays, we would leave the house after breakfast to go and play, return for lunch at twelve noon and disappear again for the afternoon, before returning home for tea. I must, however, make the point that we were never really alone; my siblings and cousins and I always stuck together. Sometimes we played happily, sometimes we would argue, but we always looked out for each other regardless.

Occasionally, my mother and my aunt would take us all out for the afternoon, for a trip to the local park, or to a nearby small farm and nursery garden to buy fresh vegetables. We loved this, as it seemed to us, through our young eyes, that we were out in the country. Such was our imagination; and the best time of all was if our grandmother came, too, because she would buy us all a raspberry ice-lolly!

On occasion, we would also go tiddler fishing. Armed with a picnic of jam sandwiches and water, fishing nets and jam jars, we would set off for a fun-filled time.

I now recall that we, the children, accompanied by our mothers, would walk quite a long way to the River Thames and spend a jubilant afternoon trying to catch tiddlers.

On one particular day, following heavy rainfall, the riverbank was very muddy, and my mother said very clearly to us all, "Be careful you don't slip and fall in." A few moments later who should slip and fall in the dirty water? My mother! We thought it was hilarious, and even she managed to laugh. However, it was a rather uncomfortable, yet humorous walk home, with her squelching all the way!

As children, we certainly managed to get up to our fair share of mischief. One day, I recall, my mother and my aunt went shopping, leaving my younger sister and my cousin in the care of the two fathers. While doing some decorating, they insisted they could keep an eye on the two girls.

On returning from their shopping trip, the mothers enquired whether the girls had been all right. "Good as gold," came the reply, "they've been playing together quiet as mice."

Much to my mother and aunt's horror, on entering my aunt's bedroom they discovered the reason for the girls' silent behaviour — they had decided to play 'Grown-Ups' using my aunt's brand-new box of make-up. They had blue lips, red eyes and the final straw — my sister had found some scissors and cut off one of my cousin's long plaits! My father and uncle were in the doghouse for weeks after that.

Another memory that I recall was a day when a neighbour was looking after us while our mother was at work. I don't know how, but my youngest brother and the neighbour's son sneaked out of her house and into ours (the back door was left unlocked). They had decided they wanted to be builders like my father. So, they took hammers from his toolbox and proceeded quite happily to knock a large hole in the hall wall! Where they found the strength from, I don't know, but they were apparently copying our father, who had recently knocked down a dividing wall in our house. When our neighbour discovered what the boys had done, she was worried sick how to break the news to our parents. However, as always, our father didn't get angry or complain; he simply turned the hole into a very attractive archway!

In spite of being hard up, my parents still tried to take us away on a summer holiday whenever possible. This took the form of a caravan in Tintagel in North Cornwall; a place I still love dearly. Our time was spent enjoying simple pleasures, woodland walks, exploring castle ruins, imagining being King Arthur's knights riding up to Tintagel Castle, or making sandcastles and swimming in the sea. This last activity was often done in the rain, as, Cornish weather being somewhat unpredictable, it was no use relying on the sun shining.

Our parents used to say, "You're going to get wet regardless, so stop moaning and get on with it." So, we swam in the rain, while they huddled under their umbrella, braving the elements, while we had fun.

An amusing incident that occurred on one such holiday, although I certainly didn't find it so at the time, was when my brothers, sister and I decided to race across a cow field, scale a small wall and the first to reach the far gate was the winner. Off we ran, laughing as we raced for the wall. Up and over we went, and as we landed on the other side, my siblings' laughter increased, while mine turned into screams of anguish. I had landed smack in the middle of a cowpat! I can still recall that weird squishy feeling between my toes, let alone the smell! Looking back, though, I can certainly see just how hilarious it must have looked.

Another holiday event that still makes me smile involved my elder brother's girlfriend, now his wife, who had come away with us. During the night, Louise had needed to use the toilet facilities, which meant crossing the field to the toilet block situated a short distance from our caravan. Off she went, wearing a lovely white nightdress and negligee; not, with hindsight, the best attire for field walking!

In an adjacent caravan to ours were a group of young men who had returned a short while earlier, a little, or if I'm honest, a lot worse for wear, after a visit to the local pub.

We woke the following morning to find that they had packed up and left. On enquiring from our other neighbours if they knew why they had left in such a hurry, they informed us that the youths had apparently seen a ghost last night, a white figure floating across the fields. In their highly inebriated state, they had mistaken Louise for a ghost!

Looking back on my childhood, the one overriding factor is that what we may have lacked materialistically was more than compensated by the unconditional love, time, support and fairness that my parents showed to my siblings and I in equal measure, and following my father's death, my dear mother continues to show us.

Chapter 5

When I was sixteen, I decided I wanted to earn some money of my own. I had been doing a newspaper delivery round since I was thirteen, but now I wanted more independence, and so I started working as a waitress at weekends in a local garden centre cafeteria. Little did I know at the time that this decision was to lead me onto a path that was to bring me more torment, grief and horror than I could have ever begun to imagine... It was here that I met John.

John was a chef who worked in the kitchens which catered for the cafeteria where I worked and also for the adjacent cordon bleu restaurant. On arriving at work, cafeteria staff entered the building through the rear kitchen door and walked through the kitchen to their work area. It was slightly unnerving, although somewhat flattering, to feel the young chefs surveying you as you passed by their workstations, and on one particular morning, while doing my usual walk through the kitchen, a voice from my left said, "Hi." I turned in surprise to see a young, handsome chef very skilfully tapping, rolling and peeling hard-boiled eggs, while looking at me with a huge smile on his face. As I looked at that smile, framed by his jet-black hair and enhanced by his bright eyes, I couldn't help but smile back.

After that first encounter, I would always stop for a quick chat when I passed by, and it wasn't long before John asked me out on a date. He told me he had wanted to ask me for quite a while but couldn't pluck up the courage. On asking him why, he replied, "Because you're so gorgeous, way out of my league."

I told him that was ridiculous, but later learned that some of the other young chefs also wanted to ask me out, so John realised he had to get on with it or miss his chance!

I must confess to feeling ten foot tall to be the talk of the kitchen! John and I started dating regularly, and it wasn't long before we were spending all our free time together.

John lived with his parents, brother and sister in a lovely house very close to where we worked. His parents were chef and housekeeper to an MP, and his family had accommodation in a wing of their house. On meeting John's parents, Pamela and David, for the first time, I recall his stepfather being very friendly and welcoming, but not so his mother. As time passed, I began to realise that no matter what I did or how hard I tried to please her, John's mum just didn't seem to like me at all. With age and wisdom, I realised that it wasn't just me; no one in Pamela's eyes would have been good enough for her son. She just didn't want to let him go.

As time passed, John and I became very close and soon fell deeply in love. He continued to work as a chef, and I kept working weekends in the cafeteria, and during our breaks we would meet outside the back door for a quick kiss and cuddle. Many a time I recall the head chef light-heartedly telling us to get a room!

In the meantime, on leaving senior school at sixteen, I started full-time employment as a bank clerk, while continuing to study in the evenings for my teaching qualifications in dance. I never really wanted to work in a bank, but I needed a secure, salaried job while studying for my dance teacher qualifications.

While working and studying, I had an amazing experience. Janine Venning was asked to provide dancers and choreograph a couple of dance routines for a Charity Gala being held at London's famous Drury Lane Theatre.

Leslie Crowther and Roy Hudd were presenting the Gala, and I was overflowing with excitement at being a part of it.

I was to perform a fast jazz routine called 'Vitality' with seven other girls. We were to wear gold sequinned tops and hot-pants.

Apart from this, I was also very honoured to be selected to perform a classical ballet solo.

To be given the opportunity to perform in one of London's oldest and most famous theatres was phenomenal.

Situated in Covent Garden, the contemporary theatre is the latest in a line of four theatres built at the same location, the earliest dating back to 1663. The most recent major interior renovation took place in 1922. This resulted in a magnificent masterpiece, a four-tiered majestic theatre able to seat well over two thousand people!

Here was I, relatively unimportant Jessica, performing on the same stage as many of the world's greatest performers.

Of particular interest to me were the musicals of Ivor Novello and also those of Rodgers and Hammerstein, such as *Oklahoma*, *South Pacific* and *The King and I*. In the present day, the theatre has hosted many long-running productions; for example, *Miss Saigon*, *42nd Street* and *The Lord of the Rings*.

As the time for my solo drew nearer, I began to realise that I was about to become a part, even if only a very minute one of this theatre's history. My heart was pounding with excitement, and I was very nervous because it was so hard to believe I had been chosen to do this, and I didn't want to let anyone down. The opportunity to dance in London's West End, let alone in such a famous venue, is awe-inspiring and something until then I could only dream about, an opportunity to be cherished and remembered forever.

I had to have a new ballet tutu made especially for this occasion, which I still treasure. It was made by one of the Royal Ballet's wardrobe mistresses. I was even allowed to choose my favourite colour — a beautiful, rich purple.

I remember with immense affection the love and gratitude I felt towards my parents, who both took on extra jobs to fund my tutu.

The cost was two hundred pounds, a lot of money; but in 1970 it was an absolute fortune!

I recall sitting in my dressing room, with make-up, hair accessories, flowers and good luck cards spread out on the unit before me.

I stared into the large mirror, which was surrounded by brightly shining lights. Staring back at me was someone I hardly recognised.

My make-up had been artistically applied, making my eyes look enormous, and my hair had been sleeked back into an immaculate bun on the back of my head. An exquisite silver tiara that my dresser attached meticulously to my hair enhanced the whole effect. I was amazed at the way I looked; just like the ballerinas in my ballet books at home.

I then rolled on my new, silky, pink ballet tights and stepped into my shiny pink satin pointe shoes. I tied the ribbons with extreme care; it would be unprofessional and possibly dangerous if they were not fastened securely and came undone.

Finally, as Mary my dresser held it out for me, her delightful smile mirroring mine, I stepped into my new tutu. I felt as if I was going to burst with excitement!

It was truly magnificent, from the gleaming satin bodice, with perfectly erect layers of purple net attached to the hip line, the glittery silver trim which edged the bodice, to the minute detail of the hook and eye fastenings running down the back.

The finished result was magical; I looked and felt like a princess in a fairy story. Now I had to do justice to the effort that had gone into my appearance and dance like never before.

"Jessica, you look stunning," said Mary.

"Thank you, Mary, you're very kind, and thank you for helping me to look like this!"

Suddenly, an announcement came loudly through the intercom.

"Jessica Storm to the stage, please. Jessica Storm to the stage, please."

This was it; the moment had finally arrived for me to make my West End debut. As I left my dressing room, Mary called after me, "Enjoy every second, Jessica, and make them all proud."

"I will, Mary; I'll do my absolute best."

As I took my position in the centre of the huge stage, it engulfed me, and I felt incredibly small and insignificant. For a moment, nerves began to get the better of me and my heartbeat increased. The curtain began to rise, and I was suddenly aware of over two thousand pairs of eyes watching me!

Some eyes were watching perhaps with indifference and some, maybe, with envy and even admiration; those young girls attending dance class who dreamed of standing where I was right now, wanting to be literally in my shoes.

Whatever the thoughts behind those eyes, they were all piercing into me; feeling almost hostile and judgmental.

Suddenly, the lights lifted and I was momentarily blinded, and as they culminated into a spotlight surrounding me, the introduction to my music began.

My body tingled with excitement and pleasure as my nerves dispelled. I stepped into an arabesque, balancing on the tips of my right toes, my left leg extended straight behind me, arms stretched out. I held the position perfectly for the choreographed three seconds and then as I flowed into the familiar movements of my dance, I experienced pure joy and exhilaration.

After a couple of minutes, as the music slowed and I melted into my final pose, there was a moment of complete silence and then, suddenly, an eruption of applause! The audience was clapping and cheering; they weren't judging me. They were expressing their appreciation for me, as I was engulfed in the tumultuous sound raining down on me. This was for me; they liked me. I had danced well.

I took my bow, the applause still resounding upon me, and then, as the curtain began to close in front of me, I was left panting and soaked in sweat, following the exertion of my performance.

I knew with complete certainty that this was what I wanted my life to be; a raging desire was burning inside me. I wanted and needed this; to allow myself to be transported to this other world. The magical world of dance; my love, my passion and later... my escape.

After my West End experience, John and I slipped back into the reality of our daily lives. I think Pamela eventually realised that John and I were not going to be parted and resigned herself reluctantly to me becoming her future daughter-in-law.

On 25th July 1971, John and I were married at St. John's Church in Isleworth in Middlesex. We were so happy. The sun was shining, and it was the most beautiful day; a day full of hope and promise for the future. John and I were indeed very young when we married, but there was never any doubt, about our true feelings for each other, and if fate hadn't dealt us the hand it did, we would have envisaged spending the rest of our lives together.

There was a plus to me working in the bank as it turned out; John and I were able to secure a mortgage to buy our first home together. However, we were short for the deposit and our only option, not holding out much hope after my previous refusal, was to approach my grandfather. To our pleasure and amazement, he agreed to lend us the shortfall and presented us with a little red book. Every Friday evening, we would go to my grandfather, with the agreed weekly payment, to repay what we had borrowed from him and he would mark it off in the book.

Our first home together! We were so excited and derived great pleasure in gradually decorating and furnishing it. We had a lounge, in which my father built us the most beautiful stone fireplace, a dining room and a tiny kitchen downstairs, a double and single bedroom upstairs and a small bathroom.

John and I, like many newlyweds, struggled financially, but we were so happy and looked towards a bright future together. In the meantime, I was still working towards gaining my teaching qualifications, intending to start, my own classes.

One evening, while John and I were at home together, there was a knock on the front door. On opening the door, I was surprised to see Janine Venning's husband Jeremy standing there.

"Hello, Jessica," he said. "I'm sorry to disturb you, but I need to discuss something with you regarding Janine, and it's rather urgent."

Filled with curiosity, I invited Jeremy in. Sadly, Janine and Jeremy's marriage had broken down, and they had separated. Janine had apparently gone abroad, and he had the responsibility of selling the dance school for her. This was a tremendous shock; I had no idea this was coming. However, on reflection, I recall that Janine had been looking drained and drawn of late, which was probably due to the difficulties she was encountering in her private life.

Jeremy's next sentence shocked me even more.

"As you are Janine's most senior student and well on the way to becoming a qualified dance teacher, would you be interested in buying her school? Also, you've been assisting in teaching the other pupils as part of your training; I feel you must know them very well. There is a strong possibility that they may remain with you if you took over the school."

My head was spinning; this is what I wanted, my own dance school, there for the taking, but then why should the current pupils remain with me? My teaching experience could never equal Janine's, so why should parents entrust their children to me? Then again, they seemed to like me and enjoyed me teaching them; maybe they would give me a chance.

I then came down to earth. It was utterly impossible even to consider Jeremy's offer — there was no way that John and I could find the sort of money that Jeremy was asking for. I wasn't even completely qualified, and I very selfishly thought to myself, with Janine gone, how was that going to happen?

Feeling extremely dejected, I told Jeremy that I appreciated the opportunity, but I couldn't see how we could bring it to fruition.

"Please don't say no straight away," requested Jeremy. "Give it some serious thought, as it will take some time for me to sell the school on the open market anyway."

"All right," I replied, "but much as I want this, I don't hold out much hope of finding a way to raise the capital."

John and I talked long into the night, trying to find a way of bringing this incredible opportunity within my grasp. By the time we left for work the next morning, we had a plan, a rather precarious one, but nevertheless a plan. As soon as I got to work, I would ask for a meeting with my bank manager. However, when I arrived at work, before I could make this request, the bank accountant told me that Mr Griffin, the manager, wanted to see me! I tapped nervously on Mr Griffin's door, wondering why I had been summoned; I couldn't think of anything I had done wrong with my work. I was by now a counter cashier, but my books all balanced, so what on earth could he want?

In response to his "Come in", I entered Mr Griffin's office, and he immediately put me at my ease. "Come in, Jessica, and take a seat. I would like your advice." He wanted advice from me, on what? I soon found out.

"I'm planning to redecorate my office, Jessica, and I feel that from the way you dress and your excellent colour co-ordination, you would be very well placed, if you're willing, to design my office makeover."

Wow, I wasn't expecting that. I quite happily agreed to take on this task, feeling very honoured to have been asked, and while we were discussing some coffee and cream and possible burnt orange colour combinations, I thought to myself, 'Come on, girl, it's now or never; pluck up courage and do it.' So, before I left Mr Griffin's office, I had told him all about my ambition to own my own school, about Jeremy's offer and if there was any way at all that he could help me.

Mr Griffin's response was unbelievable. He said it was too good an opportunity to miss, and if determination and passion could make a business venture work, I had more than enough of that flowing out of me to make it a success. He would let me have a bank loan to purchase the school!

My feet didn't touch the ground as I left his office, and I'm sure I was singing as I worked through the rest of the day!

During my lunch break, I executed part two of the plan. I telephoned the secretary of the Dance Association that Janine belonged to and whose examinations the students took and told them of my plight. They put me in touch with an examiner who I already knew, who had her own dance school about an hour's drive from where I lived. She was more than happy to finish my teacher training in the form of a 'crash course' to enable me to start officially teaching at the commencement of the new term.

I wasn't flying, I was soaring; my own dance school, it was happening, it was actually happening!

So it was that in a matter of a few weeks of extremely hard work I became the new Principal of The Kew Academy of Dancing, with the required letters after my name. Nothing was going to stop me now.

I contacted all the present parents explaining the situation; and Joy oh Joy, nobody deserted me, and they were all of the opinion that I should be given a chance to prove myself.

On that first day of the autumn term, as I stood in the studio of my dance school, I was very nervous but also very excited, and as I heard the footsteps and excited chattering of children coming up the stairs for their class, I was overcome with happiness. At that moment, a thought came into my head, and I've never forgotten it. I didn't have Janine's experience to offer these children, but I did have a lot of learned knowledge from her. I would take this knowledge and use it well. I wasn't Janine and wasn't going to try to be. I would offer these children myself, completely and utterly dedicate myself to becoming the best teacher I could be, learning more along the way and, most importantly, I was going to do it my way.

Do it my way I certainly did; from that first day there was no stopping me. The dance school went from strength to strength. Pupil numbers increased, we achieved very pleasing examination and competition results, and soon the school had an excellent reputation as one of the top schools in the area.

I had realised a dream, I had achieved what I always wanted; but little did I know that in years to come, my school was not only to be a major part of my life, it was going to be my saving grace, the thing that kept me clinging onto life.

Chapter 6

Life was moving along steadily for John and me. We had our own home, I had my school and life was good, when suddenly John was dealt an unhappy blow. He had for a while been experiencing nose bleeds while at work, and from the increased strength and regularity of these it was concluded that it was the heat of the kitchens that was causing them, as he didn't suffer at all away from work. It was with tremendous sadness that John had to leave his work as a chef, but he was left with no alternative.

He took a job driving for a tyre delivery company and soon after we had some very exciting news — I was pregnant! We were delighted with this news, our first child together. It was the most incredible and exciting feeling, to know that a new life was growing inside me. I was very lucky and sailed through my pregnancy with no morning sickness or other problems whatsoever. The only thing I did have, from the beginning, was a craving for very sour green apples, eating them day and night!

When I was about eighteen weeks pregnant, I felt our baby kick for the first time, and this was the most pleasant experience. John used to place his hand on my growing stomach to feel this sensation. Suddenly, our baby felt like a real person.

On 26th September 1972, I gave birth to Christopher, in less than two hours! I had a home delivery, very little labour pain and young Christopher just slipped into the world without any real effort. How lucky was I? He was beautiful, tiny, but perfectly formed and healthy, with a mass of jet-black hair. John and I were ecstatic to be new parents to this little bundle of joy. I was very lucky to have such an easy time but can only put it down to my muscles being so strong and toned through my dancing. Totally unprepared, therefore, was I for the births of my other two beautiful sons, later in life. They both obliged me with very long, painful labours by contrast, but without question were worth every minute!

John and I were blessed. Christopher was a happy and contented baby, and I fully embraced motherhood. After Christopher was born, I gave up working at the bank. The dance school was providing a real income, and to subsidise this I accepted a post as a part-time dance teacher in a local Convent School on a couple of afternoons a week. This allowed me to be at home most of the time with Christopher during the day, and while I was at the Convent my aunt cared for Christopher. While I continued working at my own school, John and my mother shared the care of Christopher.

As Christopher grew and blossomed, so did my school, and I was by now hiring assistant teachers and producing some large productions. I loved the choreography, and these productions let my creative juices run free and were also a great source of enjoyment for my pupils and their families.

One of my favourite productions was a quirky version I produced of the *Pied Piper of Hamelin*, called *Rats*.

In case you don't know this story, it is set in the fourteenth century in the German town of Hamelin. Rats plague the town and a colourful character called the Pied Piper, dressed in red and yellow, rids the town of the rats. He does this by playing hypnotic pipe music and luring them to the River Weser, where they fall in and drown. However, the story has a sad ending, as the mayor of the town refuses to pay the piper the agreed amount for ridding the town of the vermin. The piper, therefore, proceeds to play his music again, this time luring the town's children away, never to be seen again.

This production was such fun. Apart from playing the town's inhabitants, the children also had to be dressed as rats, in quite an unusual way. They wore leather clothing enhanced with chains, very colourful leggings and t-shirts covered in graffiti, black Doc Marten boots, brightly coloured punk hairstyles and had their faces painted like rats. The children loved it.

A good friend of mine, a very talented young man who worked as a cruise ship entertainer, very kindly agreed to play the role of the Piper, and he was phenomenal, working in a very generous and supportive way with the children.

It is with tremendous admiration and affection that I remember my father and the hours he spent building and painting the scenery and sets for these productions. I certainly gave him some challenges over the years, but his incredibly skilled hands always produced amazing results. One of his masterpieces that particularly sticks in my mind was a giant naval ship. While I was staging a large naval-themed production, I wanted a frigate built to cover the entire stage, and my father obliged! The result was incredible. Besides my dad and his support, I always also had my mother's.

Whether it was selling tickets, making coffee, trudging endlessly round material shops with me, finding fabrics for costumes, or even feeding the stage crew during rehearsals, my mother was always there and continued to be so right up until I retired in 2003.

The rest of my family have also always been incredibly supportive; my brothers and in later years my sons worked backstage as scene shifters, and my youngest brother, Dennis, apart from stage managing many productions, would often appear on stage himself. He played various characters, doing a great job and often reducing the audience to tears of laughter while playing a comedy role.

When Christopher was three, significant changes came about. My parents had a big falling out with my grandfather, my mother's father, who owned the house they lived in. The outcome of this was that they were forced to move out. This was horrendous — how could he do this, put my parents on the street?

John stepped up to the mark. We decided to sell our house and use the equity to buy a property large enough to house our family and my parents. Fortunately, we found the perfect house in Hounslow in Middlesex. It was a large, detached property, currently used as two flats, which would provide ample accommodation for us all, but would still enable us to live separately, which was crucial. We all loved the house, and so it transpired that we sold up and very happily made the move.

As you entered through the bright red front door of the house (I always wanted a red front door), you encountered a square hallway, which proceeded to narrow to its left and lead to the kitchen at the back of the house. To the right of the front door was a wide staircase that turned to the left at the top, to a landing that ran in two directions, with rooms leading off on each side. These upstairs rooms were to be home for John, Christopher and me, while my parents were to have the downstairs rooms.

Downstairs was a large living room and another reception room, which was to become my parents' bedroom. As you continued into the kitchen, there was a bathroom on the left. The back door from the kitchen led out into a vast and beautiful garden.

We were all very happy with our new home and decided that in due course we would build a partition as you came in the front door so that my parents and I had our own separate entrances. I thank God to this day that we didn't rush into doing this straight away.

Chapter 7

We settled very happily into life in our new home. Christopher started at a local day nursery, which he loved, and John started a new job as a security driver. Every morning on his way to work, John would take Christopher to nursery, and I would look out of our upstairs kitchen window across the garden. I would wave back to them as they turned and waved to me before going into the nursery. This moment every day filled me with such contentment and well-being and is the picture, later in life, that I choose to keep in my mind when I think of John.

Why is it that when life seems to be going along well and happily, fate steps in and decides to upset the apple cart?

I received a phone call a few weeks later advising me that John had been involved in a road accident. There had been a collision with his firm's vehicle and another. He was supposedly okay, but I naturally dropped everything and rushed to the hospital. On arrival, I discovered that, fortunately, John was not seriously injured. Apart from cuts and bruises, he had sustained concussion. The news was such a relief, but it was nevertheless decided that he should stay in the hospital a short while for observation, so I returned home to collect Christopher from the nursery, safe in the knowledge that John was going to be okay.

On the day that John was released from hospital, he was by all accounts fine; but little did we know how very wrong that diagnosis was.

The first alarm bell rang upon arriving back home. John went to switch on the light in the hallway, and he missed it completely. Two or three times he tried to push the switch on and eventually managed to do so. I thought no more about it, assuming that it must be the after-effects of a concussion, and this was normal behaviour. However, with hindsight, it wasn't normal, and there was indeed a problem preventing John from carrying out this simple task without such difficulty.

There were some events during the year that followed which continued to endorse the fact that there was something very, very wrong with John.

I remember waking one night to find that John was not in bed, and on getting up to see where he was, and if he was okay, I found him in our living room. He had a pot of pale blue paint and was quite happily painting blue zigzags around the walls! I was flabbergasted. I smile to myself now, but it certainly wasn't funny at the time. It was weird, surreal, and on asking him why he was doing this, he replied that he thought we needed to decorate. Pale blue zigzags weren't what I would have chosen if we had indeed planned to paint the living room, which we hadn't.

What I don't understand — or rather, didn't at the time — was how I accepted what he had done so easily. There was something inside me that was ringing alarm bells. This feeling made the hairs on the back of my neck stand up. Subconsciously, I knew I couldn't argue with him, but I didn't know why. I just think I realised on some level that I was being confronted by something I didn't understand, and fear of the unknown was engulfing me. Not knowing what the outcome of this fear would be, perhaps caution was the best way forward.

I remember saying to John, "Wow, that looks great!" What a crazy thing to say when you're looking at a room with this bizarre graffiti around the walls. But I just knew it was the right thing to say, and consequently I went back to bed and left John painting his blue zigzags.

However, the following morning, while I was in the kitchen preparing breakfast, I suddenly heard John's raised voice coming from the living room. I went to see why he was shouting, and as I walked into the living room, he turned on me.

"You stupid imbecile, what have you done?" he shouted, pointing at the walls.

"I didn't do it, John. Don't you remember, you painted the walls last night?"

John glared at me and yelled back, "You liar! Don't try and blame me for your stupidity. I'd never have done anything so ridiculous; it looks awful!"

With that, he stormed out, leaving me speechless at his outburst and feeling very concerned at the realisation that, again, he didn't remember what he had done. To keep the peace, my father very quickly helped John to redecorate the room for us, but John was still adamant that I had painted the blue zigzags.

It was at this point that I made the first of many visits that year to our GP, Doctor Knight. I desperately needed to seek some advice; how I should deal with this ghastly, horrendous nightmare I was caught up in.

On explaining to Doctor Knight what had happened with the light switch, the wall painting and the slaughter of the pigeons, he agreed that something was indeed very wrong with John. He advised that John needed to see a doctor immediately. I thought that wasn't going to be quite as easy as it sounded, as in John's eyes he hadn't done any of these things. However, I was determined to try, and so I told John that perhaps he wasn't as well as he should be after his accident and that it might be beneficial to visit Doctor Knight for a check-up. His response was exactly as I had feared; as far as he was concerned, there was nothing wrong with him and he point blankly refused to see the doctor. He went further than that and told me I should see Doctor Knight, as I was the one with the problem; it was all my fault! My fault. What exactly had I done?

According to John, I must have done all these things and therefore I needed the help, not him.

I returned despondently to Doctor Knight. "It's just as I feared," I told him. "John insists he is not sick in any way and will not come and see you."

"This is a dreadful situation for you to be in," replied Doctor Knight. "Unfortunately, although John's denial of his erratic behaviour compounds the problem, unless he can be persuaded to seek medical help there is nothing I can do. Unfortunately, help can't be forced upon John without his consent. Please keep trying, Jessica you may eventually find a way to get through to John. I'm so sorry I can't be of more help."

I left Dr Knight's office feeling extremely downhearted. What was I supposed to do now?

That was the first brick in the wall that was slowly built during that year, trying to get help from every angle I could find, but getting nowhere.

My face had become a 'Mask'. I smiled falsely and tried to appear in control as if everything was okay. I was so afraid of upsetting John and risking antagonising him further. I couldn't let him know how I was feeling. My true feelings of despair and desolation had to be disguised.

John and I had two dogs at this time. Pepe, who was a Golden Labrador who John was training as a gundog, and then Sheba, a little Jack Russell terrier, who was my dog. Although I'm not an ardent dog lover, something was appealing about little Sheba. When John brought her home to me, I immediately fell in love with her.

One day, John was working in the garden when he came in and told me he was taking the dogs for a walk. Nothing unusual there, I thought, except that when Christopher asked to go, too, John refused to take him, saying that daddy had to go by himself this time. I found this very strange; John adored Christopher and usually took him with him to walk the dogs.

In spite of the very strange behaviour, we had been experiencing from John, I somehow knew that Christopher was never in danger. Christopher was John's life, and I was sure he would never harm him.

Up went the hairs on my neck again, and my heart started beating faster as I wondered what this change in routine meant. But I didn't argue with John, as by now I realised it was futile to do so; it only made him angrier. I took Christopher inside and played a game with him while waiting nervously for John to return.

Eventually, he did so and on entering the house he told me he had some bad news. The news he imparted was that Sheba had disappeared.

"What do you mean, gone?" I asked. "The dogs were out with you; how could she have disappeared?"

John then replied, without any emotion, "She's gone, she's just gone, I know she has; you won't have her any more."

I don't know how, it's impossible to explain, but I just knew at that point that John had taken Sheba; where or what he had done with her I didn't know, but I was afraid to question him further.

"You go away now; I'm going to play with MY Christopher!"

I was completely devastated and very confused, and leaving John and Christopher playing happily, I went downstairs, knocked on my parents' living room door and went inside. Dissolving into floods of tears, I told them about Sheba's disappearance and my growing feelings that John now hated me.

They suggested going back again to speak to the doctor, but I knew it wouldn't get me anywhere. I knew I desperately needed to find help for John... but where was I to go?

My mother made me a cup of tea and we sat together, while my father went outside in an attempt to hunt for Sheba. About half an hour later he returned, and I could tell by his expression that all was not well.

"I'm so sorry, Jessica" he said. "I've found Sheba... but she's dead; her neck is broken."

"Where is she?" I screamed.

My father reluctantly replied, "I found her in the dustbin."

" No, no, no!" I cried. My mother hugged me as I sobbed, not only for my pet but also for all the despair in my life. I felt completely lost and helpless.

Leaving my mother to comfort me, my father went into the garden to bury Sheba for me. While he was doing this, John came downstairs and asked what my dad was digging for.

"He's burying Sheba; she's dead!" I shouted at him, unable to control my feelings.

"How did that happen?" he asked. "Jessica, what have you done now?"

"As if you don't know, damn you. It wasn't me!" I screamed in reply.

"Who's upset you?" he said sarcastically and walked away; returning to finish his game with Christopher. John again had no recollection of what he had so obviously done.

As he walked upstairs, I heard him saying a phrase that I was hearing a lot by now. "Leave me alone, don't speak to me, I'm going to my Marble Palace." Marble Palace? What Marble Palace?

I learnt a long time later that this Marble Palace was a place in John's head where he wanted to be. Maybe somewhere deep down, at some deeply subconscious level, John was also in turmoil, and this Palace was a place of respite, where he found some comfort.

Why, though, did he have to destroy my little Sheba, why? Did he want in some strange, warped way to hurt me? I didn't know. All I knew was the grief, emotional pain, confusion and desperation that enveloped me at the time, and little Sheba was gone forever. Was there never to be an escape from this hell in which I was trapped?

As time progressed, John became more impatient, and angry and would fly off the handle at the slightest thing. I remember one particular incident; I don't even know what triggered it off. It was obviously not very important, but it angered John to the point where he threw his dinner up into the air, and pork chops and vegetables hit the ceiling!

All he said after this was, "Don't you speak to me, leave me alone, I'm going to my Palace!"

One inexplicable fact that to this day I don't understand was that John's attitude to my parents and me was the same, angry, disinterested, accusing, hurtful and indifferent, while as far as his relationship with Christopher and his work colleagues went, nothing seemed untoward.

Apparently, I later learnt, his brain was engaging a different mind-set, but this didn't make it any easier to understand or cope with, and, in the meantime, John still refused to seek any medical help.

He started to stay out late at night and come home at odd times during the day. Often, he would pull up outside the house at lunchtime, with women I didn't know in the car with him. On one occasion this happened, Christopher was at home, and on hearing his father pull up outside, he ran to the front door and opened it. John beckoned Christopher to come down the path and proceeded to introduce him to "Daddy's new lady friend".

Another time, I returned home from work to find John knocking down the wall between our dining room and kitchen! Why he was doing this I had no idea, but I just had to accept that, in his mind, he had to do it. Of course, the next day I was very audibly accused of knocking the wall down without consulting him, and the usual pattern continued of him storming out in a rage and leaving me struggling to deal with the aftermath.

I expect you're probably wondering by now why I put up with this behaviour; why did I tolerate it? The simple answer was that I loved this man. I wanted back the John I married, the John I knew, and I was determined to do anything in my power to help him, to cure him. But sadly, the support just wasn't there and, in the end, in sheer desperation, I confided to his parents what was going on. While John's stepfather was very sympathetic and offered me any help at all that he could give in any way, his mother took an entirely opposing view.

Pamela, you may recall me saying, took an instant dislike to me when we had first met. I don't know why I couldn't think of any reason why this was the case. Nothing had occurred between us to instigate this opinion; she just didn't like me. However, I wanted to get along with her, and I tried to speak to her about John's behaviour and the effect it was having on the family. I asked her if she would try and persuade John to listen to her and receive some help.

Her response was, "Don't blame my son; it must be your fault!"

Why was this my fault? I didn't cause the car crash; I didn't hit John on the head.

However, Pamela would not or could not accept that John was ill. Maybe with hindsight, as a mother, she couldn't bear to accept what John was doing; to think that he was capable of doing these things. Or perhaps to accept that he was sick enough to behave in this way involuntarily, I don't know. But what I do know is that she just went on blaming me, accused my parents and me of lying and refused to accept John's behaviour.

From that point, I used to meet John's stepdad, David, once a week in a local park to give him an update. We would sit and talk, and while he was very understanding and comforting, we were nevertheless both full of despair. David could not even get his wife to listen to him. She completely shut down and at the end of the day all David could do was support me, as my parents were doing continually, while at the same time feeling helpless.

Desperation was setting in; I didn't know what to do. As time went on, John and I were arguing more and more, because I was still trying to tell him he needed help. He continued to blame me, as his mother did, he still denied his actions, and it was wearing, very wearing. I was exhausted and frightened. I was very young, and having to cope with an unbearably heavy load, and yet I couldn't give up on this man. I guess I hoped that something would happen to make things change, and that would turn everything around.

One Saturday, John had taken Christopher down to visit his parents. Later that afternoon, I received a phone call from Pamela. She told me that John was in hospital and, of course, I was to blame, even though I wasn't even there. While they were at his mother's, John had gone into the bathroom. He was gone quite a while, so Christopher went looking for his daddy and he found him, he thought, asleep on the bathroom floor. John wasn't asleep; he was unconscious. He had taken an overdose, and it confirmed that somewhere deep down in his subconscious mind he was confused and desperate enough to be driven to do this.

I naturally went straight to the hospital and was very relieved to discover that John was awake and okay. On asking him why in God's name he had done this, his reply was, "I don't know. I just wanted to go to my Marble Palace. You keep telling me I'm sick, and I'm not!"

It was then that I decided to try a different approach. I told John that perhaps I was ill and could we go together to seek help. It didn't work. He was adamant. "No way!" he declared. I should go, but he wouldn't.

While he was actually in the hospital, John was offered a consultation with a psychiatrist. Thank goodness, I thought, at last — a ray of hope was shining in front of me. Not for long, though, as John refused the treatment. Why? There was nothing wrong with him.

Dear God, how was I supposed to get through to this man, how could I break down his denial?

His mother was furious with me, believing that I must have driven him to take the overdose. How could she have been so blind and not seen what was staring her in the face? She just didn't want to see, and my pleas for help fell on deaf ears.

When John was discharged, Pamela took him home with her to her house. I didn't have the strength to object, so I just let him go. He stayed with his mother for a few days, while I took Christopher home to comfort him and try to pick up the pieces.

By October of that year, I was at the end of my tether, and I made the difficult decision that unless John agreed to seek the help he needed, I would have to leave him. I couldn't cope with this horrendous burden any longer. Telling John my decision, though, terrified me, not knowing how he would react to this news. However, to my amazement, he just said that if I wanted to go, then I should go, he didn't care; but he wouldn't let me take Christopher with me.

John said he wouldn't be going anywhere; he just wanted to stay in his Palace, and he didn't need me. His attitude added to the immense hurt I was already feeling — that he didn't care whether I was there or not. What had happened to my husband whom I loved so much and who had loved me in return? Somewhere along the way he had disappeared, to be replaced by this man who

I just didn't know any more and who didn't want to know me.

I told John I was planning to speak to a solicitor and seek some advice as to where we went from here. John's response was to tell me to please myself what I did, just let him know when I was leaving. With a reaction like this, I had to ask myself the question, "What on earth had I been fighting for during the past year if I meant so little to this man?" The decision was made, and I planned at the earliest convenience to seek advice and somehow move away and take Christopher with me.

However, before I was able to seek legal advice, disaster was once again destined to strike, and I was about to undergo the most horrific and terrifying experience of my life... so far.

Chapter 8

Whilst all this turmoil was happening at home, I was still continuing to run my dance school. It actually did prove to be a blessing. For those few hours each week, I was being provided with an escape, of sorts, from the hell I was living at home.

Through my dance work, I met a young man called Mark. He was involved in a production I did the choreography for, and we became acquainted during that. Mark then continued to take part as a guest artist in a number of productions I produced myself, and over a period of time we became very good friends. Nothing more than that; Mark was gay, and our friendship was therefore purely platonic. I was very fond of Mark's mother; a lovely lady who always made me very welcome whenever I visited. Sadly, she seemed unable to accept her son's sexuality and continued to try and bring Mark and I together in a romantic way. I will always remember Mark and his mother with great affection.

On the evening of 2nd November 1976, I was going out for a job interview. Mark was involved in a local production of the musical *Carousel*, and the company concerned was looking for a choreographer. Mark asked me if I would be interested in applying for the job. Of course I was, and Mark arranged to take me along to the rehearsal on this evening for an interview. He picked me up from home at about six thirty and off we set, leaving Christopher playing happily in his father's care in our part of the house, while my parents were downstairs in theirs.

I need here to remind you of the situation regarding our living arrangements. My parents, John, Christopher and myself had moved into a large house, which was two flats, one upstairs, one down, but there was currently only one front door. Once inside the front door, the staircase was situated on the right of the hallway and led directly up to our accommodation, while my parents had the rooms downstairs.

I thank God again that we hadn't yet completely separated the two flats by installing another separate front door. If we had done that, I wouldn't be here today to tell this story.

Mark brought me home after my interview, which I'm pleased to say was successful, and I was looking forward to starting work on the show. He pulled up outside our house at about ten o'clock and for some inexplicable reason an incredibly uneasy feeling came over me. I couldn't explain it, but something didn't feel right. I, therefore, didn't invite Mark inside, but thanked him for the lift and waved him on his way.

As I approached the front door, the inexplicable, uneasiness increased and I felt that something really was amiss. I turned the key in the lock to let myself into the house. A cold shiver ran through my body. I made my way upstairs, feeling nervous but not knowing why. I looked round the living room door to say hello to John and saw that he was sitting on the sofa cleaning his shotgun. This in itself was not at all unusual. John loved many country pursuits and would often go clay pigeon shooting with an uncle of mine, and therefore cleaning his gun was a perfectly normal occupation.

However, the sight of John calmly cleaning his shotgun while Christopher slept peacefully beside him on the sofa was chilling.

My tongue had turned to cotton wool, and my mouth was dry, but I forced myself to speak.

"What's Christopher doing here? He should have been in bed long ago."

John didn't look at me. He was examining the barrel of his shotgun intently.

"What do you think he's doing? He's ill. Leave him alone. Go to bed."

"Does he have a fever? Is he in pain?" I began walking towards the sofa. I needed to know that Christopher was all right. Perhaps that's why I felt so anxious when I arrived home. Maybe I'd instinctively realised that Christopher was unwell.

"I said leave him alone! Get out!"

My concern for my son gave me a brief moment of courage. Ignoring John, I bent over Christopher and put my hand on his forehead to check his temperature. It felt normal.

Instead of reassuring me, this made me even more worried. Something was definitely wrong. By now, a trail of sweat was trickling down my spine and my heart was thumping. I knew I should confront John and ask him what was happening. But I couldn't. I daren't. He was too volatile. Too unpredictable. He completely petrified me.

Satisfied, at least, that Christopher was okay, I decided to take myself off to bed. As I made the very brief three-second walk along the landing to our bedroom, I was shaking like a leaf, my heart pounding faster and faster. What was it that I was so afraid of? What was happening here? The feeling of impending danger was beginning to overwhelm me, as if I knew something was about to happen, but I had no idea what. Was this the latest brick in the wall which had by now grown so high in front of me, the wall which I now knew was not going to fall or disappear unless I completely walked away from it?

I went into the bedroom and before I had a chance to get beyond the side of the bed, which was facing me as I walked in, the door crashed open behind me with such force I physically jumped. There, stood John, shotgun in hand, pointed directly at me! The whites of his eyes appeared bloodshot and he stared wide, looking straight through me. His expression was completely blank, but piercing... piercing. Yet seemingly without seeing. So full of hate. I will never forget that look in his eyes at that moment. I was frozen to the spot where I stood; complete and utter terror enveloped my entire being. My worst fears were coming to fruition. I tried to speak, and after a couple of seconds managed to croak out, "John, what on earth are you doing? Put the gun down and…"

My words faded away as he interrupted me in a very cold, calculated tone. Whilst speaking, he continued to point the gun straight at me and yet stare straight through me with no emotion, except hatred.

"I'm… going… to… kill… you."

My adrenals kicked in and I realised in an instant that this man was deadly serious. He was indeed going to shoot me! This was crazy, like a horror film one would see on television or at the cinema. Things like this didn't happen in real life to ordinary people. But it WAS happening; this horror was actually happening, the culmination of a year of terror.

There was no use in pleading; I was faced with fight or flight. I realised in under a second that flight was not an option. I had to fight or… DIE.

Without thinking, I grabbed the barrel of the gun in an attempt to push it up and away from myself. I was pleading in desperation to John, "Stop it, please stop it! Let's talk!" It was to no avail. He tried to point the gun towards me, while I tried to push it up and away from me; but, of course, my strength was no match for his and I was failing miserably. In desperation, I screamed at the top of my voice, "Dad, dad, come quick, help me, help me, PLEASE!"

My father and mother instantly rushed up the staircase and along the landing towards us, immediately grasped the situation and stepped into the fray, also trying to relieve John of the gun. Our pleading was still to no avail. The four of us fought. Desperately we sought to prise his fingers away from the weapon. His strength was unbelievable. A man possessed.

At that point, amidst all that was going on, young Christopher, hearing the noise, awoke and ran out on to the landing. He screamed at the top of his voice, "STOP IT, DADDY! STOP IT! DON'T SHOOT MY MUMMY!"

My son's screams pounded upon my ears, while falling deafly upon his father's. Still the horror didn't stop. Christopher was crying and screaming in terror. Still, we fought on. Suddenly, I don't know how, my parents and I all lost our grip on the gun! John fell backwards into the bedroom and onto the bed. He immediately leapt up and slammed the door shut.

A second later... BANG! He had fired the gun. My parents and I froze for an instant. I then grabbed Christopher, who on hearing the shot had instantly stopped screaming. We thought that John had probably shot himself.

My dear, beautiful, brave father, who I owe my life to, then took control and commanded, "Stay where you are. I'll go in!" He pushed the handle of the bedroom door downwards and slowly opened the door wide, and there was John. He was standing on the far side of the bed, his back to the wardrobe, in which there was now a large round hole. He hadn't shot himself, he had shot the wardrobe! Before we had time to think... BANG! He fired the gun again, only this time he didn't shoot the wardrobe. He shot... MY FATHER!

The impact lifted him off the ground, carried him backwards through the air and he landed at our feet, outside the bedroom. There was a large, splintered hole in my father's stomach, from which blood was gushing out.

"DEAR GOD," I cried, "PLEASE MAKE IT STOP!" as John rushed round the bed towards us, still pointing the gun at me. As he reached us, my mother and I grabbed the gun and started to struggle yet again. Then my mother somehow, I think with God-given strength, managed to push John back onto the bed. My father, still bleeding profusely from his stomach, the insides of which were splattered on the landing walls, struggled to his feet and fell towards my mother and John, back into the fight. I watched my parents struggling with John, fighting for our lives. I listened to my four-year-old son screaming as he waded through pools of blood and body tissue. I prayed harder than I've ever prayed before.

At that point, the most amazing thing happened. A white mist suddenly enveloped me. I became completely detached from the horrendous scene unfolding before me. All I could feel was this warm, comforting, protective mist, and then suddenly... I heard a voice. It was the voice of a man; which I can only describe as velvet. The voice was so smooth, so warm, so soft, so kind and yet so commanding. I had to acknowledge what the voice said, and that was just four words. "GET... THE... CHILD... OUT!"

I was still frozen to the spot where I stood. The voice came a second time, stronger. "GET THE CHILD OUT!"

As the voice spoke a third time, I could do nothing but obey. I scooped Christopher up into my arms, fled downstairs and grabbed the receiver on the phone, which was situated on the hall wall. I dialled 999 for police and ambulance. As I was just about to replace the receiver, there was a loud CRASH, followed by the sound of splintering glass. It was my mother. She had somehow managed to get hold of the gun and, smashing the window at the top of the stairs, she hurled the gun out through it, into the garden below.

The next second John and my father appeared at the top of the stairs in a clinch, and then THUD, THUD, THUD, THUD, THUD, they tumbled together down the stairs and landed at my feet. John instantly stood up; my father did not. He lay motionless where he had landed.

"DEAR GOD," I said, "NO MORE, PLEASE, NO MORE! PLEASE, PLEASE HELP US!"

At that point, as my mother made her way downstairs towards my father, John took a step towards me. He looked straight into my eyes; no emotion, nothing. We stayed like that for a few seconds and then he turned away, opened the front door and ran out. I slammed the door behind him with such force it shook and thrust the bolt across it. I was shaking uncontrollably, my heart pounding so hard I thought it was going to burst, and yet I still gripped my son tightly to me.

Shortly afterwards, the police and ambulance arrived.

God was on our side that night. The ambulance crew that came — two fantastic men who saved my father's life — weren't, in fact, meant to be on duty that night. They were standing in for another crew, and it turned out that these two men had the previous week been on a course to study a new tourniquet system. By using the technique, they had learned on the course, they were able to stem the flow of blood from my dad's stomach. He had, however, lost so much blood — it was spattered on the walls, along the landing and down the stairs — that things were looking very bad. "Dear God," I prayed, from the very depths of my being, "please don't take this incredible man who has saved my son and I. Please, PLEASE let him live!"

My mother accompanied my father to the hospital, and I stayed behind and prayed while my father was in surgery. His heart did stop beating that night in the operating theatre. However, those brilliant, incredibly skilled surgeons brought him back, his heart started beating again, and he survived; he was very sick, but he was alive. God had answered my prayer.

Meanwhile, I had a young police officer being violently sick in my front garden, because of the horrendous site that greeted him on the stairs and landing of our house — blood and body tissue... carnage. Other policemen chased after John; while I was convinced, he was still coming to get me. I will never forget the immense kindness and consideration that was shown to me that night by two police detectives. They arranged for an officer to come to the house, the largest man I have ever seen in my life! The investigators said that he wouldn't leave my side and that nobody would get past him!

Of course, there was no way that John was going to get back into the house as it was surrounded by police, but I was so traumatised and frightened that I couldn't accept that I was now safe.

A short while later, one of the detectives and a policeman came into my parents living room where I was sitting. He said he had some news for me about John. He told me that he had been spotted running across a railway bridge, which was just around the corner from our home. The police had given chase and as they chased him down onto the platform, John jumped onto the railway line and was killed outright, electrocuted. When I heard this news, I replied, "Thank God. I'm so glad he is dead." What a dreadful thing to say, but all I could think was that he couldn't harm me any more.

Then the detective handed me the only cigarette I've ever smoked in my life. "Here, smoke this," he said, and I obeyed. I was on autopilot, robotic, following instructions without question. I became aware later that I was in complete and utter shock and at that time unable to really think for myself; I was quite happy to be guided.

The detective then asked if he could contact anyone to be with me, and following my response, he called my best friend Julie, and she was at my house within ten minutes.

Shortly after that, a police doctor arrived and suggested giving me a sedative, which I point blankly refused. I wasn't going to sleep until I knew that my father was okay. I felt such immense relief when my mother phoned later to say he was out of the theatre, was critically ill but, thank God, he had survived.

Christopher, however, had completely shut down. He was sitting on Julie's lap, motionless, not speaking, not crying, not doing anything, just staring straight in front of him. The police doctor told me that my young son was completely traumatised, and the advice he gave at that point in time was to try, God knew how, in spite of everything that was going on around me, to carry on as near to normal as possible with Christopher's daily routine. I was not to enter into any conversation with him about the events that had occurred that night, and if he asked any questions, I was to try to answer as best I could, relating to his age.

At about eight o'clock that morning, my grandfather arrived at the house; I think perhaps my mother must have called him. I remember I was sitting on the sofa; Christopher was still sitting on Julie's lap in the armchair by the fireplace, and all of a sudden, I started screaming. Screaming and screaming and screaming at the top of my voice, screaming until I thought my lungs would burst, screaming with fear and anger, with every fibre of my being, releasing the pain, hurt and fear of the last year, and then SLAP, my grandfather's hand made contact with my cheek. I stopped screaming and broke down in tears. I sobbed uncontrollably as my grandfather put his arms around me.

The police doctor was called back, and he gave me some Valium to help calm me down, and I sat in silence, a complete physical and emotional wreck.

Chapter 9

Once my father had been taken off to the hospital and I was told the news of John's death, there was nothing to do but sit and wait. Wait nervously for the news of my father's progress. So that's what Julie and I did, we just sat and waited. Christopher eventually fell asleep on Julie's lap, and I don't remember even speaking; we just sat in silence.

As John was now dead, none of the carnage that trailed through the house was needed as evidence. To my amazement, the two detectives who were at the house that night armed themselves with buckets of soapy water and set to cleaning the house. The bedroom, the landing, the stairs and the hallway, removing any physical evidence that would remind us of the horror we had just been part of. I had such respect and admiration for those men. To think that they would do that grim task so willingly to help me and for realising that no way could I have carried it out myself.

A short while later, when Julie and I were still just sitting, drinking tea and more tea, one of the detectives came in and said they needed to know if I thought John might have left a note.

"What sort of note?" I asked.

"A suicide note, perhaps," replied the detective. "A note of his intentions; anything that may throw some light on why he behaved the way he did."

I knew why he had done it. He was so sick and nobody could help him. It was the culmination of his desperation.

I had no idea whether there was a note or not, and so it was that a young police officer was instructed to search our bedroom for a possible note, and I was asked to accompany him while he searched through our drawers, cupboards, etc.

I filled with panic. "No way, no way am I going back up that staircase ever again!" I exclaimed.

The detective was sympathetic, but, unfortunately, I had no choice. "I understand how hard this is for you, Jessica but it is necessary. It would be most helpful if it could be done now, rather than later."

"Okay, I'll go and look," I said reluctantly, "but don't leave me!"

"Don't worry, Jessica; Gary here won't leave your side for a moment."

So I began, slowly, fearfully, creeping up the staircase. I insisted that Gary walked behind me, as I was afraid John was going to leap out at me from behind.

Such was my state of mind. I knew John was dead, but I still believed in some way he was there waiting for me.

I reached the top of the stairs and stopped. My legs had turned to jelly and fear swept over every part of me, as I was suddenly 'swept back' into the horror of a few hours before.

Gripping onto the bannisters for support, I gasped out loud as Gary took my arm. "Here, please let me help you."

With Gary's help, I moved very slowly along the landing towards our bedroom.

Breathing deeply to calm myself, I allowed my mind to tell me I had nothing to fear any more. Everything looked normal; there were no signs of what had happened just a few hours before. But then, on entering the bedroom, I saw the hole in the wardrobe door, and I realised I was still completely overcome with fear. I collapsed onto the bed, panting. Gary sat down beside me. "It's okay, Jessica, nothing can harm you now; just try to relax."

With my permission, Gary then started to look through the drawers of my dressing table, which was situated beneath the front window of the room, but he found nothing. He then moved to the tall chest, which stood by the bedroom door, and started to search through the drawers.

Please hurry up, I thought. I just wanted to get out of this room and back downstairs as quickly as possible so that my heart would stop pounding so fiercely.

As Gary opened the top left drawer and lifted a few of John's clothes, there it was, a long white envelope! I don't remember if there was anything written on it; I was too stunned, too shocked to take in what was happening.

"Do you know what this is, Jessica?" asked Gary.

"No," I gasped in reply. "Now can we please go back downstairs? I can't stay here a second longer!"

We made our way back downstairs, Gary behind me to protect me from who knows what — fear, memories. I didn't know; I just needed protecting.

Gary took the letter to his superior officer, while I went back into the living room. A few minutes later, the detective came in and asked if I would like to know the contents of the letter, which, of course, I did. John had intended that night to shoot me, both my parents and himself and leave young Christopher alive and alone!

As my jaw dropped to the floor, I thought, 'Dear God, what state must that man's mind have been in, to contemplate such an idea and then to leave our son alone in the horrific aftermath.' Why, oh why was his brain injury left undetected; why would he not accept help?

The letter went on to say those words yet again. "I can now go to my Marble Palace; there's nothing to stop me any more." I couldn't even begin to imagine what John was thinking or feeling.

It is only now, many years later, that I can acknowledge that poor John must have been in hell. I have, on investigation, learnt that during the car accident John sustained an injury to a particular part of his brain. This, in turn, had triggered off schizophrenia, and because John refused help the condition went undiagnosed.

Apparently, John's bizarre behaviour during the year preceding his death would to him have been perfectly reasonable. Tragically, because his condition was undiagnosed and untreated, it culminated in the horrific climax of the events of 3rd NOVEMBER 1976, a date that will stay etched in my mind forever.

John was not to blame for what he did; he was sick, very sick, and it's taken me a lifetime to realise this and be able to acknowledge and accept why what happened on that dreadful night… happened.

Chapter 10

Early in the morning, following the night of terror, there was a loud knocking on the front door and the sound of voices outside. It turned out to be journalists from the national papers. How on earth had they heard about us, and so soon? The police quickly sent them packing and told me that I was completely within my rights to refuse to speak to them. I didn't at that time wish to talk to anyone, least of all newspaper reporters.

I was behaving like a robot, completely non-animated, numbed with Valium and going through the motions of daily living, but not really being aware of doing it.

So, with Julie's help, I got Christopher ready and took him to nursery school that morning. Oh, how hard that was, how terribly, terribly hard, to let go of my son, to leave him. He seemed totally unaware that anything amiss had happened.

As we entered the nursery, he turned and hugged and kissed me goodbye, and off he went laughing with his friends as if the trauma of the previous night just didn't exist. He had completely blanked it from his memory.

As instructed by the police doctor, I briefly confided in the nursery supervisor what had occurred during the night and asked her to remove any toy weapons from the toy boxes, as apparently a visual stimulus at this stage may have caused unwanted difficulties for Christopher.

When the supervisor's jaw had been 'recovered' from the floor, she confirmed that, of course, the doctor's request would be carried out without question. She put her hand on my arm and told me to try not to worry; that Christopher would be watched very carefully, and if he showed any sign of distress emotionally or physically, she would call me immediately. So it was that, my heartstrings tugging, for all I wanted to do was hold my child close, Julie steered me out of the nursery door and took me home.

Julie took complete charge during the weeks that followed — a true friend. She shopped, cooked, organised, and moved me from point A to point B as required and back again. What I did, I did without question; I just did what had to be done, without any thought or feeling.

When we collected Christopher from nursery that first day, I was told that he had been fine, his usual friendly, cheery self. I was thrown into complete confusion; how was it possible that this little boy had completely erased that awful memory from his mind? I later learnt that sadly it had not been deleted, just hidden, too painful, too horrific to acknowledge. He had unknowingly hidden the horror deep in his subconscious. At some time in his young life, it had to resurface, but we would face that when it happened; for now, he was my same little Christopher. He bounded home happily, skipping along with Julie, while I followed slowly behind, struggling to make sense of any of this mess; totally unable to relate to this state of carefree happiness I was watching.

I felt as if I had a key in my back, a clockwork key that had been wound up to make me move, stiffly, one foot in front of the other. My eyes looked straight forward, not seeing, not thinking and not feeling, just robotically following instructions.

When we arrived home, and Christopher had had a snack and watched a cartoon on television, he suddenly turned to me and asked, "When's daddy coming home, mummy; is it time yet?"

Oh, dear God, I hadn't thought about this; I wasn't prepared for this. What was I supposed to say? I took Christopher to my knee, trying to control my body, which was shaking involuntarily, looked into his big, beautiful eyes and with my heart heaving up into my throat and feeling Julie's consoling hand squeezing my shoulder, I took a deep breath and, in a quivering voice, spoke.

"Darling, mummy's very sorry, but daddy won't be coming home any more."

"Why, mummy? Doesn't he like me any more?"

Oh, help me, I cried silently.

"Of course, he does," I replied. "He loves you very, very much, just as mummy does, but he can't come home any more because Jesus wanted him to go to Heaven and live with him. Daddy was so special that Jesus needed him."

"Can I go and visit him then, mummy?" Christopher asked. The innocence, the pure, sweet innocence coming from that child's lips.

"Not at the moment, darling, it isn't possible, but one day, one day you will see him again."

Imagine my complete surprise when Christopher jumped off my lap, said, "Okay", and went off to play with his toys. The easy acceptance of any given situation that children display continues to amaze me.

Christopher never mentioned his father again until he was about fourteen, but that's a story to be told further down the line. The only obvious factor which showed that something was amiss with Christopher was that from that day he refused to accept the colour red. If you showed him red, he would say it was green; and if he was, for example, painting a picture, and you suggested he used red, he would automatically use green. He saw both colours as green. Our doctor suggested that the sight of so much blood had terrified Christopher so much that he was unknowingly erasing red from his memory. Over time and with help, this problem did disappear, but it certainly endorsed the enormity of the horror my young son had endured.

It evolved that my refusing to speak to the press was, in fact, a mistake, as they had, I assume, talked to neighbours and written their versions of what had happened. I was painted as the scarlet woman who was out having an affair and had driven her husband in his misery to lose his mind and commit suicide!

How dare they? How dare they say these things when they had absolutely no idea of the facts? The hurt and pain they caused my family and me, on top of what we had just experienced, was totally and absolutely unforgivable. I hated them and have never since then and will never again read a newspaper as long as I live.

Chapter 11

In the days and weeks that followed, we began, with Julie's incredible help and support, to reclaim some kind of order to the family routine. My father was eventually allowed home from the hospital. A bed was set up for him in my parents' living room so that he could convalesce in comfort, surrounded by his family.

Christopher, my mother and I all slept together in my parents' bedroom. I could neither bear to be alone, irrationally fearing that John was still coming after me, nor could I contemplate setting foot upstairs again to my rooms. It was a different world up there, a world of fear, of horror, and the world that seemed destined to haunt me forever. I could not step back into that world. Therefore, we all lived together downstairs in my parents' part of the house.

My father slowly began to recover, although he was for the rest of his life destined to experience the pain and discomfort of the shotgun pellets which were embedded in his body. They would slowly work their way to the surface and he would feel the agony as the surface of his skin was broken and another pellet was released; another reminder of our night in Hell.

However, my inspirational father never once complained, and he never once blamed John for what had happened. He continually said to me that John was very sick, and the real John would never have intentionally harmed anyone.

In my mind, though, if he had written down what his intentions were, then he must have planned it, so how could I ever be expected not to blame him and go even further and forgive him?

I have such respect and admiration for both my parents for finding forgiveness within themselves so readily towards John for what he did, and that changed our lives so dramatically.

Again, I have later learned that he wasn't in control of his faculties at all and what made sense to him when he put pen to paper wasn't the true intent, not the John that we knew. It was the demon John that had put its grip on his mind and forced him to behave in the way he did.

I remember my dad asking me one day to do something for him; he said, "Jessica, please don't blame John, don't hate him; forgive him and remember him as he was." That was such a difficult request from my father. Here was a man carrying all the emotional and physical scars of what had happened, and yet he had the power to forgive, so why couldn't I? But I couldn't, at that moment in my life, I was filled with hatred. I couldn't forgive any more than I could begin to forget.

I then started to carry the guilt of what had happened to my father on my shoulders, and it didn't matter how many times my parents told me I wasn't to blame, I believed I was. If I had left John sooner, if I hadn't married him... if... if... if — so many ifs! However, I am older and wiser now, I hope, and I'm sure that the 'if game' is one we probably all play at some time in our lives. I couldn't have done anything to change what happened; I can see that now, but at the time and for many years after, all I could do was carry this heavy burden. My father was hurt and in pain and there was nothing I could do to ease his suffering.

My mother also suffered as a result of the shock she sustained. She had a mild heart attack, followed later on by a more serious one. She now lives her life as a sufferer of angina. My beloved parents who saved my son's life and mine were suffering and would carry these scars forever, and I felt that the blame rested entirely upon my shoulders. I wore the guilt like a heavy black cloak; two sick parents and a traumatised son, and all I could think was that I should have found a way to prevent it. After all, I introduced John into the family, so how could anyone else be to blame? To me, it seemed the guilt, the burden, the shame, were the punishment I should carry forever.

During the many conversations my dad and I had after that, he confided in me about an experience he had while in the operating theatre, and I would like to share it with you now. I'm sure many of you will have heard this before but hearing it from my father and the expression on his face while he was reliving his experience made it real for me and totally plausible and believable to this day.

My father told me that he suddenly felt very light and free, as if he was floating. He was totally free of pain, and it was the most incredibly joyful feeling. Suddenly, he felt himself being lifted, lifted higher and higher, and there below him was his body. He was looking down upon his poor damaged, pain-ridden body, but he didn't want it, he didn't need it. As my father floated higher and higher, he became aware that he was enveloped in a beautiful white light. He was floating weightlessly through a tunnel of light, in which he became aware of many more people doing the same thing, just floating, floating effortlessly along, people he knew, people he didn't know. All were moving along, heading towards a light that was becoming brighter and brighter as they progressed along the tunnel.

My father felt no fear, just complete and utter joy and peace. He described the light ahead of him like a magnet, pulling him towards it, giving him no choice other than to succumb. He didn't want to stop; he desperately wanted to reach the brightness ahead of him. Suddenly, he was there; he was at the culminating point of this exquisite, indescribable light. He reached for it; he wanted to touch it, but as he did, a hand appeared in front of him. He wanted the hand to beckon him; he wanted to go forward into the nucleus of this divine, comforting light, but he couldn't — the hand pushed towards him in a stop motion, and my father stayed still.

It was then that he heard the voice. When he described it to me, I knew exactly what he meant. The voice I heard while we were fighting John was the same voice, I believe, that spoke to my father. THE VOICE of GOD. "Peter," it said, "not yet, not now." It was with the most extreme reluctance that my father allowed himself to be sucked back away from this glorious light. He didn't want to go back, he wanted to go towards it, but he had no choice.

He woke in the recovery room of the hospital.

Slowly and very gradually, life in our household regained more normality. My father was recovering, albeit slowly, my mother eventually went back to work, Christopher carried on with his little life as if nothing had ever happened. Meanwhile, Julie had by now moved in with us permanently. Without her I don't like to imagine what would have become of us; she was marvellous.

We then reached the stage when it was time for me to go back to my work. Julie would put me in her car, drive me to the studio, where I would teach, and then Julie would drive me home, because that's what she said I had to do.

I have very little memory of the year following John's death; snippets here and there, but what I do recall is the first day I walked into the dance studio after being away for a while. I made my way slowly up the stairs, opened the studio door, my emotions all over the place. There was an element of comfort being back in this place I loved so much and yet at the same time I felt detached, I didn't feel as if I was completely here. Then I heard the voice of someone coming up the stairs. It was Jane's voice, one of the parents. Here she was, loyally bringing her children for their class, a few more children following behind her, and as they made their way up the stairs to the studio, I heard her say, "Now remember, be on your best behaviour for Miss Jessica, work hard and smile." How my heart went out to Jane that day; she was trying to bring some normality to my life. All the parents at the school were obviously aware of what had occurred because of the newspaper headlines, and Julie, who had been running the school in my absence, had also confided in them. Outside the studio door, more parents and children gathered; they were chatting, laughing, living.

I was in a bubble, and there was life going on outside the door, going on around me as if nothing had happened, nothing had changed. I wanted so much to be a part of that again, and yet somehow, I just couldn't seem to connect — life was continuing in front of me, and I was on the outside looking in.

Jane walked into the studio, came over to me, put her arms around me and enveloped me warmly. "Just remember," she said, "we're all here for you, we're all here," and then she turned and went. A feeling of intense love and care flowed over me. These people weren't judging me, as I feared they might. They were accepting me, supporting me. How blessed I felt at that time; I appreciate the tremendous love and support shown to me by these people.

The school was to be my escape from the hell that was revolving in my mind; the anguish, the fear, the memories, round and round and round, no stopping, no respite, continually haunting me. Here, with my work and my students, I could escape from my mind for a short time, even though I could never escape entirely.

So it continued. Julie took me to work, I taught, she took me home, where I carried on with my regular household duties. If, however, I was asked if I remember doing any of this afterwards, the answer would be no.

The most amazing thing of all is that later that year I produced, choreographed, designed costumes and did all the necessary things required to mount a large-scale production for my students. I did this, but afterwards I couldn't remember doing it!

It was only much later in life, through conversations with Julie and others, looking at photos, that snippets of memory started to return and are still doing so to this day.

Chapter 12

Although my father was recovering well, it soon became apparent that there was no way he was going to be able to return to the full-time employment he was in before the 'Accident', a name we chose for the devastating events of the night of John's death.

None of us wanted to stay in our house any longer, with all the ghastly memories surrounding us, so the decision was made that we would sell up and move on.

My parents and I, you may recall, loved North Cornwall, and so we decided that was where we would move to. It was to be a fresh start for everyone and a place to help my father recuperate. I, however, decided that, as much as I wanted to, I could not move with my parents on a permanent basis. I was not ready or able to let go of my dance school; it was my stability, emotionally and financially, and it was keeping me focused while desperately trying to get my life back on track.

I then made the hardest decision of my life. After much soul-searching, I decided that I was in no fit state, on my own, to provide Christopher with the care he needed at this time. I was struggling to function myself on a daily basis and couldn't yet take on full responsibility for giving my child the security he needed.

I therefore asked my parents if they would take Christopher to Cornwall with them; new environment, new start, secure surroundings, that's what he needed. On confirming to my parents that I was sure this was right for Christopher, they willingly agreed to take him. My love for him, more than for life itself, and wanting the best for him, to give him the opportunity to heal, were far more important than the pain and anguish I would suffer from letting him go. It paled into insignificance; I had to be strong to give my son a chance to recover.

Thus, with a heavy heart, I said goodbye to my parents and Christopher as they moved into a beautiful bungalow in a picturesque hamlet in Cornwall, with the most fantastic views from the lounge windows over the hills and moors of this exquisite part of England.

In the meantime, I moved into a shared flat in Sunbury in Middlesex.

I can still feel the pain of the night before they left, when I had to leave Christopher with my parents, ready for their move the next day. I couldn't bear to watch them drive away, so this seemed the best course of action. Christopher was very excited and happy at the prospect of living in the country, by the seaside. He knew that I would be spending half of each week in Cornwall with him and the other half in Sunbury, and he accepted this arrangement very readily.

As Julie and I walked away from my parents and Christopher that evening, my heart broke into a million pieces; I felt as if it was being wrenched out of me. Julie and I sat together on my bed that night, and I sobbed uncontrollably, as if my world was coming to an end, and in a way it was. I felt as if I was losing everything in my life that I had ever loved. I knew, of course, that I wasn't losing Christopher or my parents, and I still maintain to this day that the decision I made, in spite of a lot of adverse opinions, was the right one for my son. It was just so hard to bear.

It was Julie's strength that got me through that night. She agreed with my decision and I had asked her, under no circumstances, however hard I begged, should she let me change my mind, and she didn't.

A couple of times during that night I told Julie that I couldn't let Christopher go, but showing real strength and determination, she stopped me from running to my parents and bringing him back. She knew I would regret doing that, and I was so grateful for her resilience.

Christopher thrived in Cornwall with my parents; he started at the small, local village school, where he received a very warm welcome. He became great friends with a young boy (the community police officer's son!) of the same age, who lived in the same hamlet. My parents and Christopher embarked upon what turned out to be one of the happiest times of their lives. After school, they would often go to the beach or for a picnic, and Christopher also enjoyed helping the neighbours on their freeholding, spending many happy hours feeding the chickens and collecting the eggs.

I continued to try to rejoin the human race. I carried on working, and every Saturday evening after classes had finished, I would jump into my car and drive down to be with Christopher. There I would stay in that lovely environment until Wednesday morning, when, after taking Christopher to school, I would drive back to Sunbury in time for Wednesday afternoon's classes.

Life gradually became a little easier. I threw myself into my work, continued to visit Christopher and during the school holidays when the dance school was closed, I spent many happy weeks with Christopher and my parents.

While I was in Cornwall, in this sheltered, safe environment, immersing myself in having fun with Christopher, the horrors of the past year sank a little deeper into my hidden memory. Unfortunately, though, they never completely disappeared, always ready to creep up on me when least expected, triggered by the simplest of things. For example, seeing a programme on television in which someone may be holding a shotgun would send me into a panic attack. I would cry and shake and forcibly punch my cushion in anguish, as it seemed as if I was to be haunted by my past forever.

Chapter 13

Unfortunately, problems arose at my Sunbury flat, and I decided to seek alternative accommodation. It was while doing so that the next major trauma of my life occurred. I went to look at a room to let in a house in Chiswick. The room turned out to be very pleasant, as was the rest of the house, which I would have full access to if I took the room. The room was spacious and bright and very pleasantly furnished, and I felt sure I could be very comfortable here. Paul owned the property; he was a very personable young man, and after a second visit I decided to rent the room from him.

The evening came when I was due to go to the house to sign the necessary papers, make arrangements with Paul to move in and also meet the other tenant; another young woman who rented Paul's third bedroom.

On arrival, Paul offered me a glass of wine and apologised on behalf of Caroline, the other tenant, but she had been delayed at work and would hopefully join us soon. Looking back, I realise how vulnerable and naive I was, but at the time I was totally unaware as to what was really going on here.

Paul seemed genuine, and I felt very relaxed in his company. As we sat on the sofa, chatting and drinking our wine, Paul suddenly moved closer to me. Slightly perturbed, I moved away a little, but he still moved closer to me. I began to feel nervous and uncomfortable, but before I could say anything he was upon me, trying to kiss me. I was horrified and scared and tried to push him away, but to no avail. My pleas to Paul to stop were useless; he just ignored me.

All of a sudden there it was, again, that same feeling of fear flooding over me, sweat trickling down my back, my shoulders rising towards my ears, my heart pounding against the wall of my chest. What was I to do? I was helpless, no match for Paul's strength.

"No!" I screamed. "Stop, Paul. STOP!"

Ignoring my pleas, he held me down and with his full weight upon me I was completely helpless. In terror, I tried to scream, but no sound came out of my mouth, and as silent tears rolled down my cheeks... HE RAPED ME.

When his evil deed was over, he stood up, while I lay there sobbing uncontrollably, shaking with fear. As he adjusted his clothing, Paul just looked at me and said, "For God's sake grow up. What's the big deal anyway?"

I couldn't speak. I felt terrified, violated, humiliated and I just had to get away. As I stood, grabbed my bag and, still trembling, ran towards the front door, Paul called after me, "Oh, by the way, the room's no longer available."

I opened the front door, fled to my car and, trying to control my shaking hand, opened the door. I fell inside and locked it again, fumbled with the key in the ignition and as soon as it made contact and the engine fired, I fled.

I drove blindly, cursing myself. How could I have been so stupid? how could I be taken in so easily? But I was. Paul had completely won me over while taking advantage of my vulnerability.

On returning to Julie's, where I was currently staying, I scrubbed and scrubbed myself in the shower. I just felt so dirty, but I couldn't seem to wash away the vileness of this man's actions. I then climbed into bed, buried myself under the duvet and I was transported back to our Hounslow house. John, the 'Accident', the fear and terror once again crushing me, mingling with the new emotional pain of what had just happened. I cried myself helplessly to sleep.

I just wanted to die, to escape from this hell which had become my life. I never told anyone, except Julie, about the rape, and in spite of her pleadings, I would not inform the police. I still felt humiliated, violated, dirty and foolish, but I couldn't go there again, facing the police, the questions, and the stigma. So, I kept my silence, but my faith and trust in men was completely shot to ruins.

Chapter 14

I had for a while now been doing the choreography for a local Operatic Society in Twickenham whenever they produced shows. I sometimes performed in the shows as well. It was here, during one of their productions, that I met Daniel. He was playing the part of Jud Fry in *Oklahoma*, and during a ballet sequence we had to dance together. The dance scene led to us getting to know each other better and eventually we started dating, somewhat tentatively on my part, as I still wasn't able to put my trust in men and couldn't see myself ever doing so again. Daniel, however, seemed to accept my tentativeness and never questioned me. He was great fun to be with, and we enjoyed each other's company.

Daniel was born in Yorkshire, beautiful dale country, and when he took me to visit his parents, who still lived there, I was able to appreciate the sheer beauty of this part of our country. I have always preferred bleak, rugged countryside to pretty green fields, and the dales, like Cornwall, offered this in plenty.

On one occasion Daniel came down to Cornwall with me to holiday with Christopher and my parents. He was attentive to Christopher, which pleased me tremendously. He would willingly play with him —

football or cricket on the beach — and seemed to enjoy doing so, which, of course, Christopher loved, and we all had a very enjoyable time.

My relationship with Daniel, however, eventually ran its course. I was afraid of getting too close to anyone, and so we mutually went our separate ways, but we had had some fun together, and he had helped me to smile again. I will always remember my time with him with fondness.

In 1980, the Operatic Society staged the musical *Camelot*, and apart from doing the choreography, I was asked to dance the part of Nimue, a water nymph. Every Wednesday evening, I would go along to rehearsals, accompanied by Julie, with whom I was still currently living.

One particular evening, as we walked into the rehearsal room, my eyes were drawn to a very handsome man whom I had not seen before. It transpired that his name was Michael, and he was playing the part of King Arthur. I was somewhat smitten, and later in the evening, on learning that he had enquired as to who I was and whether I was unattached, I admit to having felt quite flattered. I also learnt, though, that on discovering I was the choreographer, Michael wondered whether I could actually dance the steps, as well as choreograph them.

On the evening in question, I was, at the producer's request, planning to dance my Nimue solo. Right, I thought, I'll show King Arthur!

After changing into my dance gear, I proceeded to perform, and as always, on hearing the music, I was swept away to that magical place I loved so much and danced as if my life depended on it.

Michael apparently turned to Julie and said, "Wow, she really can dance!"

After the rehearsal, as was the usual routine, we were all in a bar, drinking and chatting, when Michael approached me. We started talking, and before we parted that evening, he had invited me out for a meal. He told me a while afterwards that it was the lilac pencil skirt I was wearing as I walked into rehearsal that first caught his eye!

I felt very excited, in a way I hadn't felt for a long time. I was looking forward to our date the following evening, and when it came about, I wasn't disappointed. Michael took me to a restaurant in Hampton and was the perfect gentleman. He opened doors for me, pulled out my chair and made me feel rather like Royalty. I felt very comfortable and at ease in his company. Conversation flowed smoothly between us, and before we parted that evening we had learned quite a lot about each other.

Michael was an only child, he was ten years older than I was, which at the time didn't present any problem for me, and his parents lived in Gloucester. He had his own business, which appeared to be very successful. The theatre was one of his primary interests, and I thought it marvellous that he had this in common with me. I was also fascinated to learn that he had been treading the boards in Amateur Dramatics, acting and singing, since the age of thirteen.

The thing that pleased me most of all was that on learning that I had been married and had an eight-year-old son, Michael didn't turn and run, as many men would have done; instead, he asked about him with genuine interest. Christopher was my life, and no man was going to come between him and me, and at that time I felt that Michael understood this and respected my feelings. I had a lovely evening and accepted the offer of a second date without hesitation.

Michael lived in a picturesque cottage set in woods in Ottershaw in Surrey, and on our second date I went to his home for dinner. For some inexplicable reason, I felt completely confident in doing so; I didn't feel at all nervous or threatened by him. Was I beginning to regain some trust in human nature?

I recall Michael had prepared a delightful chicken casserole, and as we ate, drank wine and chatted, I felt very calm and at ease. Perhaps, I thought, this was a sign that I was beginning to move on with my life. Michael and I continued to see each other, both at rehearsals and outside of them, and soon became a couple.

I quickly learnt that he was an incredibly skilled actor and singer, culminating in him being a tremendous success as King Arthur.

During the years that followed, I continued choreographing many shows, and Michael would invariably have been playing the principal male role. Tevye in *Fiddler on the Roof*, Henry Higgins in *My Fair Lady*, Robert Browning in *Robert and Elizabeth* and Emile de Becque in *South Pacific*, to name but a few, always performed with great skill, finesse and success.

Chapter 15

Life was, at last, beginning to move in the right direction for me, but unfortunately my parents were encountering problems. They were still really enjoying life in Cornwall, and for a while my father had been doing some light work again, which had provided them with financial stability. However, sadly the work dried up, and nothing materialised for either of my parents. Regretfully, the eventual outcome was that they had to sell their bungalow and move back up country. Although they were very sad that this was necessary, my parents were nevertheless happy that they had enjoyed the last few wonderful years in the West Country. They handled things in a very pragmatic way, a skill I am pleased to say they passed on to me and which has helped me tremendously in dealing with the many difficulties life has thrown at me.

Christopher took the move in his stride and saw it as the next exciting adventure in his life.

My parents and Christopher moved to a new house in Finchampstead in Berkshire, and I was thrilled to be able to move back in with them and be with Christopher permanently again. We all settled happily into our new home, and it thus followed that I introduced Michael to my parents and Christopher.

Initially, Michael and Christopher seemed to accept each other very readily, and as time progressed, Michael began to take Christopher and I out together.

I recall on one occasion the three of us went to a funfair. We had a splendid time, but what sticks out in my mind was Michael's attire that day. In an attempt, I think, to appear cool, he dressed in jeans and a denim shirt, which was open from just above the waist, and around his neck he wore a large gold medallion! Although far away from his usual style of dress, I thought he looked great. However, in later life, on being reminded of how he dressed that day, poor Michael just cringed in horror!

On moving to Finchampstead, I started teaching dance on a couple of afternoons a week at a local primary school situated literally a few minutes' walk from home. It was ideal, and I thoroughly enjoyed these classes. In fact, one of the young children I taught there also joined my school in Richmond. Sandra had a medical condition which made movement difficult for her, and medical opinion was that dance would help to keep her mobile. Her very dedicated mother, Joan, drove Sandra up to Richmond a couple of times a week to attend my classes, and Sandra positively thrived. She continued at my school until early adulthood, when, on marrying, she moved away and the journey became impossible. I developed an extreme fondness and respect for Sandra. She always worked so hard, in spite of her difficulties, enjoyed everything she did, and her ultimate achievement was performing in a group ballet dance in one of the school productions, wearing Pointe shoes on her feet. I remember shedding tears of joy as I witnessed the sheer grit and determination of this girl.

However, Sandra leaving my school didn't mean the end of her connection with it. Right up until I retired in 2003, Sandra, her lovely mother Joan and a friend of theirs whose daughter also attended my school, worked tirelessly backstage at every performance. They would drive up to Richmond so they could dress and chaperone the children, making sure they had everything they needed. Their help was invaluable, and I will always remember them with tremendous affection, gratitude and love.

Sometimes while I was teaching at Finchampstead, Michael would come over with his red setter Oscar, collect Christopher from home and they would take Oscar for a walk together or sometimes play football on the school field. On occasion, they would press their noses against the windows of the school hall, where I was teaching, and pull strange faces. The children in my class thought it hilarious, but I would send Michael and Christopher packing, pretending to be cross, while also smiling!

As time passed, my affection for Michael grew, and I fell deeply in love, something I thought I could never imagine happening again. He was very generous and affectionate, and his acceptance of Christopher was the icing on the cake.

One evening while Michael was visiting and my parents had gone off to bed, Michael produced a small box containing a ring, held it out to me and proceeded to propose to me! I was so excited, completely swept up in the moment, "Yes," was my reply. "Yes, yes, yes!" I realised this is what I wanted, a new husband who I loved and who loved me in return, security for Christopher and myself, a future that looked full of promise. In that moment I was so happy!

In the spring of 1981, Michael and I were married in a beautiful, small country church in Eversley in Berkshire. Christopher made a charming pageboy in his bottle green Edwardian suit. His smile was a picture, as he was, in his own words, "Getting a new daddy today."

My sister Joanne, my sister-in-law Louise and her young daughter Mary, who were my bridesmaids, wearing long, pale green dresses and straw hats, accompanied him.

My car came to a halt outside the church, and I gleefully watched as some of the guests strolled down the path. They were all chatting and laughing, and my excitement on this day's wonderful occasion heightened. Everyone seemed to be feeling the joy that this day was bringing — my wedding day.

The sun was shining high in the sky as I walked down the pathway to the church, feeling like a princess in my exquisite Edwardian ivory wedding dress. My father, looking very debonair in his grey top hat and tails, escorted me proudly towards the church, my arm affectionately linked through his. I offered up a silent prayer. "Thank you, God, for my wonderful parents, without whom I would not be here now, beginning life anew."

We entered the church, and my eyes beheld Michael waiting for me, looking incredibly handsome in his morning suit. He turned and smiled at me, and my heart melted. I was convinced that this was indeed the beginning of a new start in life for Christopher and myself.

One particular highlight of the ceremony was when a close friend of Michael and me sang 'Ave Maria', a song we both loved. As her exquisite voice rang through the rafters, I felt goosebumps down my spine.

After the church ceremony, we held the reception at The Hawley Hotel in Blackwater. The grounds here were so beautiful that this was where we had the photographs taken with all our family and friends. Then followed a delicious meal — avocado prawns, chicken wrapped in bacon, and, of course, wedding cake! Amongst family and friends were Julie and some of my most senior students from KAPA This felt so relevant that they were here supporting me. My work had kept me going through many tough times. We spent many hours that evening dancing, listening to music and socialising with our guests.

Michael and I then left to begin our honeymoon together. As we drove away, I looked back and waved at everyone with an enormous smile on my face. I settled back into my seat, feeling relaxed and safe for the first time in a very long time. I glanced across at Michael, who turned and flashed me a loving smile in return, and my heart overflowed with happiness. We were starting off at the beginning of our new adventure together.

Chapter 16

Michael and I honeymooned in the beautiful Highlands of Scotland, staying in some amazing venues and having a grand time together. On the drive to Scotland, we stayed overnight at an impressive Country House Hotel and stayed in the bedroom that William Shakespeare slept in. It was a lovely room, full of character, with original oak panelling around the walls and even a four-poster bed. On arrival, champagne and flowers awaited me, and I felt so happy and hopeful.

During the evening, an extremely amusing, but at the time very scary, thing happened. I had slipped out of our room and on my return, Michael was nowhere to be seen. I thought this very strange as I hadn't passed him on my way back from the hotel reception and couldn't think where he could have gone. Suddenly, a voice called my name, and I realised that Michael was hiding from me, somewhere in the room.

"Jessica, are you there?" the voice spoke again, and on looking around the room and not finding Michael, I began to panic. What started out as a joke suddenly became quite serious. I was sure I heard Michael's voice, but he was nowhere to be seen! I was spooked, and I started shouting for him, when bang, the wood panelling on the wall by the bed suddenly slid open and out stepped Michael! He had found a secret passage and was hiding in there. I laughed and cried at the same time, and I think I actually punched him for scaring the life out of me!

Another unusual and absorbing place we stayed at was historical Borthwick Castle. The place was a castle in the true sense of the word and having always had an interest in historical buildings and the stories surrounding them, I was thrilled to be staying in such a beautiful place.

The 1st Lord Borthwick built the twin-towered fortress of Borthwick Castle in 1430 as a stronghold for withstanding attacking invaders, particularly the English. King James I, had awarded Lord Borthwick a charter to build the castle as thanks for his assistance in bringing the King back to Scotland, after being imprisoned in England for eighteen years.

The castle had enormous walls, which were twenty foot thick at the base and over a hundred foot high, and originally there was a moat, drawbridge and portcullis.

As Michael and I approached the castle, the first thing that caught my attention was a large cavity in one of the external walls. I was filled with amazement and anticipation to discover how this had occurred, and also what we would find once inside.

The first surprise was when a small gentleman, who was huddled over and dressed in black, opened the heavy black door which made up the entrance to the castle. Michael and I found his appearance rather strange, but nevertheless he greeted us warmly and showed us into the Great Hall.

Wow, what a sight greeted us! The room was so vast and high, and at the far end, to our left, was a wonderfully large, hooded fireplace. Suits of armour stood in great alcoves on either side of the fireplace, and there were sofas and armchairs arranged around it. At the opposite end of the room there was a minstrels' gallery, to the right of which was a winding stone staircase.

The gentleman who had welcomed us invited us to sit by the fire, and he would serve us tea. As we sat, my eyes still taking in this amazing place, my mouth still open in wonder, our host disappeared behind a black curtain situated opposite the entrance door.

Without being disrespectful, I must confess that Michael and I likened him to a member of the Addams Family!

When he returned with our tea, I couldn't wait to question our host. We learnt that the damage to the outside wall had occurred when Oliver Cromwell had laid siege to the castle in 1650. Cromwell, on accusing the ninth Lord of Borthwick of harbouring people responsible for the murder of his men, offered Borthwick the opportunity to walk free from the castle, thus relinquishing it to Cromwell. Lord Borthwick didn't respond immediately, and therefore Cromwell bombarded the castle, destroying the east parapet and tearing the large cavity in the wall. Lord Borthwick did then agree to leave the castle with his wife and child, and Cromwell took up residence.

We also learnt that the castle had played host to various historical figures over the years, the most fascinating being Mary Queen of Scots, whose bedchamber we were to be staying in!

Our host then proceeded to inform us that the castle was haunted and that we were the only guests currently staying there. Help, I thought, I'm not so sure about this latest information, and as we climbed the spiral staircase, I felt a strange cold sensation running through my body, which wasn't at all a pleasant feeling. This moment turned out to be the start of the development of sensitivity and susceptibility to certain energies I have gained over the years.

As we entered Queen Mary's room, it was fantastic to be standing where she had stood, but when I moved to the area by the window, I experienced the same cold feeling and was quite perturbed by it. My emotions were all over the place; the thought of sleeping in the Queen's bed was thrilling, but at the same time I experienced inexplicable feelings of reluctance.

Michael and I then decided to explore the rest of the castle, which turned out to be as fascinating as what we had already encountered. While moving through the remainder of the rooms, I felt perfectly comfortable and was filled with fascination; it was just like stepping back in time. However, on entering the Red Room, with its red-flocked walls, four-poster bed and heavy red velvet curtains, I again felt cold and unsettled.

We returned to our room to dress for dinner, and as Michael was ready before me, he asked if I minded him going down to the hall to have a drink before dinner while he waited for me. Of course I didn't mind, but as soon as Michael had left, I felt very uncomfortable. I didn't know what I feared, but it certainly felt as if I wasn't alone in the room. Feeling vulnerable and totally inexperienced in matters relating to the paranormal, I dressed at breakneck speed and proceeded to join Michael as fast as I could. I hurried down the spiral staircase, cold flowing over me again while I looked over my shoulder; how I didn't fall and break my neck I don't know!

On joining Michael in front of the glorious fire, my fears quickly subsided. We were served a fabulous dinner in the Great Hall, just the two of us, feeling like Lord and Lady Borthwick. Michael, I recall, ate venison, and I ate veal. Our host, it appeared, was also the cook, and an excellent one he was, too!

As we left Borthwick the following morning, in spite of my strange experiences I was elated at having been to this marvellous place and was so grateful to Michael for having brought me here.

The rest of our honeymoon continued happily, as we travelled further north, enjoying lovely walks through the Highland heather and visiting the Isle of Skye, which was, at the time, covered in mist!

Unfortunately, during the last couple of days it poured with rain incessantly and so we decided to return home early, a decision that was to lead me to do something I will regret for the rest of my life.

It had been arranged that when we returned from honeymoon, Christopher was to come and live with Michael and I in Michael's cottage in Ottershaw. Christopher was as excited as I was at the prospect; he was coming to live with mummy and his new daddy, and it was to be the next great adventure in his life. Little did we both know at that time how very wrong we were.

My mother had arranged to go away on a mini-break to Amsterdam with Louise's mother Phyllis, with whom she was great friends. While they were away, we were to collect Christopher, with a view to lessening, albeit a little, the wrench she and my father were going to experience. Having had Christopher living with them for four years, it would be hard that he was going to be moving away from them.

On our journey back from Scotland, Michael suggested we should collect Christopher on our way home that day, two days earlier than planned. Initially, I was reluctant, thinking that we should keep to the arrangement, but Michael, I soon learnt, could be incredibly persuasive.

His opinion was that he was still my son, and I should be able to do as I wanted. True, but I felt I had given up that right when I asked my parents to take Christopher after John's death. However, Michael was excited and adamant; he couldn't wait to settle his ready-made family into his home. I understood that I also was excited at the prospect of Christopher and I being together again in a loving, secure environment. Becoming so swept up in the joy and emotion of what was to happen, I became blinded to the reality of what we were planning to do. I therefore conceded and gave in to Michael's wishes.

When we arrived at my parents' home, my father and Christopher were there, while my mother was still at work. We explained to my father why we were back early and that we would like to take Christopher with us. Once again, my father was incredible. He could see how excited Christopher was and therefore made no objection. I know now that he was keeping his true hurt feelings to himself. So we left with Christopher and a few of his belongings, the rest to be collected later, and headed home to Ottershaw.

Christopher telephoned my mother that evening; he was so bright and cheerful, and my dear mother was wonderful and shared his excitement with him, as he told her about his new bedroom. Nevertheless, she was so angry with Michael and me. She was angry because we had taken Christopher before the agreed time, as while she was away on holiday, she was hoping to prepare herself for the fact that when she returned Christopher would be coming back to me. Imagine how she felt when, on returning home from work that evening, she discovered he had already gone.

When my mother spoke to me, it was like a cold slap of reality hitting me. What had I done? How could I have been so selfish to have committed such a cold, insensitive act? How could I not have even considered how my poor mother would feel when she arrived home from work to find Christopher gone? She wasn't going to feel our elation and excitement. All she was going to feel was the pain, the calculated coldness of what we had done, the pain of 'losing' a child, and who better to have understood that feeling than myself.

My elation quickly disappeared. I was angry with myself for listening to Michael; I was mad at Michael for his suggestion in the first place, and yet I couldn't express that anger. I realised that I couldn't tell Michael how cross I was and that what I wanted to do was take Christopher back to my parents for another two days. I knew that was totally impractical because Christopher wouldn't understand why. Why was I unable to express my feelings? Why couldn't I say that I disagreed with what we had done?

Slowly, realisation dawned on me. I was afraid to get angry; I was scared to make Michael angry. During our courtship, I had witnessed Michael's anger on a couple of occasions, but nothing major, so I told myself that everyone gets angry sometimes, and that's a normal, healthy thing if the anger is controllable. But not for me; I couldn't do anger. I had already experienced with John the devastating effects of extreme violence, and no way could I risk making

Michael angry to the extent when, in my mind, I didn't know what might happen.

I must point out that in no way did I at any time liken Michael to John. John's actions were the result of a mental condition; Michael was perfectly healthy both physically and emotionally.

However, I had to acknowledge that I was afraid, afraid of anyone getting angry, and, closer to home, afraid of Michael getting angry.

So I kept quiet. I apologised to my parents for my actions and gradually things settled down. I hope that over time they have been able to forgive me, but to this day I still can't forgive myself for the dreadful thing I did to them.

Chapter 17

Michael, Christopher and I settled down to life in our new home. Christopher enrolled at the local school, and I thought that life had turned a corner and things were looking promising.

Soon after Michael and I married, I fell pregnant. Although not planned, we were elated. We both wanted another child to join our family and a brother or sister for Christopher.

However, during this pregnancy I was extremely unwell, continually sick and exhausted much of the time. This, in turn, began to add to the pressure that was already building at home.

I became aware that, previously unbeknown to me, Michael's business wasn't flourishing in the way I had been led to believe, and he was experiencing problems. He had tried to keep this from me, to save me from worrying, which, of course, I understood and appreciated. On reflection, though, when it's obvious that something is amiss, and you don't know what, you begin to worry regardless. Furthermore, Michael had to help out a lot at home because I was so unwell, and so the pressure he was under was exacerbated.

Michael became very irritable, short-tempered and intolerant, and although I understood the reasons why, it didn't make it any easier to accept or live with. Things gradually got worse, and Michael started to become impatient, not only with work and general problems, but also with Christopher.

One day, Christopher was laying the table for dinner and he was trying to fold napkins in a way that Michael did. He was struggling, understandably, as it was something new to him, but instead of simply helping Christopher with the task in hand, Michael snatched the napkins and proceeded to fold them himself, while asking Christopher if he was entirely stupid! Wow, where did that come from? Frustration rose up inside me, my skin bristled and prickled, I felt the hairs stand up on the back of my neck; he had no right to speak to Christopher like that. I desperately wanted to tell him so, and yet I couldn't; if I said anything, I would risk increasing Michael's anger and making things worse.

My mindset was that anger resulted in sheer devastation. I believed that speaking up to Michael would make him angrier, and if he became more inflamed, what was going to happen? After all, look at what happened to John. I hugged Christopher, telling him I also found it challenging, and with regards to Michael, I kept silent.

As the weeks turned into months, I was still very unwell; Michael was becoming angrier and intolerant, and I was beginning to realise that there were two completely different sides to him. Concern grew, as I hadn't been aware of this before we married. It rather reminded me of the nursery rhyme, 'There was a little girl who had a little curl, right in the middle of her forehead; when she was good, she was very good, but when she was bad, she was horrid.'

Life became like this now with Michael. When I saw the Michael I had fallen in love with, he was kind, loving, and generous to a fault. Life felt wonderful. I was able to forget the bad times very easily. Conversely, the other side to Michael was horrendous. He was angry, unpleasant; he would throw objects in temper, and above all he was frightening. I hated it. This wasn't how it was meant to be; everyone has a few bad times, of course, but we were experiencing far too many.

Christopher had now started to withdraw into himself, although I admit that I was slow to acknowledge this at the time. I so desperately wanted things to work that I didn't allow myself to see everything as clearly as I should have done. Christopher would come home from school and instead of spending his time with Michael and me, he would go straight to his room and play by himself. It was so hard and confusing for me, but also, I realise with hindsight, for Christopher. One day Michael would take Christopher out with our dog Oscar and play hide and seek, build dens in the woods or play football with him. The next day, Michael was ranting and raving. How was a child supposed to understand that?

Michael loved and still does love sailing, and so he thought he would introduce Christopher to this activity. He gave Christopher a little mirror dinghy — as I said, generous to a fault — and my parents and I would go along and watch them sail. Materialistically, Christopher and I wanted for nothing, but this wasn't really what we so desperately needed. We lacked consistency, a daddy and a husband who we understood.

One Sunday morning, Michael and Christopher were preparing the dinghy's sail for their afternoon sailing trip. Michael went down to the newsagents to buy a newspaper, leaving Christopher to finish what needed doing to the sail. I was inside the house when Christopher came in, looking very tearful and upset. I asked him what was wrong, and his reply knocked me for six.

"Daddy told me to finish the sail, and I don't remember how to do it. Please help me, mummy; I don't want to make daddy cross."

Dear God, I thought, what on earth is happening here? The penny suddenly dropped. Not only was I afraid to anger Michael, so was my son, but he was also walking on the same eggshells that I was!

I took a deep breath and told Christopher that I didn't know how to help him, but he wasn't to worry. I would explain to daddy, and he could show him again, so Christopher disappeared up to his room to await Michael's return.

When he did come back, things didn't go as I had hoped. On discovering that Christopher hadn't finished the set task, Michael turned to me.

"What is your son, an imbecile, or what?"

I felt as if something had pierced my heart. How could he say such a wicked thing? How dare he speak about Christopher like that; how dare he? From somewhere deep down inside me, due to the sheer injustice showed to my son, I found a voice, a very small, nervous voice, but nevertheless a voice. I told Michael that he shouldn't be cross with Christopher, and I wouldn't accept him insulting him in the way he had. Why couldn't he just help him, and however frustrating that might be, show him again how to prepare the sail?

I was shaking, I was scared. Michael proceeded to call Christopher downstairs, told him to go outside and wait, and Christopher obeyed, moving like a pre-programmed robot, utterly devoid of emotion, just following instructions without question. I wanted to scream and shout, I wanted to shake Michael and make him realise what he was doing to us, but I couldn't; it was already bad, and I couldn't risk making it any worse. For Christopher's sake, I once again withdrew into myself and stayed silent. Michael went outside and together they completed the task. Before we went off sailing, Michael did apologise for what he had said, but even so, he was still angry and so was I. The damage had been done; another layer of hurt and disappointment added itself to the already growing ball of desolation which was growing inside me. I felt isolated, hurt, let down and above all scared, scared of how this was all going to end.

When we arrived back home, Michael's demeanour changed. He fixed us all a drink, and we sat down together chatting and laughing, and he played rough and tumble with Christopher as if nothing negative had occurred earlier. This was lovely; this was what I so longed for. When moments like this happened, I did what had by now become second nature to me — I pushed away the memories of the Michael I disliked and soaked up the times we had with the Michael I loved.

I was in turmoil, very confused, but still determined that things would change for the better. I loved this man so much, and if love can conquer anything, then surely it would go some way to solving our problems.

Chapter 18

On 21st December 1981, after a very long and arduous birth, our son Nicholas came into the world. He was born prematurely, being about six weeks early, and although small, he was perfectly healthy and beautiful, with a mass of jet-black hair. Worth every minute of the hard time he'd given me!

My labour was very long and after about thirty hours the midwife popped out for a cup of tea, telling me not to do anything while she was gone! However, I wasn't able to oblige; it was at this moment that Nicholas eventually decided to make an appearance and Michael caught his head in one hand while pressing the emergency call button with the other.

We were overjoyed, and Christopher held his new brother so tenderly and looked at him with such love and affection, I thought this was the best Christmas present ever. Once again, my thoughts were filled with joy and hope.

I returned home with Nicholas in time for Christmas, but only just. Following a substantial snowfall, it was impossible to get the car out of the track leading from our cottage to the main road. My brother-in-law Ben kindly came to assist, and he and Michael had to dig a passage out so that I could be collected from the hospital.

Christopher was playing Father Christmas in the school play and my mother-in-law, Dora, made him a beautiful costume to wear. After the play, Christopher proudly showed off his collage of the nativity, made from different coloured tissue paper, which was displayed on the school wall. Incidentally, over thirty years later, I still have this and display it with immense pride every Christmas. I felt happy. We had a quiet, but enjoyable family Christmas; things were going to be okay, or so I thought.

My happiness lasted until New Year's Eve, when I suggested to Michael that we invite our parents over to spend the evening with us, which he agreed to. As we waited for our parents to arrive, Michael became very quiet and subdued. He poured himself a drink and sat silently in an armchair, without having lit our open fire, which he usually did in the evenings. I asked him why he hadn't done this, and his reply was that it wasn't cold so he wouldn't bother. Usually, this would not deter him, as it made the room cosy and I thought it would be very welcoming for our parents, but to no avail; he didn't light the fire.

Our parents arrived, were warmly greeted by Christopher and me, but Michael completely ignored them! We all sat down in silence and, feeling extremely embarrassed, I tried to start up a conversation while thinking, 'Why hasn't Michael even offered anyone a drink?' The atmosphere could have been cut with a knife.

After a short while, it was my father who took the initiative and approached Michael.

"Is it okay to make everyone a drink?" he asked.

"Fine," Michael replied, without even looking up from his drink.

Dad proceeded to do just that and made us all a drink. Some host Michael was turning out to be!

Following a very awkward hour, during which Michael still hadn't spoken, my father suggested that he and my mother should make a move to go home, which they promptly did, with Michael's parents following close behind.

I felt awful, awkward and embarrassed; the evening had been a total disaster. I asked Michael why he had been so rude and inhospitable, and he told me that he had wanted to spend New Year's Eve alone with Christopher, Nicholas and me and not with our parents. Why on earth didn't he just say so? I might not have been particularly thrilled with his request, but at least the dreadful evening we had just been through could have been avoided. Michael and I didn't speak for the remainder of the evening, but by next morning he was his usual cheerful self again and I was expected to brush the unpleasantness of the previous evening under the carpet as if it hadn't happened.

Michael wanted me to breastfeed Nicholas; he was adamant it was best for him, and, of course, in theory I agreed. I am sure many women understand that in practice it isn't always so easy.

Nicholas cried continually before and after he was fed, and I began to suspect that he wasn't getting enough milk from me. But because Michael so wished it, I continued to try feeding Nicholas myself. One morning, when the health visitor came to see how we were doing, she looked at me (Nicholas was still screaming) and told me I looked exhausted.

"Are and you Nicholas sleeping okay?"

"No, we aren't," I replied. "He continually wants to feed and won't settle."

On learning that I had, in fact, just fed Nicholas before her arrival, she took complete control of the situation. "This is ridiculous," she said. "I know you want to feed him yourself, but this child is hungry!" So, without any hesitation, she produced a carton of formula and proceeded to give it to Nicholas.

I watched as he gulped the milk down and then — peace, silence, he had stopped crying. I placed him in his cot, and he slept! After that, even Michael had to agree, albeit reluctantly, that Nicholas needed to be bottle-fed. He became a far more contented baby, but even so, Michael's mood changes still continued.

One day he was lovely, the next he would fly into a rage over what seemed the smallest thing. When Michael was in one of his rages, that feeling from the past came back to me. I started to shake; sweat trickled down my back; intense fear enveloped me, but of what,

I didn't know. I just felt that I should keep the peace and not make matters worse by adding fuel to the fire.

One of Michael's outbursts, which scared me more than any other, occurred at a time when we were both involved in another Musical Production, *Robert and Elizabeth*, in which Michael was playing Robert Browning, the poet. While we were at rehearsal one evening, Michael went over to his leading lady and kissed her on the neck. I was young and naive, and I didn't like this. A peck on the cheek I could handle, but I felt this contact too intimate. I nervously ventured to tell Michael this later and he said I was ridiculous, there was nothing at all in it, that he and Paula were just good friends. I realised afterwards that I was rather silly, and I didn't have any cause for concern. At the time I was feeling very unsettled and confused because of our situation at home and feared anything that could potentially threaten Michael's and my relationship.

On the day of the final performance, Michael turned up at lunchtime at KAPA, where I was teaching that day, and presented me with a beautiful new outfit to wear at the performance that evening, and he reiterated that my concerns over him and Paula were completely unfounded. I felt great; I had my lovely, kind Michael back that day and I looked forward to the evening performance with pleasure.

Michael, as always, played his part superbly and I must admit, so did Paula. However, when at a certain point in the show the two of them had to kiss passionately, I dissolved into feelings of self-doubt again. I knew I was irrational, but I couldn't help it. I couldn't bear seeing Michael in that situation, when at home that type of intimacy was becoming more infrequent. I felt threatened.

As he drove us home, following the after-show party, I told Michael I had enjoyed the show very much, and he was superb as always. I then retreated into silence, my thoughts whirling around in my head. Michael's enquiries as to whether I was all right were answered with, "Yes, fine, thank you", even though I wasn't. I couldn't tell him what I was really feeling; I didn't want to risk making him angry.

Michael persisted. "For God's sake, Jessica, what is it? You look so miserable and you've hardly said two words since we left the show."

"I told you I'm fine." I didn't have the courage to tell Michael what was wrong with me, as I feared his reaction.

"That's great," he yelled at me. "You seem hell bent on spoiling my evening…"

"I'm not," I interrupted, but Michael just continued his verbal onslaught.

"You're so selfish! I'm sick and tired of this; just bloody well tell me what's going on!"

Michael was becoming more and more irate and as I tried to sink lower into my seat, he screamed louder into my face.

"Michael, keep your eyes on the road, you're scaring me!"

"Good," came his reply, and he accelerated even more.

"Okay, Michael, I'll tell you, just please slow down!" He looked so angry and I was shaking in fear, afraid of Michael and afraid of dying in a car crash. "I just found it so hard to see you kissing Paula so passionately in the show; it made me feel insecure."

"I was acting, you stupid bitch. How many times do I have to tell you? There is nothing going on between Paula and me!" Michael was screaming so loudly now that I just wanted to open the car door and jump out. I so desperately wanted to get away from him, but I had to finish what I needed to say.

"If it was only in the show, it would have been all right, but you do tend to flirt with Paula during rehearsals and…"

"You fucking stupid bitch! I'm not taking any more of this. I'm warning you, you've pushed me too far."

He completely lost control of himself and proceeded to drive home at breakneck speed!

I was absolutely terrified. "Michael please stop, you are scaring me. You are going to kill us both!"

"I don't care!" he screamed with rage and continued to drive like an absolute maniac.

How we made it home safely I don't know but thank God we did. Michael skidded the car to a halt, leapt out and kicked his door closed with such tremendous force that the glass in the window shattered!

Please, no, I thought, as it hit me again, the fear, the shaking and trembling as the tell-tale sweat trickled down my back, the enveloping terror of the unknown outcome of anger.

Michael stormed into the house, fixed himself a drink and flopped down into an armchair, face like thunder, while his parents, who had been babysitting, realising something was amiss, left quietly. They, too, were afraid to intervene.

I was shaking like a leaf; I didn't know how to resolve this terrible situation. I just quietly took myself upstairs, looked in on the boys, who were both sleeping, and then, climbing into bed, I buried myself under the duvet, trembling with fear as I drifted into a restless sleep.

The next morning, Michael gave me the silent treatment, while he banged and crashed around the house. His parents were coming to lunch, and I was feeling very anxious as to how he would behave. Dora and Joseph arrived and Dora, who I was very fond of and got on well with, joined me in the kitchen to chat as I prepared lunch. Joseph joined Michael, who was still in a bad mood, in the lounge.

Dora, having picked up on the atmosphere, insisted on knowing what I was wrong, and as began to tell her what had happened the previous evening, Michael suddenly stormed into the kitchen. "What the hell are you doing? Keep your mouth shut!"

"Your mum was just asking me if I was okay."

Michael suddenly threw his arms across me and pushed me against the kitchen cupboard. Holding me there, his arm across my throat, he continued to yell at me.

"Don't involve my parents, you fucking bitch!"

"Joseph, Joseph!" Dora screamed for her husband.

Joseph hurried to her aid, a look of horror on his face. "Let her go, Michael," Joseph commanded.

Michael ignored Joseph and continued to pin me against the cupboard, anger oozing out of every pore of his body.

I was unable to speak, overcome with terror that he was going to strangle me.

"Let. Her. Go." Joseph stepped in to break Michael's hold on me. Michael released me, but he was still wild with anger. Through sheer temper, he ripped the two cupboard doors from their hinges and threw them forcibly into the back garden! He followed the doors outside and remained there, I hoped to calm down until lunch was ready.

After I had stopped crying and shaking, I attempted to serve lunch, which, although Michael joined us, was eaten in complete silence. As I was about to clear the plates away, the room suddenly started spinning; I felt very dizzy and the next thing I knew, I was upstairs in our bed. Apparently, I had fainted, and Michael had carried me upstairs and put me there. I got myself up, aware that the house was completely silent, and started to make my way downstairs, noticing en route that Nicholas was in his cot and Michael was in his upstairs office. Where, I thought, was Christopher? I soon found out.

Michael's parents had gone home, and my dear, sweet Christopher was still sitting at the dining table, sitting in silence, looking down at his hands, which were clasped together in his lap. He must have been so frightened when I fainted. How long, I wondered, had he been sitting there? How on earth could Michael have just left him there in that situation, left him to soak up the anger and traumatic behaviour he had earlier witnessed, without any comfort or consolation? The answer was beyond me.

What was happening now? What was happening was that my eyes were beginning to open; I was starting to look beyond the rose-tinted glasses and see what was going on around me. I was afraid of my husband, and it was heart-breaking to realise that so was my son. I immediately comforted Christopher and then together we started to clear away the dishes.

Later that afternoon, Michael reappeared and offered to make me a cup of tea and started chatting to Christopher as if nothing untoward had occurred. I was then, as had become the pattern, completely swept up in the feelings of joy and contentment I felt when Michael was displaying the wonderful loving person he could be.

I wanted these moments to become our reality, happiness and peace, with the bad times being isolated incidents. Sadly, it was the wrong way round; for us there was too much misery with pleasant interludes occasionally slipping in. How could I possibly go on coping with this erratic behaviour?

Christopher was unhappy, I was unhappy, I suspected Michael was also unhappy; I had to do something.

Chapter 19

Often, we hear of, or are made aware of, invariably through the media, many cases of domestic violence, be it physical or emotional. I must confess, and I'm sure many of you would also, to failing to understand why the aggrieved party tolerates the behaviour which is unacceptable to them and doesn't just simply walk away from the situation. Now I do understand. If you love someone in the way that I loved Michael, you so desperately want the relationship and the family unit to work. An image forms in your mind of how you want things to be, how they should be.

Over time you begin to believe that if you want it and keep trying hard enough, everything will come right in the end. This longing becomes so overpowering that you continue tolerating what you feel is unacceptable, because of an overwhelming conviction which keeps telling you that things will change, what you desire will come to fruition.

Now, many years later, I am aware of the sheer naivety of that belief. I realise that for a negative situation to change, the root problems of that negativity must be addressed to promote improvement, it doesn't just happen by itself.

But I was so young, so vulnerable, I had been through so much and so desperately wanted, needed my relationship with Michael to work, that I eventually began to switch off from what was going on around me. I tried to focus on what I wanted, convincing myself that if I believed hard enough things would improve, and I began to allow the negative issues to become an accepted part of everyday life.

When Michael was calm and happy, we had enjoyable times together as a family; but sadly, it never lasted. Michael's intolerance and anger would rear its ugly head, often over something quite trivial, and I would then usually withdraw into myself, trying to keep the peace, rather than anger Michael more, in an attempt to protect the boys from these unpleasant experiences. On occasions when I did speak out, Michael and I would invariably enter into very heated arguments. Michael seemed to think he was always right, but deep down inside me I would always be trembling and erring on the side of caution for fear of pushing Michael too far. The sad and simple truth was that I was afraid of him.

I was also afraid of the effect that his mercurial behaviour and the all too many arguments were having on Christopher, who was becoming more and more withdrawn. I feared that Nicholas, who although far too young to understand what was going on around him, must have sensed the stress and unhappy atmosphere when things weren't right.

While I was struggling to find a solution, an incident occurred which gave me the answer to my dilemma, but unfortunately also forced me to make the second hardest decision of my life. One day while we were at home, Michael working and I going about my daily routine, we received a phone call from the head teacher at Christopher's school. Apparently, Christopher had been fighting. I was completely taken aback; this was so hard to believe, being completely out of character for Christopher. I was in a state of shock, stunned, trying to absorb this extremely disconcerting news.

While I was trying to make sense of what was happening, Michael sprang into action and hastened to the school to discover what had occurred and brought Christopher home. When they arrived home, Michael ordered Christopher to go to his room and told me that he had indeed been involved in a fight at school, and such behaviour could not go unpunished. Before I could ask any further questions, Michael rushed upstairs, put Christopher over his knee and spanked him. As I ran upstairs, I heard Michael hit Christopher four times.

I reached Christopher's bedroom and screamed at Michael, "What the hell are you doing?" How the words came out, I don't know. I stood looking at this angry man and this bewildered child. He had hit my child. Caution was thrown to the wind, and I vented my feelings without any thought for the consequences. Michael pushed past me, hurried downstairs and out of the house. Confusion then enveloped me. While I comforted Christopher, he was apologising for getting into trouble and thus making Michael angry, but no one had stopped to listen to his side of the story. He was being goaded at school and had indeed retaliated, but he hadn't started the fight.

Instead of finding out the facts first, Michael had reacted like a bull in a china shop, leaping into action, invariably causing devastation along the way, and the result being a dreadful mess left in his wake to be cleared up. Sadly, this was something that Michael often did, acted before giving a situation due thought and consideration.

A couple of hours later, Michael returned. I froze as I heard him open the front door, not knowing what to expect. However, he came in, went straight to the kitchen and made us all a cup of tea. He lifted Christopher onto his lap and started to speak to him. He told Christopher that he had spanked him because it was unacceptable to fight other children and it mustn't happen again. Christopher nodded acceptance and then Michael hugged him.

My mind was whirring, my emotions all over the place. How can a man change so dramatically? How can he be so horrible one minute and so loving and caring the next? No sooner had this incident passed, than another phone call came from Christopher's school. He had allegedly hit a girl with a roller skate. How, what, why? A million questions reeled around my head. Why was Christopher rising to the bait and getting involved in these incidents at school?

Later, I understood what the answer was. It was a cry for help from Christopher; he would rather receive negative attention than no attention at all. He was feeling swallowed up in this mess of a family. The new daddy that he had looked forward to having, with joy and happiness, hadn't turned out how he had hoped. Instead, the good part of his new daddy was heavily overshadowed by his anger and intolerance, and his mother was weak and afraid, and all Christopher could do was cry out for help in the only way he knew how. I told Michael I would go and collect Christopher, but before I had a chance to get my car keys, he had rushed out of the house, leapt into his car and proceeded to speed off down the driveway, leaving a trail of flying gravel in his wake.

Nicholas started crying, and as I prepared his feed, I was aware that my hands were physically shaking, as was the rest of my body. As I sat in the dining room, feeding Nicholas, my heart pounding, I couldn't stop shaking; my palms were soaked in sweat as I struggled to hold the bottle to Nicholas's mouth, and pure terror enveloped me. What was going to happen, what was Michael going to do now?

As Michael and Christopher arrived back home and Michael flung open the front door, it was evident he was in a rage. He ordered Christopher to go upstairs and remove his lower clothes. Oh no, no way was this going to happen again. Christopher turned at the top of the stairs and asked whether Michael meant just his trousers or his underpants as well. Michael's reply was both. My eyes still fill with tears when I remember the picture of that innocent, frightened little boy, knowing exactly what Michael was going to do to him. I immediately tried to reason with Michael, suggesting we should sit and discuss what was happening. I wanted to try and calm him down and hopefully defuse the situation. However, Michael was deaf to my pleas. With anger flowing from every pore in his body, he ran upstairs to Christopher's room. "No, Michael, stop!" I pleaded.

Where the strength and courage came from, I don't know, but I did know that I had to stop Michael somehow, and I leapt into action. I quickly put Nicholas in his bouncy chair and ran upstairs after Michael. As I did so, I heard his hand make contact with Christopher's bare skin, once, twice, and as I reached the top of the stairs, he struck Christopher a third time. Christopher screamed, as I fell into his room and yelled at Michael, "Stop, stop it now!" The scene before me will remain with me for the rest of my life.

Michael froze, his hand in mid-air, about to strike again; Christopher was lying over Michael's knee, sobbing, and the green valance that draped around the base of Christopher's bed was wet with urine. Pain and fear had made Christopher urinate!

"Let him go!" I yelled, and Michael stood up, released Christopher and ran downstairs out of the house. I was crying, downstairs Nicholas was crying, but young Christopher was silent. As I hugged him to me, he spoke, "Please don't cry, mummy. I promise I won't be naughty again and make daddy angry."

I told him that this wasn't his fault and that I would ensure that it would never happen again. As I helped Christopher to dress, I was horrified to see the marks on his buttocks where Michael had hit him so hard that the skin had been broken.

How dare he, how dare this man do this to my son? "I hate you, Michael, I hate you, you cruel, insensitive BASTARD!" But my words of anguish didn't reach Michael; he had already left the house. Dear God, how could I have let this happen, how had it come to this? Wasn't it bad enough that Michael had emotionally abused Christopher since we married, and now he was abusing him physically? I put every ounce of trust in this man; I placed my child in his care, and he had let me down, really let me down; but, more importantly, he had let my son down. My emotions were in overdrive. This man, who I loved so much, had hurt my son and in doing so had hurt me so, so deeply. How would he have felt if someone had done the same to a child of his?

I took Christopher downstairs, lifted Nicholas out of his chair and as I sat in the armchair hugging my children to me, I vowed that never again would this happen to Christopher. Whatever it took to remove him from this nightmare, I would do it. As I sat there, motionless, with the boys held tightly to me, I knew what I had to do — I had to remove Christopher from this unsafe environment.

Once again, my world was crashing down around me. Everything I had hoped and dreamed of had been destroyed in one cruel blow, quite literally, when Michael hit Christopher. I will tolerate a lot of things and cope with many burdens put upon myself, but nobody harms my children in any way and gets away with it. My sons are my life, and my life is dedicated to their safety and wellbeing.

I am not saying for one minute that Michael intentionally set out to hurt Christopher. However, he was obviously unable to control his anger and therefore I could take no more chances where Christopher was concerned. Who knew where it might end?

I firmly believed that Nicholas was in no danger from Michael. He was Michael's biological son, and he had the same sense of protection towards Nicholas as I had to both my sons; I knew he was under no threat. However, Christopher was.

I made the decision for the second time in my life to ask my parents to take Christopher back into their home. There was no way that they could accommodate Christopher, Nicholas and myself in their beautiful but small cottage, and as I had nowhere else to go and no money of my own, I accepted that Nicholas and I would have to stay with Michael and Christopher would have to leave.

Before I had the chance to approach mum and dad, fate stepped in and lent a hand. On the Wednesday evening of that week, Michael and I went to rehearsal for the show we were currently involved in, leaving the boys in my parents' care at our home. When we returned home, the air could have been cut with the sharpest of knives, as my mother opened the front door, before we had even put the key in the lock.

"How dare you?" she cried. "How dare you?" She was enraged, and as my father tried to calm her down, he suggested we sit and listen to what they had to say. While we were at rehearsal, my mother had, as usual, prepared the boys for bed. After settling Nicholas, she went into the bathroom and chatted with Christopher, which he enjoyed, while he soaked in the bath.

As Christopher went to step out of the bath, mother passed him a towel, and in doing so she noticed the marks on his buttocks where he had been hit. She was horrified and on asking Christopher how it had happened, she learnt that Michael had inflicted it. Full of outrage, she said she was going to take Christopher there and then and report Michael to Social Services for child abuse. My father stepped in and advised remaining calm for the boy's sake. Although also furious, he was able to be less emotional and accept that what had happened, although unforgivable, was not necessarily done with malicious intent. He was aware that if a report was made to Social Services, there was a strong chance that Christopher and also Nicholas may be taken away from us. I explained to my parents that I had already decided to ask them to take Christopher back.

Mother was so angry with me for not speaking up before, and therefore the decision was made that the next morning I would pack up Christopher's belongings and take him to live with my parents for the second time.

After I had left Christopher at their house the next day, I drove to a local wood and parked the car. I sat there, alone, and completely crumbled. My heart felt as though a thousand knives had been thrust into it and broken it into a million pieces; my body was wracked with emotional pain. I shook uncontrollably as I sobbed for my son. I wanted him, I wanted him so much, but I couldn't have him, not if he was to be safe and happy. "Why, God, why? Haven't I suffered enough? First John and now this, losing my child?

"My poor Christopher, why did he have to suffer so, to witness that horrific night his father died and then to suffer abuse at the hands of his stepfather? He's just a child! Why, God, what on earth were you thinking?"

At that moment I was so angry with God for allowing these atrocities to happen to Christopher. I had failed my eldest son; I hadn't seen just how unhappy he was. How could I have been so blind? He'd been taken from the security of his grandparents' home with the promise of a new life with mummy, a new daddy and his baby brother. What he got was a stepfather who hadn't had any previous experience with children or had any idea how they behaved. Of course, I don't blame

Michael for this lack of knowledge, but one can learn, and, unfortunately, everything had to be done Michael's way, whether he was right or wrong.

Instead of the new family life that Christopher was promised, what came to fruition was a stepfather who was incredibly intolerant of anything that Christopher did that didn't come up to Michael's exacting standards. His new daddy was often infuriated, and his mummy was a walking wreck. The emotional torment that Michael inflicted upon Christopher and therefore me was totally unacceptable and unforgivable, but nevertheless still doesn't equate to the sheer disgust I feel at the physical abuse that Michael inflicted upon my innocent child. I felt as if I was in a suffocating, dark void, with no way out of this new hell I was forced to live in.

Would Christopher ever be able to forgive me for not being able to prevent the dreadful experiences he had suffered? Would he ever be able to understand why I sent him back to live with his grandparents? Would he ever accept that it was not a case of choosing between him and Michael? There was no choice; Christopher had to go, but I couldn't, it just wasn't a viable option. I did what I had to do, what was right at the time, and I pray that now, much later in life as Christopher raises his little daughter, he will understand what real love for a child is. Yes, I made many mistakes along the way, but everything I did, every decision I made, I made through love for my child.

In time, my parents began to understand, not necessarily accept, but figure out why I hadn't spoken of the problems before, why I wanted to be with a man who could behave like this. The simple truth was that I had nowhere else to go. How was I supposed to survive with a young baby on my own? Putting this aside, God forgive me, but a part of me still loved Michael. How, why? I don't know; I just did, and therefore I couldn't just throw everything away and voluntarily subject Nicholas to an unstable and unpredictable future.

Most importantly, I now knew that Christopher was going to be safe and happy with my parents, and perhaps with not having to worry about Christopher's safety on a daily basis, things may even begin to improve at home. Maybe, Michael might calm down, maybe. Who knows what the future had in store, but at this moment I had to be content in knowing that Christopher was safe; Michael couldn't harm him any more.

A number of people, so-called friends, berated me for my decision to 'give Christopher away'. "How could you give up your son?", "You should be ashamed of yourself" were some of the comments I had to bear. However, it didn't matter what other people thought; they were, after all, in no position to judge — unless you have personally experienced something, you can't possibly understand and therefore have no right to throw stones.

I love my children more than life itself; I live for their happiness. I gave Christopher to my parents as an act of pure, unconditional love. As long as he was all right, my feelings didn't matter; they paled into insignificance, and they are a cross I bear willingly forever for the sake of my son, a cross of guilt I bear to this day.

Having said that, I need to stop the story for a moment and let you, the reader, know something. I am sitting with my son Nicholas, who is now thirty-five years old and amazingly helping me with this book. He has just read and edited this chapter and raised issues I am now sure you the reader also feel. I am not ashamed to say he brought me to tears, and we had a heated chat about parts of this chapter and others, and we both feel I need to go further in explaining to him and you what I find so hard to explain.

Nicholas in no way blames me for anything that happened to him, and I know full well, despite being an amazing, headstrong young man, he is emotionally scarred deep down and today has a very poor relationship with his father. However, he still wants an answer as to why I remained with Michael for so long and put us all through so much.

In his words, "Mum, I don't blame or hold it against you in any way, ever! No one, not even your children, can judge or understand fully that part of your life. You were young, naive, in an impossible situation. You wanted desperately to have a family unit, more so for me after losing your first husband and Christopher. You wanted it to work so badly that you felt you had to stay with Michael and make it work. I get this, mum; I know that you would do anything for your children, and you did what you thought was best at the time for all of us. I love you for that; I respect you for that, and I will never hold it against you.

"However, reading this book again and helping you edit it, you have to know this morning I am pissed off at you! Having said all I have just stated, I still can't see how it took so long for you to realise enough was enough. Why did you not leave sooner? Did you not see it was affecting me mentally, in a different way to the physical abuse Christopher had faced? Why would you go back to a man that could hurt you so much? Was it not worth the risk of going it alone with Christopher and me? Why didn't you?

"I need to understand what you thought then and how you think now. I feel you owe it to your children and your readers to try. So I am going for a coffee, and you have to write again. I know it hurts, and you find it impossibly hard to reason out what happened forty years ago, but tough, mum, get on with it!"

My son has spoken, so here goes. I can't give a one-sentence answer to this question, as there isn't one simple reason why I stayed with Michael. All I can do is try to offer some reason behind the choices I made.

I spoke to Sarah, my counsellor, after asking myself the same question many years ago. She explained to me that it is very common, although somewhat inexplicable, for some people, more often women, to stay in an abusive relationship, even when they know it is wrong. Firstly, there is an inbuilt conviction, which, if you want something to succeed and you keep trying hard enough, you will eventually achieve the result you desire. Very often this isn't the case, but it nevertheless remains an involuntary belief that you can't let go of. This does, of course, offer some explanation why so many women — and some men, of course — stay in abusive relationships. Even though you know you should walk away, a reflex message in your brain keeps telling you not to. Tomorrow or next week or next month may be the day when everything changes for the better.

I have recently read four books, all with a common thread running through them — stories of women living in various abusive relationships. In all cases, these women knew that they should have walked away, but none did so. They all believed that things would change for the better. Interestingly, in all of these stories, staying in an abusive relationship proved to be the wrong decision.

I had already had one disastrous marriage resulting in the death of my husband and me living away from our son. I dreaded history repeating itself. I didn't want Nicholas to be the child from another broken marriage; I wanted him to have a normal family life. So deeply did I desire this for him, that I was blinded to the fact that the chance of achieving it was virtually impossible.

Secondly, when you are in an abusive relationship, your partner dominates you. You know this is happening but are powerless to change it. If you speak out or stand up to your spouse, you are afraid this will ignite their temper, so you spend your life trying to keep the peace. This doesn't mean that I never tried to stand up for myself against Michael, but when I did it always produced a negative result. Look at the time, for example, when I spoke out after his show and almost got myself killed for it!

Finally, there is that unyielding emotion of LOVE. I was a vulnerable young woman, recovering from a traumatic past, that had been given a second chance of happiness. We all crave to be loved, and I selfishly wanted this also. I desired security, affection and attention. When Michael wasn't in one of his rages, he gave me this. This made it even harder to walk away. If you truly love someone, it is like having a magnet deep inside you that continually attracts you to that person. It is such a wonderful feeling that you don't want to destroy by breaking the magnet. It, therefore, becomes a head versus heart battle. Your common-sense head, is telling you to go, to walk away. Your heart, supported by the innate sense that things can change, is telling you to stay.

In many relationships, including mine, you do find the strength to walk away, but the pull of the magnet is so strong you then find you can't function away from the person you are being drawn to. This often results, as in my situation, in couples separating and reuniting a number of times.

If I had had my sixty-three-year-old head on my shoulders forty years ago, I would be telling an entirely different story now. What I didn't see at the tender age of twenty-three, that is now with age and wisdom, staring me in the face, is that I was, even though perhaps not intentionally on Michael's part, being played.

By being so kind and loving to me after one of his outbursts, Michael was in effect emotionally blackmailing me. "If you leave, look what you'll be missing; my behaviour isn't that bad, is it?" You then start to question and doubt yourself. Is our relationship so bad; is our family life so terrible?

The answer today is emphatically YES! However, forty years ago, being in a completely different place emotionally, nothing was so clean cut and dried.

I thought that the right thing for Nicholas was to try and create the 'perfect' family environment. How very wrong I was. I desperately wish my eyes could have been open then as they are now. I failed to see that in my effort to give Nicholas what Christopher had been so cruelly deprived of, I, in fact, ruined Nicholas's childhood. I was blind to the fact that emotionally he was becoming deeply scarred by the environment he was living in. Because Nicholas appeared to be a happy and outgoing child, I didn't question that he may not be feeling this way inside.

Indeed, he wasn't. It breaks my heart to make this discovery. While I was doing what I thought was the best, I was, in fact, doing the worst. I can't justify my inadequacy any other way than the reasons I have stated already. Today I can look back and see that the fears stopping me leaving Michael could have been overcome. I anticipated being homeless, but wisdom tells me that surely Nicholas and I could have found a couch somewhere within the family. I couldn't work longer hours as I had Nicholas to care for, but my family wouldn't have let us starve. The irrational fears and concerns of a twenty-three-year-old seem so easily resolvable with age and wisdom.

However, there was one major concern; the one above all others that kept me with Michael. He threatened that if I left him, he would take Nicholas from me. He made it quite clear that he was prepared to fight tooth and nail through the courts to get Nicholas. His ammunition was that I had no permanent home, no means of supporting Nicholas, and the worst thing of all — I was an unfit mother. I still have a letter he wrote containing many lies about my inabilities to be a good mother to both Christopher and Nicholas. What defence did I have? How was I supposed to win that fight? I was certainly prepared to try, but knew that if I lost the fight, I also lost Nicholas. No way was this man having my son. I would suffer anything to prevent this happening. Tragically, my decision resulted in Nicholas having a dreadful childhood, but I truly thought it was better for me to be in that childhood completely, rather than risk being pushed away.

How I wish I had been able to rationalise things better then and see what I can now so clearly see.

Having said all this, everyone has his or her limit. After varying amounts of time, sometimes, as in my case, many years, the pattern you have become so used to changes, quite involuntarily. The simplest of actions can, in a reflex action, change your mindset. It's as if a blockage has lifted from your mind and the reality before you, becomes clear. This is when one usually receives the message in the brain that "Enough is enough".

Next, the guilt creeps in, and you become aware of what you didn't see before. You realise how your choices and actions have affected those around you; in my case, my sons. I still stand by my decision that it was right to place Christopher in my parents' care, even though losing out on him growing up and being with him is the price I will always pay for this action.

Nicholas, though, is a different story. I now see that I got it so wrong. Any life away from his father, however hard that life would have been, would have been the better decision and would have spared Nicholas the terrible scars he now carries as a result of my decision.

I can only reiterate that I did what seemed right at the time. I now understand that my decision was wrong for Nicholas. However, I still stand by my main reason for making it — I could not risk losing him to his father or the care system.

There are no right or wrong answers. Until one is faced with a situation, it is impossible to judge whether the actions a person takes are the correct ones or not.

My children always were and always will be my priority and reason for living. Perhaps Nicholas is right; maybe everything would have worked out all right if I had walked away when he was young. I don't know. All I do know is that I have to live with that decision, and one of my biggest regrets is the scars my son now bears because of it.

I will ask you to close your eyes, try to imagine having lived my life and formulate your views on this.

I won't ever be able to dispel the guilt I have over the wrong decisions I made, but at the time they were made out of love and the perhaps naive belief that I was doing the right thing. People have tried to tell me I have nothing to feel guilty about, but they are wrong and are not in a position to say this. The guilt I carry is the price I must pay for the bad decisions I have made, and it is only right that I carry this for the rest of my life.

I can't turn back time and change my sons' childhoods, but if I could I most certainly would. All I can do is offer Christopher and Nicholas, and later my third child Oliver (not yet in my story), my heartfelt and sincere apologies for all they have suffered and hope that one day they may be able to find some understanding and eventual forgiveness.

Chapter 20

I left my parents' house, drove my car to the woods and cried until I could cry no more. I was completely spent; there were no more tears left to cry. I was exhausted, drained of all energy. I felt empty.

As I arrived back home and opened the front door to let myself in, Nicholas started squealing with excitement. My heart overflowed with love for him, as I picked him up and smiled back at him. At this moment, I began to understand how my life was now going to be. I would be living two separate lives, one here with Nicholas and Michael and the other entirely separate with Christopher, on the occasions that I was with him.

I tried to throw myself into my new life, determined that something good had to come out of all the misery that had gone before, but it was so hard. A chasm had opened between Michael and myself, a chasm that could never be bridged; a line too far had been crossed.

When times were good, and Michael, Nicholas and I were having fun together, I would allow myself to be totally absorbed in the moment, and all the bad would disappear, and I would feel relaxed and happy. Sadly, it was short-lived; involuntary thoughts would invade my mind. "You have no right to be happy, and neither does

Michael; after what has happened all you deserve is misery" or "Christopher wasn't happy, why should you be?" were the type of thoughts that would confront me.

I was in turmoil and decided to confide in my mother; I desperately needed some help. Her advice was incredibly wise. Nothing could change what had happened, and therefore I had to learn, however hard, to accept the hand I'd been dealt. I had to build a life with Nicholas and Michael, give it my all for Nicholas's sake. The pain I carried inside, I would have to bear silently; there was no choice. Berating myself and denying myself any pleasure was a pointless exercise. I had to focus on my new family, safe in the knowledge that Christopher was going to be okay and devote myself to 'the family' I was with at the time. If I didn't, then Nicholas would also begin to suffer, and that was unfair and unnecessary. I returned home, feeling far more hopeful — it was almost as if I had been given permission to try and move forward, to be entitled to enjoy the good, to lessen the burden of enduring the bad.

Consequently, I tried, really tried to pick up the pieces and move forward. The pain of Christopher not being with me never went. It was a physical gnawing pain, always there, ensuring I never forgot the dreadful atrocities he had had to bear. I don't think Michael will ever understand the pain and misery his actions caused, the debilitating agony of losing a child.

Life gradually settled into a pattern; it was like a roller-coaster. We had fun, and we had bad times. I continued to walk on eggshells every single day, waiting for someone or something to upset Michael and send him into one of his rages; then his mood would change, and we would enjoy happy quality time together.

One lovely time I recall was when Michael, Nicholas and I went on holiday to Denmark when Nicholas was about fourteen months old. Nicholas was a happy, bubbly child, and as we made sandcastles and played on the beach, it felt splendid. Michael was loving and attentive, and we had an enjoyable time. The only downside was when Nicholas decided to choke on a piece of pork during a beach barbeque, rather hair-raising at the time, but soon sorted by a finger down his throat to relieve the offending object!

Back at home, we enjoyed simple pleasures, taking Nicholas to the park, feeding the ducks at the local river or picnicking on sunny days. These were lovely times, and I wished our lives could run more consistently in this vein, but I knew it couldn't be, so I relished these times as I did the occasions when Michael and I spent time together as a couple. If we were out together, Michael would be attentive and protective; he would treat me like royalty and show me respect, which made me feel special, and I truly adored being with the man I fell in love with. However, it made it so impossible to understand how this lovely man could turn so ghastly, so quickly. Michael's anger could be triggered by something very simple, someone on the telephone who didn't respond as he wanted, a lost document, struggling to unwrap difficult packaging, his computer going wrong, and many other simple things, including me!

His response to these aggravations would typically start with very audible and verbally abusive expletives, which could then lead to punching or kicking an unfortunately placed inanimate object, slamming doors, etc; and at worst, throwing something across the room, usually the offending object.

Until much later, when we were seeking the advice of a marriage guidance counsellor, Michael never understood how frightening it was when he behaved like this. The simple truth was that I might have loved Michael, but I loathed his behaviour, and I was genuinely afraid of him.

On the occasions when I would retaliate or confront Michael, albeit very nervously, it would just increase his anger and make the situation worse. Michael would never be wrong, so more often than not it was best to remain silent. It took me twenty-five years to realise that I had become a sponge; I soaked up everything that was thrown at me and allowed myself to become oppressed and controlled. Decisions were made for me; I was always on edge in company, for fear that Michael would say something embarrassing or critical. I lost my independence and self-worth. In fact, without realising it, I lost my true self.

Although living back with his grandparents, Christopher continued to attend the same school, which was near to us, as we felt that another change would cause unnecessary upheaval. So, every morning, accompanied by Nicholas, I would go to my parents and collect Christopher and take him to school, and every afternoon I would reverse the process, collect him from school and bring him back to my parents' home. How my heart leapt for joy when I saw him each morning, but how it broke every afternoon when, on my parents' return home from work, Nicholas and I would leave Christopher and go back to my other life. This arrangement continued for a while until, eventually, it began to take its toll. I was exhausted both physically and emotionally. The coming to and from school was wearing me down, and on top of that, I felt as if I was on a piece of elastic. When I was with Christopher, Michael would be pulling on the elastic, wanting to know how long I was going to be away and when I would be back home; and when I had to leave Christopher, he would plead for me to stay longer and question why I had to rush back to Michael. I was desperately trying to find an alternative solution to this problem, when, one day, the answer was unexpectedly presented to me.

It was during a school holiday. I was at my parents' visiting Christopher and my younger brother Dennis was also there. Dennis went to boarding school, which he loved, and while he was home, he told Christopher all about life at his school. Christopher decided he would like to go away to school like his Uncle Dennis, who he worshipped. Initially, I thought that Christopher was just copying Dennis, but as time went on, he was adamant he liked the sound of boarding school life and all the extracurricular activities that were on offer. Although Christopher was very happy being with his grandparents, by the time they came home from work there wasn't a lot of spare time for Christopher to pursue out-of-school activities. Therefore, after a lot of thought had been put into the suggestion, it was decided that Christopher would enrol at a very carefully chosen Boarding School on a trial basis. My mother and I were to visit him every Sunday and take him out for the day, and during school holidays he would return home to my parents. Between them taking their holidays at the same time as Christopher and me visiting him regularly, Christopher would be taken care of.

Christopher soon settled into life at his new school, and he loved it. He thoroughly enjoyed the sport, and there was ample opportunity to take part in many disciplines — football, cricket, cross-country, athletics, tennis and horse-riding, to name but a few. The staff were wonderful, and Christopher soon began to make new friends. Of course, it was hard for both my parents and me to have Christopher even further away from us, but we savoured the visits and holidays when we were always greeted by a very happy, relaxed child, and if Christopher was content, then so were we.

During the school holidays, Christopher and Nicholas would spend time together, but on my Sunday visits to Christopher during term time, Nicholas would stay with Michael. I felt that as I was with Nicholas every day, it was important for Christopher and me to also have some quality time together. This was when the elastic band came back into play. When Sunday mornings came, Michael always managed to make me feel torn. "Do you have to go right now?" and "When will you be back?" were his usual questions. This was my one precious day a week with my son, and I didn't want it to be monitored; but unfortunately, I never felt that Michael gave it to me readily.

The pattern of our lives continued in this vein. Christopher away at school, Michael and I still riding our love hate roller-coaster, I running a home and my Dance School and Michael continuing to operate his own business from home.

On reflection, I feel that this contributed to our problems. Michael and I were together almost twenty-four seven. Any business problems arising during the working day, I was also subjected to the outcome, as I was there. If, however, Michael had worked away from home, this wouldn't have been the case. I would have been able to be myself during the day, and when Michael came home from work, we would have been happy to spend time together in a less stressful environment. Unfortunately, this wasn't so, but when I look back, I really think it a great shame that this situation couldn't have been different.

I threw myself into my work at the dance school. Apart from the general classes for adults and children, I would produce open days, concerts, workshops and, every two years, a major musical production in which every pupil was involved. This was when Michael came into his own, and I could always rely on his unflinching support. Whether it was designing programmes and tickets, shopping around for backcloths, props, etc, driving all over the place to collect such, or filming the actual production, at which he excelled, Michael would be there for me. Although I felt that Michael didn't feel I excelled at much, my dance work was one thing that he always praised me very highly for. Michael would also at times appear in some of my shows in his acting/singing capacity, and here again his talents would shine through.

The rest of my family were also very supportive during Showtime. My mother would sell tickets and make coffee and refreshments. In later years, Dennis would stage manage for me and also appear on stage in various guises; and my very skilful father would make scenery. I remember many a cold winter's day when father would be in the studio, which wasn't the warmest place in the world, painting and bringing to fruition my ideas; nothing was ever too much trouble for him. I certainly did set him some challenges over the years. However hard, Dad always obliged. The looks of sheer amazement on the faces of the children when their eyes beheld the wonderful scenery, accurate to the smallest detail, were beautiful to see. The perfect memories and video recordings of these wonderful times will remain with me forever.

Chapter 21

When Nicholas was about a year old, I had a very strange experience while on holiday in Wales with him and Michael. We had rented an old farm cottage for the week. As we arrived and saw this very quaint cottage nestled comfortably in a quiet country lane, I felt myself relax. I looked forward to a pleasant holiday with my husband and youngest son. We drove through the gates at the side of the cottage and Michael parked the car in the designated area behind. We climbed out of the car and enthusiastically made our way inside the cottage, to explore our new home for the week. The entrance was through the kitchen, a newly built extension which ran along the back of the cottage. The kitchen led into a dining room, and this was like stepping back in time. The room was cold, as was the rest of the cottage, with very low ceilings and very thick, uneven stone walls. The things that made me gasp, however, were the very large butcher-type hooks that hung down from the ceiling.

I was overcome with a strange, uneasy feeling. What were these hooks used for, I wondered, what had gone on in this place many years ago? All I knew was that I didn't like this room and didn't want to be here.

We continued out of the dining room and turned left into a small passage which led to the front door. Off this passage to the left, next to the dining room, was a living room with an open fire. Upstairs we discovered three bedrooms, a double for Michael and me, a smaller room for Nicholas and a third, spare double room. As we went to enter this room, I stopped in the doorway; it was as if I was frozen to the spot. I couldn't go inside. I was afraid to go any further. Michael went into the room with Nicholas and asked what I was afraid of. "There's nothing here," he said. "What's the matter with you?"

I didn't know, was the simple answer. I didn't understand these irrational feelings I was experiencing. I took a deep breath and slowly edged my way into the room. As I approached the foot of the bed, a cold draught blew across my face and upper body, as if someone had just opened a window, which they hadn't. I was terrified and ran from the room trembling.

Michael was perplexed; he didn't understand my reaction any more than I did. I think he believed that I was just letting my imagination run away with me, as he wasn't experiencing any negative feelings in the room at all. However, I knew that what I felt wasn't imagined, it was real.

I had heard somewhere that animals are especially sensitive to paranormal presences, so I asked Michael to bring Oscar, our red setter, up to the bedroom. Michael humoured me and did as I asked. He went into the bedroom and called Oscar to follow him, and lo and behold, Oscar would not go in. He whined and tried to shy away, and no amount of beckoning would make him enter.

I insisted that we shut the bedroom door, and it was to remain shut while we were here. I was scared something was happening here that was beyond my comprehension. The spare bedroom and the dining room held secrets that didn't bear thinking about. I told Michael that I was terrified. I didn't like this place at all, and I just wanted to go back home and put as much distance between myself and the cottage as possible.

Understandably, Michael didn't agree; this was a family holiday after all, and it wasn't fair to him or Nicholas if we cancelled it just because I didn't feel comfortable where we were staying. So we stayed, and we had a lovely time together, but as soon as we returned to the cottage after being out, feelings of fear flooded over me. I would rush through the dining room as quickly as possible and would not go upstairs without Michael. I didn't know what I was afraid of; I just knew that I was.

The day before we were due to return home, something happened which gave substance to my fears. We had returned to the cottage after being out for the day, and Nicholas had fallen asleep in the car. As the car was parked right outside the kitchen window, we decided to let him sleep on. I could see him from the kitchen window while I prepared dinner. I stood at the sink, washing vegetables and peeling potatoes, while

Michael went up the lane behind the cottage to collect wood for the fire that evening. In the cottage kitchen, I felt fine; this was an added extension to the cottage, and none of the negative feelings ran into here. As I prepared dinner, though, I knew I would not be venturing into the old part of the cottage until Michael returned!

A short while later, as I busied myself cooking, Michael called me from inside the cottage. "Jessica, come here, I need you." I assumed he had entered by the front door and was lighting the living room fire.

"Hang on a second," I replied.

Michael's response was, "Jessica, come here, I need you now!"

Michael's impatience irritated me, and as I replied, "All right, I'm coming," I placed the saucepan I was holding onto the draining board. I glanced at the car to ensure Nicholas was still asleep, before going to see what Michael wanted. My jaw practically hit the floor. As my eyes looked beyond the car and fell upon the lane where Michael was earlier collecting wood, there, walking back towards the cottage, his arms full of firewood, was Michael!

"Jessica, Jessica, I need you!" As the voice from within the cottage called me again, I screamed, ran out of the back door and sat huddled on the doorstep. My head buried in my hands, I sat shaking like a leaf, and that is where Michael found me when he returned. It wasn't Michael calling me as I had assumed, so who or what was it?

I didn't want to know; I was terrified. Although Michael couldn't understand what was going on, on seeing how upset I was, he agreed that we would head back home that evening, instead of waiting until the next morning.

Obviously, I never did discover what it was I had experienced in that remote Welsh cottage, and in time I put the experience behind me and tried to accept it as one of life's unexplained phenomena.

However, it was to be the start of a new path that opened up in my life. A fascinating path on which I was to discover a susceptibility to energies surrounding us and abilities I had to hone into those energies. The experiences I was to encounter became fascination instead of fear.

If I could remember where the Welsh cottage was, I would go back now and rather than succumb to the paralysing fear of thirty years ago, I would ask the 'Voice' what it wanted of me. I would like to put it to rest, but unfortunately, I can't remember, so this isn't possible.

I just hope that whatever was there is now at peace.

Chapter 22

When Nicholas was about eighteen months old, things at home took a turn for the worse. Michael was having business problems, which sadly was often the case. The problems with his work ended up making him angrier and more impatient. I don't think Michael ever really thought I understood his problems and the strain he was under, but I did, at least to the best of my ability. However, understanding the issues didn't make it any easier to live with them.

Young Nicholas was, of course, although involuntarily, being subjected to this unhappy atmosphere. I was just about ready to run away. I couldn't go on any longer, living under this dark shadow of having to be wary and on guard the whole time. Unbelievably, that is what I did. I didn't know where I was going or what I was going to do. I just had to leave, taking Nicholas with me.

On Tuesdays, Nicholas would spend the day with Michael's parents, and therefore, on one particular Tuesday, I took Nicholas to Dora and Joseph as usual. I then returned home, to rapidly throw some clothes into a couple of black sacks for Nicholas and myself. I was planning to leave while Michael was working in his home office, as I didn't want any confrontation. Unfortunately, this didn't work, and Michael appeared just as I was walking out. He became infuriated and threw my two sacks out of the front door, telling me to go and not come back.

I was trembling as I climbed into my car, but knew I had to finish what I had started. I drove to Michael's parents' home and knocked on the door of their flat. They didn't open the door but told me that Michael was on his way over, and they were not to let me take Nicholas. I was incensed, furious. How dare they keep my son from me? Nicholas was crying and calling for me through the closed door.

"Let me have my son," I screamed. "You have no right to keep him from me!" My frustration increased. Nicholas needed me; he was upset. Without further ado, I rammed my shoulder into the door, again and again. I was desperate; I had to get inside to Nicholas. "Open the door!" I screamed, and as I felt the door begin to give way, Joseph opened it, just as Michael appeared.

I snatched Nicholas from Dora and held him to me, but I was no match for Michael, and he prised my arms away from my son and took him from me. "You can't do this," I screamed at Michael. "Your actions have made me lose one son; I'm not losing another!"

Michael told me I needed to calm down as I was upsetting Nicholas. Calm down, calm down? How was I supposed to calm down when my child was being withheld from me? Nicholas was indeed still upset, and this was the last thing I wanted. So I kissed him and told him I would see him soon, and I left. I ran back to my car, shaking and trembling, not knowing what to do. I sat in my car, trying to calm myself and decide what course of action I could take to get Nicholas back. I then remembered a solicitor friend of mine I had dated for a while before I met Michael. As we had remained friends, I decided to ring him for some advice. Russell was amazing. He told me to drive straight to his office; he would free up his time and see me straight away.

When I arrived at Russell's office, and he had sat me down with a cup of coffee, sheer relief made me break down. After I had cried out my fear and frustration, he put the wheels in motion to bring Nicholas back to me.

Firstly, he arranged for the local police to go to our home and check that Nicholas was quite safe and happy and not in any distress, and this was indeed the case. I never thought that Michael would intentionally harm Nicholas, but if he became angry and went into one of his rages, I was concerned that Nicholas should witness this.

Next, Russell approached the local Magistrates' Court and drew up a petition stating that I was to have custody of Nicholas until further order and that he was to be returned to me by twelve midday the following day.

I spent a few tense hours sitting in a local cafe, waiting for this order. When Russell arrived and told me

I had been granted custody of Nicholas until further notice, I cried with relief. I thanked Russell profusely for everything he had done for me and drove back to my parents' home to tell them the news.

As I expected, early that evening Michael telephoned to inform me that he had just been served the order. If Nicholas wasn't returned to me by the stated time, Michael would be arrested. He really couldn't believe that I would go to these lengths; his words were, "I didn't think you had it in you."

I was like a mother cat protecting her young. When they are threatened, you can do anything. I told Michael I regretted what had happened, but he left me no choice; he wouldn't let me have Nicholas, so I had to do whatever was necessary. I asked him whether he was going to bring Nicholas to me the following day, or if I should collect him. Michael's reply was that Nicholas had been pining for me and therefore would I like to go and collect him straight away.

Filled with relief, my mother and I immediately drove to our home, where Michael and Nicholas were. On arrival, I asked my mum if she would please go in and get Nicholas. I was so afraid of confrontation with Michael, and Nicholas had had enough upset for one day. She returned immediately with Nicholas bundled up in his little red snowsuit and handed him to me through the car window. I held him to me and cried with relief, "How on earth has it come to this?"

She told me that Michael was very calm and that he wanted to talk to me. I left Nicholas in the car with his grandmother and very reluctantly went up to the front door, where Michael was waiting. I didn't go inside, but asked Michael what he wanted to say. "Sorry," was his reply. "I'm so sorry. I don't mean to get angry, but as you know I have zero tolerance for stupidity."

I knew this only too well, and I told Michael that being sorry wasn't enough. It was a good starting point, but something had to be done about his anger before any of us could move forward.

Before I walked away, I told Michael I would call him to arrange for him to see Nicholas at the weekend. Then I left without looking back, tears streaming down my face, as I went to my son.

Nicholas and I stayed with my parents for a few weeks, and although it was very cramped, they never complained. I knew, though, that this arrangement was only temporary. During this time, Nicholas saw Michael often. Michael was continually asking me to rethink our situation, telling me he would change. Would I please consider returning to our home, to give him another chance?

I was missing Michael, but not his anger. My mother told me I was miserable without him, and maybe we should consider trying again to see whether Michael's promises of change would, in fact, come to fruition.

So, I returned to Michael, to be greeted with roses, a candlelight supper and lots of apologies and promises. I was again caught up in the moment. This was the man I loved, and we had to make this work.

The change in Michael lasted about a week! Life once more dissolved into the old routine — up, down, good, bad. I withdrew back into myself and once more tried to keep the peace. I started walking on eggshells again, hating the anger outbursts, feeling helpless and yet relishing the times when things were good, and my loving Michael was around.

This became the routine. I chose to return, and I had to cope with that decision. However, I felt very let down and disappointed that Michael had not made any move to seek help for his anger problem. I would liken living with Michael to residing in a spider's web. When things were good, it was like being enveloped in a warm, protective, sheltering cloak; but when things turned bad, that web became constricting, suffocating and entrapping.

Throughout our marriage I would send Michael little cards or notes, telling him how much he meant to me. My sentiments were real, but I also thought, that by expressing my feelings to Michael, it might make him step out of the box and realise what was in jeopardy if his actions didn't change. Although these notes were appreciated at the time, long term nothing changed.

During the next few years, Michael and I lumbered on, with one or two more separations thrown in for good measure. We just couldn't seem to be apart, and we always came back together and somehow came through those difficult times.

In the meantime, Christopher had moved on to a Senior Boarding School and settled well, making new friends readily. Young Nicholas was now at nursery and, being a very outgoing child, thoroughly enjoyed his times there.

Chapter 23

In 1986, a different set of problems arose. Christopher started having nightmares at school. Jumbled, mixed up dreams that were occurring almost every night and causing him a lot of distress. On-going to the school and talking to the headmaster and Christopher, I learnt that he was beginning to experience flashbacks of snippets of the night his father died. When he was awake, he remembered nothing of the happenings of the night his father died, so he, therefore, couldn't make any sense of these dreadful nightmares.

I could. It was evident that the predicted time had arrived when his subconscious memory was 'waking up' and regurgitating the terrible events that, at the time, Christopher had blocked out. I always knew that one day he would remember, but I guess I hoped it wouldn't be while he was still so young. I thought adulthood would perhaps make it easier to bear. But here we were, Christopher, aged fourteen, needed to be told what had happened to his father. His questions needed answering, and I was the one to do it.

Because of the distress, confusion and unhappiness that Christopher was experiencing, it was decided between myself, my parents and Christopher that he would leave Boarding School, come back to my parents' home and attend a local day school. This way, my parents and I could be on hand to give Christopher the help he needed to deal with his problems. He was relieved and delighted to be back within the safe and comforting confines of his grandparents' home.

While Christopher settled into his new routine, safe in the knowledge that my parents were on hand at night to comfort him through his nightmares, I sought the advice of a clinical psychologist. I needed to know the best way to handle this very difficult situation for my son.

Back into play came that old elastic band. I wanted to be there to hold Christopher when he woke, frightened, but I couldn't because Michael apparently needed me there with him and Nicholas. Christopher was asking so many questions. At night he was upset and distressed as the nightmares continued. During the day he was preoccupied with, in his words, "Trying to put together the many pieces of a jigsaw puzzle, which were floating around in my head, when I didn't have a picture to copy of the puzzle I was trying to make."

I, therefore, decided, on the psychologist's advice, to carry out one of the hardest tasks I have ever had to undertake. I was to put the puzzle pieces together for Christopher.

Thus, it was, that I sat down very nervously with Christopher and told him about the events surrounding and leading up to his father's death; the car accident which caused his brain injury, his pattern of behaviour during the following year and the actual events of the night John died.

During the next couple of hours, Christopher's expression didn't change; he remained completely expressionless. He listened; he asked questions, "Why didn't they know my dad was sick? Why would dad want to hurt grandad? Why do I remember standing in so much blood?"

Every question he asked I answered as honestly as I could, and slowly the pieces fell into place. "I remember that now, mum" or "That is making sense to me now."

It was almost as if Christopher was writing a school essay. He was gathering his facts together in a very calm and calculated fashion to present a piece of work that made sense. This initially threw me off-guard. I expected distress, to be confronted with raw pain and emotion, but this was not the case. My son was in control, completely absorbed as he digested what I divulged to him. How my heart went out to him. He shouldn't have to hear this, and he shouldn't have suffered this. But there was no way out. I couldn't change what had happened and therefore had to press on with this tremendous task, feeling the utmost admiration and respect for the young man who sat before me.

As I finished relating this terrible story to Christopher, I felt my body physically sag. I was drained, completely spent, exhausted with not only having to speak to my son of these dreadful events, but having to relive them myself at the same time. However, these emotions were accompanied by a strange sense of relief.

Although I could never take away this burden that Christopher would have to carry for the rest of his life, there was some comfort to be had in knowing that now his questions had been answered he would hopefully be able to move on with his life without being haunted by the unknown.

I, of course, emphasised to Christopher that his father was in no way to blame for what had happened and that as he was very sick, his actions were totally out of character. Although tragic and sorrowful, it was not in any way John's fault.

I told Christopher that I loved his father very much and always would. That sometimes in life the most dreadful things happen and we just can't understand why. We had to be strong together and help each other to pick up the pieces and move on. I made it clear to Christopher that he must come to me at any time he had more questions, and I would do my best to answer them for him.

When I finished speaking, Christopher still showed no emotion. He simply said, "Thanks, mum, for telling me; it makes sense now", and that was it.

He has never mentioned what he learnt about that dreadful year since. His nightmares stopped and the only discussions we have had since that day were good ones about his father. We spoke about his father's culinary skills, how we met, the good times we had together and the virtues his father had both as a husband and as a father. It was so important that Christopher's image of his father was the one I choose to carry also. The John I married, the real John, the loving, caring, normal man that he was.

The end of 1986 brought more sad news. On 4th November, Michael's father Joseph died. Although Michael wasn't exceptionally close to his father, it was nevertheless a sombre time. We decided that Dora, Michael's mother, should come and live with us. Michael didn't want her to be alone any more than she wanted to be. I was perfectly happy with this arrangement, as I was very fond of Dora and got on very well with her, and so she came to live with us in our family home.

Chapter 24

Christopher settled happily back into life with his grandparents and at his new school. It pleased me to see him rediscovering himself, the happy, contented boy he used to be.

On the other hand, for me the pain continued, the silent, gnawing pain of deprivation. Although emotionally I was always with Christopher, physically I could only be a part-time mother to him, and this was so hard to bear.

Life continued in its usual pattern — good, very good, bad, very bad, up, down and into the darkest depths. This was the place where the next tragedy in my life sent me. I fell pregnant and subsequently suffered a miscarriage. Any woman (and their partner) who has experienced this will understand the immensity of the pain and devastation that is experienced. The feeling of loss was overpowering. Why should I have yet another child taken from me, and so soon? Every fibre of my being was engulfed by this sense of loss and longing. The outcome was that Michael and I decided to try for another baby, and when I became pregnant and managed to carry our baby to term, we were elated.

In July 1987, our third son, Oliver, came into the world. Like his brothers before him, he was tiny, but healthy and beautiful.

Christopher and Nicholas were both excited when they came to the hospital to meet their little brother for the first time. I will always remember that beautiful picture of Christopher sitting in a chair, gently holding Oliver to him, while Nicholas stroked Oliver's head and held his tiny hand. That picture of my three beautiful children tugged at my heartstrings. This was how it should be three sons together. Even though the boys couldn't grow up in the same household, my greatest joy in life is that an incredible bond developed between them, and now, many years later, they are very close and supportive of each other.

It was about the time Oliver was born that Nicholas, at the tender age of six, discovered an activity that was to become an ongoing passion throughout his life — the game of rugby. He joined a local club which offered 'Mini rugby' for young children and took to it like a duck to water. Not only did Nicholas love his rugby, but also it soon became apparent that he had a real talent for the game. I recall many a cold, but nevertheless thoroughly enjoyable Sunday morning, standing on the touchline, cheering him on, as he sped like a whippet towards the touchline to score another of the many tries he clocked up during his rugby career! In one season he received an award for breaking the record for the most tries scored by a player in a season. The previous record was thirty-six tries, which stood for many years. My son scored seventy-four! To this day his name is still on a plaque at the local club.

On a less cheerful note, our dear father's health was now deteriorating rapidly. He had been struggling for four years with emphysema, and it became clear that he was on borrowed time.

My father had been there all through Christopher's childhood, and I was also so pleased that he had been able to spend time with Nicholas. A particular very fond memory I have is of Nicholas being chased, although very slowly, by his grandad, around the apple tree in my parents' garden. Nicholas would shriek with laughter as they enjoyed this game.

My father also, thankfully, managed to share the beginning of young Oliver's life. A loving and devoted grandfather.

During my father's five-year illness, my mother nursed and cared for him, and as time progressed this became a twenty-four-hour labour of love. As dad became more unwell, his mood would change. He would try his best to smile, but sometimes sheer frustration and immense difficulty in trying to draw breath made him irritable and impatient. Mother was usually on the receiving end of this, but she never complained or retaliated. This amazing woman responded to her husband's needs, doing everything for him, day and night, in a genuine, loving way. I recall her sleeping on the sofa for years. It was now impossible for my father to go upstairs to bed and he couldn't be left alone, so she stayed with him. Truer love and devotion I have yet to see.

It was a very dark day for our family when, on 14th September 1988, my beloved father lost his fight and died peacefully in his sleep.

My mother went to wake him as usual with his morning cup of tea, and when he didn't respond, she called for Christopher. How proud I was of him, when I learned that, on responding to her call, he very calmly told his grandmother that grandad 'had gone'. He then proceeded to cover his grandfather with a sheet, sit his grandmother down with a cup of sweet tea and then telephone me. Christopher had taken complete control of the situation, doing what needed to be done in a very calm and mature way.

We all respond in different ways to the death of a loved one and grieve for that person, in the same way that each individual has their own faith and beliefs, or not, as the case may be.

For me personally, God had always featured in my life. The acceptance of a 'Presence' more powerful than ourselves came easily to me, and I had no doubt that 'Life' continued in some form after death.

However, my father's death changed my view entirely; I completely lost my faith. He had been taken from us much too soon, and I couldn't accept a loving God allowing this to happen. Although my faith did return later on, at this particular time I went off on a different tangent. I could no longer imagine Heaven and my father being there, but I couldn't accept either that he could just completely no longer exist. I needed answers; I needed to re-evaluate my beliefs, to try to make sense of the utterly inexplicable. I don't know how or why it happened, although it does make sense to me now, but I stepped onto the path of 'Spiritualism'. I felt lost and abandoned, and somehow this was promising to provide me with a direction that I so badly needed.

Since starting out on this journey, I have come to believe that there is no coincidence in life; people come into our lives when we need them and they need us. It thus follows that people move away from us physically or emotionally when that need has been satisfied.

Out of the blue, I received a phone call from an old friend whom I hadn't spoken to for a while. On hearing that I was very tense, frustrated and confused, she suggested I join a meditation group. I must confess my initial response, one of complete ignorance, was, "Isn't that something that people do who are somewhat strange, and they sit around making strange wailing noises together?" How very wrong I was, as my friend hastily pointed out to me. Meditation helps to relax the body and clear the mind, and you certainly didn't have to be 'strange' to engage in it. So, with my friend's guidance, I enrolled with a group she recommended.

I arrived on that first morning feeling very nervous and unsure, but I knew somewhere deep inside that I was doing the right thing. My nerves dispelled instantly when Ann, the lady who ran the group, greeted me very warmly. She showed me into her living room, invited me to sit down, and as we waited for the other group members to arrive, we chatted very easily.

A further five people joined us, and they were all as friendly and welcoming as Ann. Ann then proceeded to guide us through a deep breathing and relaxation exercise and then, while feeling very calm and comfortable, we listened to a visualisation tape.

As I let the speaker's words flow over me, I felt more at peace with myself than I had done for a long time. I allowed my thoughts to flow freely when the voice asked me to make my way through an exquisite garden, the beauty of which I had never before encountered. I saw colours that didn't exist in our world; everything was more vibrant, and I felt a genuine connection to everything around me; I could even feel the trees and plants breathing!

Joy and peace were flowing over me, and I felt such a sense of belonging that I didn't want to leave this beautiful place.

After the visualisation exercise had finished, we all stood in a circle to perform a grounding technique. Initially, I didn't understand what this was, but Ann soon explained that it was important to ensure that our feet were 'firmly planted on the ground' after meditation; that our thoughts were back in the here and now and not still 'floating off somewhere else'.

She then served us all coffee and biscuits and friendly conversation flowed between us.

As I left Ann's home after the meeting, I felt light and free, in a way that I couldn't put into words. All I knew was that I couldn't wait to return next week, to meet my new friends again and enjoy another meditation session with them.

As the weeks passed and I continued to attend Ann's meetings, inexplicable changes were taking place in my life. I became more aware of my surroundings; I found myself stopping and looking, really looking instead of just glancing, at flowers and trees and appreciating in wonderment how magnificent their formation was. The colours of nature appeared more vivid and exquisite in their brilliance, and the sheer magnitude and incredibility of the sky astounded me. I didn't know what was happening to me, but I did know that I was enjoying the experience. Something then occurred which did give me some cause for concern.

May I ask you at this point not to think me crazy and decide to close this book, because I can tell you with complete honesty and conviction that I am completely sane and as rational as you are! Please continue to read my story with an open mind, because everything I am telling you did happen to me, impacted upon my life and brought me to where I am today.

I awoke suddenly one night and saw a red light, rather like a small streak of lightning, flash across the bedroom ceiling. It only lasted a couple of seconds, so, thinking it was my imagination playing tricks in my sleepy state, I gave it no more thought and went back to sleep. However, the following night the same thing happened again. This time, I didn't put it down to the imagination. Once yes, twice no, so I climbed out of bed and looked out of the window to see if there was anything outside that could be causing this fleeting red light. As I looked out onto the back garden of the house, to be greeted with nothing but black denseness, I knew that this wasn't the case. There had to be another explanation, but what?

As this nightly event continued, I became uneasy and concerned, starting to believe that I was going 'mad' and seeing things that weren't there. However, in the cold light of day, I knew without a doubt that what I was seeing was very real to me — I just didn't understand it. Interestingly, when I began to accept that what I was seeing, although inexplicable, was there, my uneasiness and concern began to fade, and in their place came curiosity and a longing for answers.

The light began to change from being just red to becoming a rainbow of vivid colours, flashing across the ceiling above me. I began to look forward to my nightly 'light show'.

I never divulged what I was experiencing to my family or friends because I'm sure they would have thought I had lost the plot and had me sectioned! I did, however, need to speak to someone, so I went along one day to have a chat with Ann. I just felt in some way that she would be able to help me, without passing any judgement. The most amazing thing was that when I told Ann about my 'light show', she became excited and enthused as to how lucky I was!

This was the first of many conversations I had with my new friend. Ann was very knowledgeable and always tried to answer my questions to the best of her ability. She never tried to influence my thoughts or opinions in any way, which I respected. Concerning my 'light show', Ann said I was beginning to 'open up' and become more aware of the energies around us.

The Universal Energy is always there, I just never really thought about it before. Now, though, through allowing myself to be open to any new happening, emotionally or physically, I was becoming able to experience certain things on a different psychic level.

I remembered the descending mist and the 'velvet' voice that spoke to me the night John died, commanding me kindly, but firmly, to remove Christopher from the mayhem. I realised that this voice was indeed the voice of a Higher Power. For me, the Voice of God. I realised that my childhood belief of God being a little old man sitting on a throne in a beautiful garden called Heaven just didn't work any more.

I grew up, and my father's death helped me to understand this. My faith returned, but God had taken on a new persona. God was everywhere, in everything we see. We just have to look, listen and feel. God for me is the Great Universal Energy that is all around us. We all have the power to access that energy and communicate with God. We just have to ask, believe our prayers will be answered and they will, although not always in the way we would wish — and, by the way, don't forget to say Thank You!

As I continued along my path of spiritual development, my beliefs became healthy again. I once more believed in God, in Jesus, in Angels, but now I also thought that when we die our souls pass over to 'The Spirit World', for me Heaven. I believe we begin life as a soul in the spirit world that our true essence is spiritual, that we come to earth in human form to learn lessons, and when that lesson is taught, we return to the Spirit World. After rest and receiving guidance, never judgment, from our Spirit guides, when we are ready, we return again to earth to learn our next lesson. After each earth life, I believe we progress to a higher spiritual plane, and when all lessons are learnt, we eventually achieve 'Nirvana', the place of complete and utter Love; we become 'One with God'.

You may be someone who can accept and even agree with my beliefs, or you may wish to reject them entirely. That doesn't matter; everyone is entitled to his or her opinion and to have his or her views respected. However, what does matter is that it is my faith and beliefs that have given me the strength to endure and survive a life of much hardship, which ordinarily would have sent many people 'over the edge'.

I hope that by reading my story you will see that the human body is a remarkable thing, capable of the most incredible feats of physical and mental endurance. That there is strength within us that we don't realise we possess until put to the test.

As long as we have something to strive for and survive for — in my case, my beautiful sons — we can draw on that strength, and anything is possible.

Chapter 25

After Dora had been living with us for a while, we decided it would be beneficial to us all to move to a new property that would be more suited to our needs. Although Dora used our kitchen and bathroom, there wasn't a separate bedroom available for her. Also, although her own room was relatively large, it was still a combined living/sleeping space, and we felt we would like to try and find her a separate living room and bedroom if at all possible.

Also, I have to admit we all felt that our independence and privacy were being somewhat compromised, as we were often 'getting under each other's feet'.

The solution was found when we moved to a bungalow, which had a separate annexe. The main home had ample accommodation for Michael, the boys and me, and in the annexe, there was a large lounge, with patio doors leading out onto the back garden, a good-sized kitchen and bathroom and a large bedroom, perfect for Dora.

Dora loved it, and the bonus was that she had her own separate entrance to the annexe round the side of the garden, through which she would often be seen showing friends in for tea. Also, there was an internal door leading from her bedroom into our living room, so if she needed us at any time, she could come straight through to us.

Dora and I decided that while she prepared her own breakfast and lunch, I would cook her evening meal for her every day. Although she now had her own kitchen, it seemed pointless for her to cook the main meal while I was cooking for the family anyway. She insisted, however, on eating her evening meal in her room, which I respected her for, as it gave us our own time with the boys. Every Sunday, however, Dora would come and join us for a family meal together. I would often go in and have coffee and a chat with her, and she seemed really happy in her new home.

Dora was a very delicate, refined lady, unobtrusive and kind. In the mornings after Michael had gone out to work in the office he had erected in the back garden, she would come through and help with the washing-up, while we chatted together quite happily. She was excellent at sewing, and I remember with much gratitude, the numerous name labels she stitched onto the boys' school uniforms for me!

The boys were, of course, growing up before our eyes. Christopher still lived with my mother and was now working in insurance. Nicholas was progressing very well at school, thriving at his rugby and captaining his team, while young Oliver was developing quite a character. He was a lovable rascal, whom you couldn't remain cross with for long when he looked at you with his large brown eyes and flashed his cheeky smile.

Michael's mercurial behaviour continued; when he was calm life was good, and then something would happen and trigger him off into one of his anger outbursts.

One particular day, when fortunately, the boys were at school and nursery, and Dora was out, Michael was infuriated over something, and this turned into an argument between us. Michael stormed out of the bungalow, heading for his garden office; and I, rather unwisely as it turned out, followed him in an attempt to settle the argument. As I went to follow Michael into his office, he pushed me out of the way so he could close the door.

Unfortunately, he pushed me too hard, and I fell backwards down the office steps and landed on my back on the lawn.

A searing pain shot up my spine and for a few seconds I found it hard to breathe. Michael, of course, didn't intend for this to happen, but it did, and I was initially unable to get up.

Our next-door neighbour had apparently been out in her garden and overheard what had happened, so she came round, rather bravely I thought, to enquire if I was all right. Michael told her in no uncertain terms to mind her own business and sent her on her way! He then proceeded to take me to hospital as my back hurt, and while there he told me that it was entirely my decision, but if I told the doctor Michael had pushed me, he could be charged with assault. I didn't want that, no. Michael certainly shouldn't have pushed me; again, this was a result of his anger, but he never intended to hurt me, so I told the doctor I slipped down the steps.

It turned out that my back was only badly bruised, nothing more; but nevertheless, it endorsed the fact that Michael's anger was a major issue in our lives, so why couldn't he see it?

Chapter 26

In the summer of 1991, something happened which was to impact upon my life forever. Michael, Nicholas, Oliver, my mother Martha and I went on holiday to Cornwall. Mum, still struggling to come to terms with the death of my father and on the verge of a breakdown, expressed a desire to return to Cornwall, where they had been so happy together.

Christopher was unable to take time off work to grant my mother's wish and take her, and this resulted in Michael offering to take us on a Cornish holiday, inviting Martha to accompany us. She was so excited at the prospect of returning to her beloved Cornwall that my mother accepted readily, also conceding that perhaps this would be a chance to begin to close the enormous cavern that existed between her and Michael. A cavern which had opened the day she discovered Michael's abuse of Christopher. Like me, she would never be able to forgive Michael for what he had done, but for the sake of Nicholas and Oliver, who often asked why their grandmother didn't visit our home, some truce had to be made.

We stayed at the King Arthur's Castle Hotel in Tintagel and had a lovely time. Nicholas and Oliver enjoyed many happy hours playing on the beaches that Christopher had played on as a young boy. This was interspersed with taking a trip down memory lane, revisiting some of my parents' favourite haunts, hidden woodland trails, deep gorges leading down to the sea and quaint fishing villages.

After a full and pleasant time, Michael had to return home a couple of days early by train for a business meeting, and I was to drive the rest of us home a couple of days later.

On our journey back, we decided to stop off and visit Stonehenge, as the boys had never been there and expressed a desire to do so. We thoroughly enjoyed walking around the ancient stones and learning about the site's fascinating history. We set off again after this enjoyable break in the journey and then, not far from home, disaster struck.

I left the M3 motorway at junction 5, and as I entered the roundabout at the top of the slip road, there was the most thunderous bang and an almighty thud as another car ploughed into us on the nearside of my car. This car was travelling at such speed that the impact didn't stop it. Instead, it wedged itself underneath my car, and as it continued to move forward, it lifted my car onto the two offside wheels and proceeded to carry us onto the central reservation of the roundabout, where we eventually came to a halt. All of this action took a matter of seconds, and although at the time I wasn't sure what was happening, I remember saying to the boys, as we crashed towards the middle of the roundabout, "It's okay, mummy's here, it's okay!" My immediate thought was to allay their fear; but, on reflection, I somehow doubt I was able to disguise my own.

As we came to a halt, there was silence. I felt a stillness and unawareness of anything around me; it was like being inside a bubble, with the rest of the world outside. Nobody spoke, nobody moved. The first thought that came into my head was that we were dead. "Oh no, God!" I said out loud. "Not my boys, not my mum, not yet."

Suddenly, the bubble burst and in an instant, I realised I was very much alive and was being dragged from the wreckage of my car. An agonising pain shot through my back and neck, as a man I didn't know lowered me gently onto the reservation grass.

"My children — get my children!" I screamed, dragging myself painfully to my feet and struggling towards the car. The same man carried Oliver from the car, while a lady, whom I also didn't know, walked Nicholas from the car, with her arm consolingly around him. Within seconds, my mother was also helped out of the car and by now I was aware of a second young man and woman also being there.

Unbelievably, miraculously, we were all alive and seemingly okay; very shaken, of course, but it would appear, at the time, no serious injury.

The man and woman who had come to our rescue had apparently left the motorway behind me and, following me up the slip road, had witnessed the whole incident. The police and ambulance arrived, and we were all taken to the hospital to be checked out. Nicholas and Oliver suffered minor bruises, but thankfully nothing more. My mother, however, went into major shock, which rendered her unconscious and gave way to a severe angina attack. This was extremely frightening and worrying, but fortunately, thanks to the skilled medical staff and a short stay in hospital, she recovered well.

As for me, I sustained an injury to my back which was to wreck my dance career and leave me in pain and discomfort to this day.

It came to light that the young man at the scene of the accident was the driver of the other car, and would you believe he walked away, as did his girlfriend, completely unscathed! According to the police, he entered the roundabout at a speed of more than eighty miles an hour, and the wonderful man who came to our rescue confirmed that he raced onto the roundabout without any intention of stopping. I was completely blameless and couldn't have avoided the collision in any way.

Apparently, this insane young driver was driving an untaxed, uninsured vehicle and did not possess a driving licence!

As we moved on, following this accident, I became embroiled in a lengthy compensation claim. Michael came into his own and found a fantastic solicitor to act on my behalf who was determined to see that justice was done, even if only in a financial way. Because of my injury, I was no longer able to dance myself, and although I insisted on continuing to teach, I often did this from a chair, with a senior student demonstrating to the class.

My heart was shattered into a million pieces; my lifelong love and saviour had been snatched from me by a complete stranger, in a moment of utter madness.

I had foreseen myself working well beyond retirement age and had planned to become an examiner and lecturer for my Dance Association. These dreams were over; there was no way, beyond a miracle giving me back my body, that they could come to fruition. It was devastating, cruel; I did nothing to deserve this!

However, there it was, I couldn't change the situation, I had to accept it. That incredible inner strength again reared its beautiful head and made me look at the situation in a different way. Look at what you can do, focus on that, not on what you can't do. Not easy by any means, but I nevertheless, against all the odds, determinedly carried on running KAPA, as my school was now known. With the addition of drama and singing coaching, it had become The Kew Academy of Performing Arts. I taught when I could and was just there when I couldn't. Sometimes, Michael would physically get me out of bed and take me there himself, but I just couldn't give in, wouldn't give in.

Julie was incredible, as were my family, my pupils and their families. Julie took up so much of the slack for me, going far beyond the call of duty. Without her, I could not have carried on with my work at KAPA for as long as I did.

Later that same year, my poor body underwent yet another trauma. I had to have more major abdominal surgery, and this, coupled with the effects of the road accident, led to the onset of a condition called myalgic encephalomyelitis (M.E.) and fibromyalgia. However, it took a long time to get this diagnosis. The primary symptom of M.E. is extreme fatigue, and I don't mean feeling very tired. I'm talking about a tiredness that can't be fought; a tiredness that at worst means not being able to stand up without collapsing.

After my surgery, I never really recovered fully. As time passed, I became exhausted and depressed. I suffered very severe headaches and was feeling nauseous much of the time, all classic ME symptoms. I visited my GP on numerous occasions to try and establish what on earth was wrong with me, but when blood tests showed nothing obviously amiss, she was completely unsympathetic and told me to pull myself together; she often felt tired, but she just had to get on with it!

I was so taken aback by her total disinterest and lack of understanding. I wasn't just tired, I was so exhausted, and I couldn't function properly. I dissolved into floods of tears, tears of desperation, tears of fear from knowing something was wrong with me, but not knowing what. Still, this doctor sent me home, telling me to fight on and she was sure this 'tiredness' would pass.

It didn't, it just went from bad to worse. Some days I didn't even have the strength to lift a knife and fork to feed myself. The headaches continued, nausea continued, I suffered dizziness, and inexplicable bruising would on occasion appear on my legs. Things came to a head one day when I was home alone. I dragged myself up from the sofa in an attempt to go and wash the breakfast dishes, and promptly collapsed into a heap on the floor. My legs just wouldn't support me. I was terrified. I couldn't stand up, and it was as if there wasn't a skeleton in my body. I reached for the telephone, which was fortunately on the small table beside the sofa, and, sobbing into the phone, I called Michael. He was back home in no time and on seeing the state I was in said, "That's it, enough is enough, we're not being fobbed off any more." He then proceeded to pick me up from the floor, where I was still lying, put me into his car and drove to the doctor's surgery. He carried me in and demanded to see a different doctor, not my usual one. On being told that I couldn't be seen without an appointment, Michael informed the stunned receptionist that we wouldn't leave the premises until we were seen! After a very short wait, we were indeed called in to see another doctor, a man whom I had not met before.

Oh, my goodness, what a difference! He told me that he could see something was wrong by just looking at me. He examined me, asked questions about everything that had been going on, and by the end of the consultation he informed us that he suspected I might have M.E. Neither Michael nor I knew what this was, and the doctor patiently explained the condition to us. He went on to tell us that unfortunately many people, some doctors included, wouldn't accept the condition as a reality and that it was often being termed the 'Yuppie flu' and applied to people who were 'unwell' who didn't want to work.

I was horrified. What I was experiencing was certainly real; I wasn't lazy, just very ill!

The doctor went on to explain that there wasn't a conclusive test to diagnose M.E. The diagnosis was achieved by eliminating any other known conditions with the same symptoms. Once this was done it could be safely concluded that M.E. or chronic fatigue syndrome, as it has come to be known, was the diagnosis. Within a week this doctor had an appointment arranged for me with an M.E. and chronic fatigue specialist in London. This gentleman was extremely understanding and sympathetic to the way I was feeling. After discussing my entire medical history, and my current symptoms, he proceeded to carry out various tests, from blood tests to having many wires attached to my body to assess, amongst other things, muscle efficiency. The specialist's conclusion was that

I was indeed suffering from M.E. My muscle function result was very bad, and the expert explained that chronic fatigue sufferers are unable to replace the energy their body uses at a fast enough rate and hence extreme fatigue sets in. The harder you push your body, the more exhausted you become and the harder it is to replenish the energy.

The specialist was very frustrated and made no secret of his annoyance at the medical professionals who would not recognise this illness. There is no cure available; the condition can only be managed. The worst thing one can do is to 'Fight It'. This simply exacerbates the exhaustion and other symptoms. The way to manage chronic fatigue is to learn to pace, which is easier said than done, believe me. I was advised to decide what I felt I had the energy to do and only do half of that, thus conserving energy. If I had no energy at all, I should give into that fact and rest. We were told that the sooner chronic fatigue is diagnosed, and pacing begins, the more chance there is of the condition disappearing. Imagine how the specialist, Michael and I felt, knowing that I could have and should have been diagnosed many months ago. I had unknowingly made the condition worse by fighting it and now had less chance of achieving a complete cure. I was so upset by this realisation and promptly changed from my current doctor to the male GP who had been so kind to me. Sadly, the damage had been done and unfortunately couldn't be undone.

Fibromyalgia is a condition which often accompanies M.E. and causes inexplicable, often severe pain throughout the body. This is diagnosed by applying pressure, which is very painful, to various parts of the body, and the skin's reaction can confirm fibromyalgia.

Michael and I left the consulting rooms armed with the address of another M.E. specialist nearer to home, whose care I was now to be under. I was provided with much advice on coping with my illness and medication to possibly help in increasing muscle strength, pain relief and depression, to name but a few.

I sank into the darkest depths; I felt that my life had come to a standstill. I had a family to care for, a home and business to run; this couldn't be happening to me, it just couldn't — surely, I had already suffered enough.

Chapter 27

Life at home became even harder now that I was so unwell. There were many days when I couldn't even find the strength to get out of bed. M.E. is a truly debilitating condition. You want to function normally, but your body just won't let you, and because of this, you become frustrated and profound depression sets in. This, in turn, makes the condition worse, and so you end up in a vicious, unbreakable cycle.

On top of his work, Michael had to care for the boys and take on the essential chores around the house, such as cooking and doing the laundry. He would care for me, bringing me drinks and meals while I was bedridden, and this was when the kind and generous side of him shone through, and I will always be grateful for that care he showed me.

The extra pressure inevitably took its toll, and while I was resting in bed, I would hear Michael raising his voice and becoming angry, invariably with someone on the telephone who wasn't doing what he required in the way he wanted. The phone would then be slammed down, and as his frustration grew, various other objects would have his anger thrust upon them, or innocent doors would be thumped or slammed.

It was unbearably hard to lay there and listen to this. I would start sweating and shaking, and I wasn't even in the same room as Michael. Eventually, I would drag myself out of bed to go and try to ease the load and hopefully diffuse Michael's mood by attempting to take over the household tasks.

Another emotion which I, and I'm sure many M.E. sufferers, experience is guilt. I felt guilty because often when the boys came home from school, they would find me in bed, not able to be a normal mum, doing what ordinary mums would be doing. Not being able to take part in the mothers' race on sports days, not being able to 'taxi' them around, as I should have done, for example.

You may be thinking, hang on a minute; at least you were there, weren't you? Many children don't even have a mother around at all. True, but that thought didn't change how I felt. I hadn't been able to be a full-time mother to Christopher, and now I was falling short at the task for Nicholas and Oliver.

None of my boys has ever said or inferred that they felt this way. They have always — and still do — treated me with the utmost care and respect. However, in all honesty, I'm sure they must have found it hard and, like me, wished vehemently that the situation could have been different.

Stress is one of the worst things for chronic fatigue sufferers and can, in fact, be one of the leading causes of the condition. It therefore followed that when life was relatively calm and safe, I would feel less tired and be able to do more. In the same vein, as soon as the atmosphere at home became volatile, then I would slip involuntarily into an M.E. attack, and this was the pattern my life had now adopted.

I didn't think life could burden me with any more suffering. How wrong could I be!

Chapter 28

By 1993, Nicholas had moved on to senior school, and Oliver was at prep school. Nicholas settled into his new school very well and immediately became involved in the school rugby.

Meanwhile, Oliver had also discovered and showed a great affinity for the game. He was playing mini rugby at a local club, but sadly his school did not offer the sport. By the time Oliver started his last year at prep school, he was really into his rugby and playing extremely well, so he approached his sports teacher to begin rugby in school. Eventually, Oliver got his way, and rugby became part of the curriculum.

We truly admired Oliver's spirit and determination for going after what he wanted and succeeding. Oliver was one jubilant young man.

If you have ever been through the process of a compensation claim for personal injury, you will be able to empathise with the sheer pressure and frustration that is thrust upon you. If not, believe me, it can be horrendous. I was the victim of the car accident and yet the representatives of the guilty driver, whose actions caused my injury, seemed intent in wriggling out of their responsibilities.

I had to attend medical examinations for 'both parties', and on many occasions the medical examiners for the 'other side' seemed intent on proving I could move my body in ways that I no longer could. When trying to oblige and being unable to do so, they would become agitated, reducing me to tears, and I would go back home feeling extremely distressed, not being able to understand how they could act in this brutal way.

Another way they try to 'catch you out' is to have you followed by someone with a video camera, the aim being to record you on film doing something you claim you are unable to do. Now, I fully appreciate that there must be many cases where fraudulent claims are made. However, when, as in my case, it is entirely true, the pain is real, not being able to move in certain ways, and also not being able to dance any more, it is utterly devastating having people trying to make you out to be a liar. As if your injuries aren't enough to cope with, it is cruel to try and make out that it is all pretence!

My solicitor had pre-warned me that they may try to 'catch me out' on camera, but insisted I had no cause for concern because they wouldn't be able to find any incriminating evidence.

One Saturday morning, when I was due to go to KAPA and felt able to drive myself, Michael went out to defrost my car before I set off. When he came back inside, he informed me that a man was sitting in a white van just across from our bungalow and had been there for quite a while. Fearing that perhaps I may be being watched, Michael helped me into my car and loaded my work equipment as usual. He then told me to remain calm, and if the white van proceeded to follow me, then Michael would, at a distance, follow the van.

I pulled out of the driveway and set off on my journey, and immediately, on looking in my mirror, I saw the van behind me. I felt nervous; I don't know why, I had nothing to hide, but it was a horrible feeling having someone trailing you.

As I pulled up at the dance school, the white van passed me and stopped a short distance further up the road. I was shaking and started to breathe deeply to try and calm myself. I pressed my horn, which I always did, and right on cue Julie and a couple of students came out as usual, and Julie helped me out of the car while my students unloaded the equipment. Michael had phoned Julie so she was aware of what was happening, as he knew I would be somewhat upset. We made our way into the school and prepared to start the day's classes, not knowing what to expect from the 'video man'.

Jane brought me my coffee, as she always did, and in case this man tried to enter the school I confided in her what was happening. The children's safety being paramount, Jane would always greet and question any unexpected visitors.

I was sitting on my chair inside the door, operating the music player, while Jenny, one of my student teachers, began to teach a junior ballet class.

Julie, meanwhile, was on guard, while teaching a tap class in another room, ready to be called if needed.

Michael, who had followed the van, parked around the corner and entered the school through the rear entrance, and was waiting in the kitchen.

The class had only been running for about fifteen minutes when Jane, who handled the situation brilliantly, popped her head around the door and said "Jessica, sorry to interrupt, but I have a gentleman here who is enquiring about dance classes for his daughters."

The man came in, and I invited him to take a seat at the table where I was sitting. As he sat down, he 'accidentally' knocked a packet of biscuits off the table and they went everywhere. Tracy, another student of mine, immediately came to my aid. "Don't worry, miss, I'll get them for you." Tracy knew I wasn't able to reach down to the floor to retrieve the biscuits, but the video man's little plan had failed because now he also knew I couldn't!

This 'creep', as I choose to call him — because, in my mind, he was — then proceeded to tell me he had two daughters aged six and eight and asked what classes I could offer them. I explained the different dance styles, singing and drama that we could provide 'his children' and suggested he leave his name and address and I would see that a prospectus and enrolment form were sent to him. He went on to say that perhaps his wife would be better placed to deal with this and suggested that she might call me to discuss such. Tracy fetched him one of my business cards and he then left the school, crossed the road and climbed back into his white van, watched by Jane!

It wasn't at all funny at the time and what the 'creep' did was despicable; but when Jane, Michael and Julie came into the hall where I was, we all dissolved into hysterics because he had failed miserably. He left with no incriminating footage and with his tail between his legs! His camera had obviously been under his coat.

Guess what? I never did receive a phone call from his 'wife', but then I never expected to!

As my case continued, various offers of settlement were made, but my solicitor insisted on refusing them, as I was entitled to much more. There were, however, more than a few occasions when I just wanted to throw in the towel. However much money I received, it wasn't going to give me my body back or make me able to dance again; but his insistence that the money would help me in many ways, such as my future medical bills and loss of earnings, made me hang on.

As the compensation claim was nearing its end, something I found very amusing happened which entirely proved that my solicitor was right about the compensation I was entitled to.

Apparently, one lunchtime, one of his office juniors met a friend from another legal firm for lunch. They did, during lunch, unthinkingly break the rules and discuss a current case that the friend's firm was engaged in. He told my solicitor's junior that they had a very big case going on regarding a young dancer whose career had been severely affected and an ongoing injury sustained following a road traffic accident. Their client was totally to blame, and that as 'video footage' and many examinations had proved that her injuries were real, they were looking at an enormous pay-out!

My solicitor's junior then told his lunch partner that it was a real coincidence as their firm was also involved in a big case about a dancer!

Although totally out of order, these somewhat irresponsible young men had done us a favour by confirming what the 'other side' expected to pay out, so we hung on till the last minute, insisting we would take the case to court if they didn't pay the required settlement.

The afternoon before we were due in court, I was sitting at home working my way through the enormous files my solicitor had given me, feeling very nervous about what the next day would bring. My solicitor still insisted that the other side would not let it get to court, even at this late stage, because they knew that it was highly likely that the judge would award an even higher settlement than my solicitor was requesting.

My man certainly knew his stuff. At five o'clock that afternoon, he rang me and told me to put the files down, it was all over. Settlement out of court had occurred, as he knew it would, and the requested settlement figure had been agreed upon.

I dropped the file I was holding onto the floor and, when I'd recovered my composure, thanked him profusely for bringing this case to such a successful end; I was overjoyed it was finished. However, when my settlement payment arrived in the post, I expected, metaphorically speaking, to be jumping up and down with joy. In reality, I just stared at it blankly. Although I had to acknowledge that it would, of course, make life a lot easier financially, enabling me to pursue treatments which may bring some pain relief, but beyond that I felt nothing. No emotion at all; what I wanted most, this piece of paper I was holding couldn't give me.

Chapter 29

I have, for as long as I can remember, had a great love for North Cornwall. Since spending family holidays there as a child, I have always felt a great affinity for the beautiful landscape it has to offer and the power and majesty of its breath-taking coastline. I also love the folklore and fascinating legends which are entwined through this mystical place.

It therefore made perfect sense to me that once I had come to terms with the help my compensation could bring me, I decided that some good should come out of this, something which would benefit the entire family; and so I decided to purchase a small cottage to serve as a holiday home for us all.

The cottage nestled in a tiny hamlet on the edge of Bodmin Moor, a perfect location for revisiting all our favourite haunts. The place that topped the list for me was Nectan's Glen, a place of ultimate peace and beauty, situated in Trethevy, near to the very magical Tintagel. What is so special about this place is that it houses, hidden from the outside world, a spectacular sixty-foot waterfall. Gaining access to the waterfall involves walking through a beautiful, dense woodland valley, along the Trevillet River, necessitating crossing a few rickety wooden bridges en route, thus taking you back and forth to both sides of the river. This walk itself is remarkable and somewhat unworldly, as you encounter lush tree ferns, quartz stone, incredibly strange trees, and in May a magical carpet of bluebells awaits you. Eventually, the walk culminates at some ancient stone steps, leading up to 'The Hermitage'. This is where the Glen owners reside, and there is a small teashop providing refreshments, gratefully received by all on arrival!

The Hermitage is a late nineteenth century, half-timbered building, which is said to be constructed on the remains of a Celtic chapel, supposedly built by St. Nectan in 500 AD. St. Nectan is one of the West of England's most celebrated saints, being the eldest son of the Celtic king, Brychan. On receiving a vocation to become a monk, he sailed from Wales to the Cornwall-Devon border. On landing here, he settled by a spring at Stoke in the dense Hartland Forest, north of Bude. He lived here as a hermit, tending the sick and the poor throughout Cornwall and Devon.

Legend claims that the Knights of King Arthur's Round Table came to St. Nectan at the chapel he built at Nectan's Glen, to be anointed by him before undertaking their quest to find the Holy Grail. Believe it or not as you will, but still a fascinating story.

Next to the teashop is St. Nectan's Cell. Slate steps lead up to this small chapel, and the rear rock forms a natural altar. The shrine inside is quite beautiful, decked out with various donations from local artists, including statues of water goddesses, mermaids and fairies, along with rocks, crystals and other trinkets. Pieces of paper containing prayers of thanks or from those in need are scattered around the shrine, and there is a display of photographs showing 'Spirit Orbs" taken in the Kieve, which is situated at the bottom of a majestic sixty-foot waterfall. It is assumed and I choose to believe, that these represent the spirits that dwell in this place, but there are, of course, a number of theories; moisture or water reflecting on the camera lens, for example. Kieve is the Cornish word for basin and this particular kieve is twenty feet deep and is rounded smoothly; rather like a very large sugar bowl.

The waterfall itself is accessed through a gate by the teashop, down some old stone steps. As you descend, the steam rising from below surrounds you and the thunder of the falls is heard before encountering them. As you round the corner, you then behold a sight that will truly take your breath away! The waterfall is said to have healing powers and is known as one of this country's most spiritually significant places. The water crashing down from above, into the kieve or basin at the base of the falls, overflows into a beautiful healing pool, in which many visitors stand or bathe to receive the healing properties, and when you look up at the top of the falls, it almost appears to be bathed in an ethereal glow.

The flora and fauna are also fascinating, and the damp shade supports a few rarities, amongst which are two rare liverworts. There is a rich wildlife here amidst a mysticism of fairies and spirits, all enveloped with the beautiful sound of birdsong.

Whether, like me, you believe in angels, fairies and other spirits of nature, whether you are a keen horticulturist or animal and bird lover, or if you simply wish to enjoy a visit to an outstandingly beautiful place, then I would highly recommend visiting Nectan's Glen.

Another favourite Cornish landmark of mine is Tintagel Castle (King Arthur's Castle), which is a medieval fortification on the Peninsula of Tintagel Island, close to Tintagel Village. The Castle has a long association with Arthurian legends, dating back to the twelfth century. In history, King Arthur's time would have been the fifth century, and although it is impossible to prove whether he did exist, known history identifies him to a great Celtic chieftain in the West of England who had a known fortress where Tintagel Castle is today. The original fort has now gone, but archaeological digs have produced proof that fifth-century citizens lived on this site.

A new castle was built on the site around 1230 by Earl Richard of Cornwall and is now nearly eight hundred years old. After two hundred years the castle was in ruins and remains so to this day. Legend says that in the fifth century, Tintagel Castle was the fortress of Gorlais, husband of Ygerna.

Merlin the wise man disguised King Uther to look like Gorlais and tricked Ygerna into making love to him, resulting in the conception of King Arthur.

Many believe that Tintagel was Camelot, and when you think of King Arthur, it's very easy to imagine Queen Guinevere by his side, the wise man Merlin, Lancelot — his most trusted knight — along with the other knights of the Round Table, the magical sword Excalibur and much more.

Whether the legend is right, we can never really know. It is up to the individual to believe what they wish. However, much evidence has been discovered to support the legend of King Arthur, and it certainly gives you food for thought.

In 1998, a sixth century stone slab was discovered, which I have seen, at Tintagel. The slab bears the inscription, 'Pater coli avi fecit Artognov', meaning 'Artognou, father of a descendant of Coll, has had this built'. The name Artognou was most likely pronounced Arthnou. Arth was a Dark Age prefix added to the name of a ruler. This confirms that a wealthy person, with a name like Arthur, lived here in the sixth century. Quite fascinating.

Significant amounts of expensive pottery have been found on the castle site, which would have been imported from the Mediterranean, thus suggesting that an important chief controlled the fortress. It is highly possible, therefore, that this man was Gorlais, Duke of Cornwall and King Arthur's father.

A final example exists which is so overwhelming it is difficult to warrant any opposition. There have been thousands of reported sightings of the ghost of Arthur at Tintagel. In my mind, it follows that these can't all be the visions of the neurotic, charlatan or just attention-seeking time-wasters. More than two hundred of these people have been interviewed by a very reliable source, and this person claims that many of the interviewees were very 'ordinary, down to earth' people.

If we are therefore prepared to accept that King Arthur's ghost has been seen at Tintagel, then we must surely presume that he once lived.

Interestingly, over eight centuries ago, Geoffrey of Monmouth, a Welsh monk residing in Oxford, wrote the first bestseller in the history of British publishing, entitled *History of the Kings of Britain*. Because of Geoffrey of Monmouth, the Arthurian theme came to life. As Cornwall has so many Arthur place names, and locations with a related Arthurian story, we are inevitably bound to ask the question, 'Can there be smoke without fire?'

Naturally, Tintagel and its castle make the most of the Arthurian legend to promote tourism, and there are many facilities for visitors. There is an audio-visual tour available, 'Searching for King Arthur', a shop, cafe and toilets on site, and between April and September, a Land Rover service is available down to these facilities for the less able. There is a climb of at least one hundred steps from here to reach the castle, but it can also be accessed from the church of St Materiana along the coastal path, and this in itself is a lovely experience.

Finally, a parting note before we leave this mystical place. The nearby Castle Beach is one of the safest bathing beaches in Cornwall, and Merlin's Cave can be seen at the beach. Did Merlin the magician live here?

Tintagel is a must if you are considering holidaying in the West Country.

Chapter 30

We decided to spend the Christmas of 1993 at our Cornish cottage, and we were all very excited at the prospect, as my mother Martha, Christopher and Michael's mother Dora were going to be joining us. I was hopeful that this might aid the healing process to further bridge the gap between Michael, my mother and Christopher.

Michael, Nicholas, Oliver, Dora and I went down to the cottage a few days before Christmas to make sure all preparations were in place and the cottage looked its best, while my mother and Christopher were planning to join us on Christmas Eve.

The main front door was situated in the centre of the cottage. On entering, you came into a small square room from which a door led off to the right into the living room. A staircase ran along the left wall leading upstairs, and just beyond the stairs was the door to the kitchen. Upstairs there were two double bedrooms and a relatively large bathroom.

Michael and I were to use the main bedroom, my mother, Dora and Oliver were to share the second room, containing three single beds, and Christopher and Nicholas were going to 'camp out' in the living room.

While I prepared the bedrooms, Michael and the boys set about erecting the Christmas tree and ensuring there was an ample supply of logs for the fantastic open fire in the living room. An ancient and large fireplace, one of my favourite features of the cottage, housed the fire.

Once the decorations were up and presents wrapped, it felt splendid, and I was determined that this was going to be a great family Christmas.

On Christmas Eve, Christopher and his grandmother were stopping off en route to have lunch with my cousin and her family and were expected at the cottage around five o'clock.

The fire was alight, the roast beef for dinner was cooking in the oven, and Michael, Dora, the boys and I were relaxing in the lounge, awaiting their arrival. As we waited, five o'clock came and went, then five thirty, then six o'clock, and by now the boys were becoming very restless, as they were so excited at the prospect of their brother and grandmother joining us. I could also sense that Michael was becoming somewhat agitated, insisting that they could have let us know if they were delayed. My response to this was that they would have to find a roadside phone box to do so, something not waiting around every corner in the lanes of Cornwall.

However, I was by now becoming anxious; they should have been here by now, but they weren't, and there was nothing to do but wait.

I suddenly had the idea to ring my cousin Suzanne and check what time mother and Christopher had left, so we could try and gauge where they should be. Suzanne was extremely apologetic but told us that lunch had been delayed and that they hadn't, in fact, left until about three o'clock, an hour later than planned. She was very cross with herself that she hadn't thought to let me know, although I made it clear that she was in no way to blame. We now knew that they should be arriving at any time, and although this brought great relief, I felt very unsettled, as Michael's agitation didn't disperse. He was angry that we had been put through this unnecessary concern. He was right to feel like this, but I hoped that when he knew everything was okay and our worries proved unfounded, that he would relax and 'let it go'. Unfortunately, this was something he was unable to do, so there was an unpleasant atmosphere even before our Christmas together had started.

No sooner had I put the phone down on my cousin, than the cottage phone rang, and I heard Christopher's voice on the line. He was ringing from the phone box at the end of the hamlet, as he wasn't sure exactly where the cottage was. It was well hidden from the view of the road, and he needed directions to us. Within a few minutes, we heard Christopher's car stop at the top of the garden path and Nicholas and Oliver threw open the front door, as their suppressed excitement exploded, to greet their grandmother and brother. As they came into the cottage, I told my mother that we had been worried that something had happened because they were so late and how I had phoned Suzanne to check when they had left. She was very apologetic and reiterated what Suzanne had said about the delay in serving lunch. I told her that in itself it was absolutely no problem, but she should have thought to call us. However, they were here now, and that was what mattered.

Nevertheless, things were about to go from bad to worse. Before mum had even had time to remove her coat, the cottage phone rang again; it was my sister, Joanne. She was ringing to see if Christopher and mum had arrived and asked to speak to her. I was about to explain that they had only just arrived and could mother therefore call back in a little while, when mother spoke up, saying that it was okay, she would talk to Joanne now. As I passed over the receiver my heart sank; mother had made a big mistake here. We'd just got over the stress of the afternoon, Nicholas and Oliver were desperate to show their grandmother around the cottage, and here she was sitting on the arm of the chair, coat still on, engrossed in conversation with my sister!

As the boys were halted in their tracks, I sensed Michael's reaction before I even looked at him. He stormed out into the kitchen to fix himself a drink, and I followed him, feeling the tension spreading through my body. He was furious at Martha's behaviour, and I admit, he was right to be so. She had been tactless; she just hadn't thought about what she was doing.

I asked Michael to please just let it go, as we didn't want the whole holiday spoiled, but he just walked upstairs and stayed there until dinner was on the table. Then followed a very strained dinner, with Dora and me trying to make conversation, and what didn't help also was the fact that the meal was somewhat past its best by the time it was served.

I went to bed that night with my heart in my boots. How could my dreams of a happy holiday have been shattered so easily, so soon?

Christmas morning arrived, and when we were all gathered around the roaring fire, watching the boys opening their presents, the atmosphere seemed to have lifted somewhat, and Michael appeared more amiable. Thank goodness, I thought, it's going to be all right after all. After breakfast, Michael put the turkey in the oven, as he had decided he would cook the Christmas dinner. Martha, Dora and I prepared the vegetables for him and laid the table.

Then the next problem arrived; one of the boys announced that the toilet was blocked! The investigation revealed that this was indeed the situation, and therefore Michael went outside to lift the manhole cover and hopefully find the source of the problem. As he came back into the kitchen, mother, trying to be helpful, suggested that he looked in the Yellow Pages for a 'Drain Man'. Oh, dearest mother of mine, one doesn't in a situation like this tell a fifty-year-old man what to do. Some would have raised their eyes to the ceiling perhaps and let this 'advice' go over their head, but not Michael. The look on his face told me exactly what he was thinking. He stormed out and returned a short while later with our neighbour and his drain rods in tow and they proceeded to spend Christmas morning clearing the drains — not ideal in any situation! Once the problem had been resolved, and Michael had cleaned himself up, he then proceeded to take the turkey out of the oven for inspection. As he was doing so, mother said to him, "Leave that, Michael, it's okay, I've got it all under control." Again, she didn't mean any harm; she thought she was helping, as Michael had been occupied with less savoury activities. However, as Michael stormed upstairs and I followed to try and calm the situation again, he told me that he was sick of my mother interfering in everything.

What was I supposed to do? I did appreciate how Michael felt, but I'm sure many men would say their mother-in-law interfered; surely, it's how you deal with it that matters?

We were only here for a few days, could he not try and let it waft over him? I could see that my mother did think she was being kind and helpful, so how was I supposed to resolve this?

Just before lunch, a Christmas card was pushed through our letterbox from another neighbour called Jackie, whom we didn't know that well at this time. Thinking this a pleasant gesture, Michael suggested returning a card. I wrote one and Michael told Oliver to go and deliver it. Oliver, understandably, didn't want to do this — he didn't know Jackie and felt apprehensive at going to a strange house. Michael, however, his intolerance still apparent, insisted Oliver do this. As I reluctantly handed Oliver the card, not wanting to instigate any more disharmony, which as it turned out I inadvertently did, Michael glanced at the envelope and asked, "Don't you know how to spell Jackie? You've spelt it wrong!"

I replied that this name could be spelt in more than one way and that I'm sure the lady in question wouldn't be offended if I had chosen the wrong spelling. Michael then proceeded to yell at me that it did matter, and his version was, of course, correct, so I quietly changed it and sent little Oliver on his way. Michael left the room and then it was mother's turn to be angry. "How dare he speak to you like that, and particularly in company!" I asked her just to leave it, as I was at my wits' end already and couldn't be doing with any more aggravation.

We made it somehow through Christmas lunch, after which we opened the rest of the presents and then, guess what? More problems. Michael had requested that he be able to watch Pavarotti, the world-famous opera singer, on television that afternoon, and although this wasn't anyone else's cup of tea, it was only right that he should be allowed to watch this programme in peace. Christopher and Nicholas were upstairs listening to some music together, we ladies were just relaxing in front of the fire, but young Oliver decided he didn't want to play with his new toys at that time — he wanted to watch his new *Toy Story* DVD. Michael told him that he could watch it later, so as any child would, he came to me and asked if he could watch it now. I reiterated what Michael had said and told Oliver that he could watch it later as Daddy had said to him. Little Oliver wasn't giving up that easily. He then went to my mother with the same question, and she replied, "It's fine with me, darling, but it's up to Daddy."

That was the straw that broke the camel's back; Michael stormed up to our bedroom and slammed the door. He thought mother was saying that Oliver could watch his film now, while she had meant that she didn't mind when he watched it, it was up to Michael. Looking back, I could have banged their heads together. They just seemed to be rubbing each other up the wrong way at every turn, and here was I stuck in the middle, being able to see both sides of the situation and not being able to resolve it, while my fantasy Christmas crumbled around my feet.

Michael spent the remainder of the day in our bedroom, reading, while I tried to put on a brave face — saying he had a bad headache — and get through the rest of the day as harmoniously as possible. As I lay in bed that night, I tried to make some sense of why this all had to go so horribly wrong. I was unable to do so. Was I trying to achieve something that was beyond achievement? Perhaps, but I knew I had had to try. Sadly, it had failed miserably.

As I lay in the dark, I heard coming from below the voices and laughter of Christopher and Nicholas as they chatted and laughed together while watching a DVD. This, at least, I thought was wonderful, listening to two brothers sharing time happily together. No sooner had I immersed myself in the pleasure of that vision when it was shattered. Michael got out of bed, went downstairs and told the boys to turn off the film and go to sleep, as they were disturbing everyone else. I was upset now; they weren't bothering anyone, and I told Michael so when he returned to bed. He wasn't interested in what I thought and turned his back on me angrily and went to sleep.

The next morning, as you would expect, Christopher and Nicholas were very sullen, mother and Dora remained silent, and Oliver, sensing this disharmony, decided to 'play up' and be difficult.

I'm not sure how, but we decided to go on a walk to 'Rocky Valley', another beautiful Cornish landmark. During the walk, Nicholas and Oliver cheered up a little as they climbed over the rocks, but the atmosphere amongst the adults was very strained. Following a pub lunch, we all returned to the cottage, then Michael immediately left again, saying he needed some space. That's when all hell broke loose. Mother let her feelings out, saying that Michael had made no attempt to get on over the last couple of days and that she wanted to go home straight away. Christopher, supporting what she said, agreed to take her home. This somehow turned into a very loud argument between Mother, Christopher and me, and then Nicholas became involved as he came to my defence, not wanting me to be shouted at. As the situation became more volatile, the most unfortunate thing, at that time, happened. Christopher became angry in a way I had never seen him before. He started shouting about Michael. It was as if all his pent-up emotion and anger over what had happened between him and Michael was being released involuntarily at this moment. Then, all of a sudden, he turned to Nicholas and yelled, "If you think this is bad, I'll tell you what your wonderful father is really capable of!"

Before I could try and diffuse the situation, Christopher was screaming about Michael beating him and the way he lived in fear of his anger and intolerance. "Dear God," I thought; this was the cathartic experience that was inevitable for Christopher, but why now, with his brother hearing all and understanding nothing.

Dora, meanwhile, had shut herself and Oliver in their bedroom, not knowing what to do. Christopher was crying, mother was shouting at me in desperation, saying that she would never forgive Michael for this, and Nicholas was stunned, rendered motionless.

Christopher then told his grandmother to pack quickly and within minutes they had left the cottage to make their way home.

I was shaking uncontrollably; Nicholas was asking me repeatedly if what Christopher had said was true. Oliver was crying because his brother and grandmother had left. I had to take control of the situation; I had to pull myself together for the boys' sake. They were frightened, confused, as was I, but I was their mother — I had to sort this. I told the boys to go and pack as quickly as they could because I was going home, and if they wanted to come with me, they must do as I ask without question. I told Nicholas I would try to answer his questions later when we arrived home. I then explained to Dora that I had to get as far away from the cottage and Michael as possible and that I was more than happy to take her with us if that was what she wanted.

When Michael returned, I told him why mother and Christopher had gone and that I hoped he was pleased with himself. All I wanted was a united, happy family Christmas, but even that was too much to ask. I told him I couldn't be near him at the moment and was taking the boys and Dora home. Surprisingly, Michael made no objection and decided he would stay at the cottage for a few more days and perhaps we could talk when he came back. At that moment I had nothing to say; I was too angry and upset.

I got into the car with the boys and Dora and drove away without looking back… silent tears rolling down my cheeks.

Chapter 31

By the time we arrived home, it was getting very late, so Oliver and Dora went straight to bed. I felt great sympathy for Dora, as she apologised for Michael's impatience. I gave her a hug and made it quite clear that she was in no way to blame for her son's behaviour. She had nothing to apologise for. I loved Dora immensely, and it pained me to see her upset in this way.

Once Nicholas and I were alone, he again asked me whether what Christopher had said Michael had done was true. I knew that Nicholas wasn't going to be fobbed off and thought to myself that he wasn't a lot younger now than Christopher was when I had to tell him all about his father. I decided I should be honest with Nicholas, and so we sat down together and I confirmed that Christopher was telling the truth. I went on to explain to Nicholas why things had gone so terribly wrong between his father and Christopher.

After I had finished speaking, Nicholas didn't say very much, except that he now understood why Christopher had gone to live with their grandmother. I explained that what I had told Nicholas was in the strictest confidence and was not to be divulged to anyone else. Yes, he now knew the truth about his father and brother, but that he should try to put it to the back of his mind and not dwell upon it in any way. Nicholas then gave me a big hug and told me that he would always look after me, and then he took himself off to bed. I was incredibly touched by this loving act and was left dumbfounded again at the sheer maturity and resilience that both Christopher and now Nicholas had shown.

I went off to bed myself, and as I lay there in the dark, my thoughts swirled around in my head. What was I going to do now? Mother and Christopher were angry and upset, and what was going to happen when Michael decided to come back home? The answers weren't forthcoming, and in sheer despair I buried my face in my pillow and cried myself into a fitful sleep.

A few days later, Michael returned home in an extremely contrite and apologetic mood. Now that we were both calm and had had some space between us, we were able to discuss what had gone so very wrong at Christmas. Michael told me that he felt undermined by my mother and that she interfered too much. I replied that I did appreciate how he felt and at times I agreed that mother's offers of help could come across as interference, but that surely for such a short period he could have tried to 'grin and bear it'. Michael's response was that he wished he could have, but he couldn't. He said I knew how small his intolerance level was, and he was being pushed too far. It all came back to the same issue as always, Michael's anger problem. Why wouldn't he try and get himself some help?

Now, further down the line, I know the answer. He didn't apparently realise that his anger was such a major problem, and in any way, abnormal! I still find this so hard to understand and believe.

Gradually, life slipped back into its usual pattern, Michael would do something pleasant, or say something lovely to me; he would be in a happy mood and therefore so would the boys, and once again the adverse problems would fade into the background. As I said before, Michael's generosity knew no bounds, and he would often take me on shopping expeditions. He liked me to have lovely clothes and would thoroughly spoil me on these shopping trips. Not only did he trudge willingly around endless clothes shops, but also, he would quite happily go along the clothes rails selecting things for me to try, which he thought I might like.

Times like these that we spent together were lovely, and I remember them with fondness. However, although I was very appreciative and thrilled with my lovely purchases, I would honestly have swapped them all if it meant having 'calm and happy Michael' more often.

Eventually, mother, Christopher and I got back on track, but Michael was never to be mentioned to them again.

Over the next couple of years, a change came over me, and I began to wish that there was some way I could get Michael to understand really what his actions and behaviour were doing not only to me but also to Nicholas and Oliver. They were obviously also subjected to his outbursts when they were at home. I worried about the effect this mercurial behaviour would have on them. I so wanted to confront Michael. This feeling was becoming stronger and stronger, but I just couldn't bring myself to do it. The crux of it was that I was so afraid that by confronting him I would anger him more.

Then, on 31st August 1997, something happened that was to help me overcome my fear and say what I wanted to say; something extremely tragic — Princess Diana died.

Michael and I were both strong supporters of the work that she did, and I recall on the morning of her accident Michael woke me, in a state of shock, and told me the dreadful news. We sat and watched the news on television, struggling to make sense of why this should have happened. Diana had much to cope with during her life and yet somehow, deep inside, she carried a hidden strength and emanated an aura of genuine care and support for those in need. She had the strength to fight for what she believed in. For some inexplicable reason, Diana's death had a tremendous impact on me, and I decided that the day of her death was the day I would confront Michael, and I did.

That afternoon, both Nicholas and Oliver were visiting friends, so I grasped the opportunity and told Michael that I needed to speak to him.

As he sat in the armchair, opposite the sofa where I was sitting, waiting to hear what I wanted to say, I began shaking. That same old feeling. Sweat started to trickle down my neck, and my shoulders lifted up near my ears. I was terrified of how Michael would react, and yet it was this fear that pushed me on. Being this afraid of him confirmed that there was something very wrong which wasn't getting any better, and I had to speak out. As I started to speak, my voice shook. I ventured to tell Michael that I didn't think he understood how the boys and I felt when he became angry and impatient, and that we needed it to stop. As Michael listened intently, I began to relax a little and thought to myself, "You've come this far, girl, keep going!"

Taking an enormous deep breath, I then went on to explain, which I had never done before, just how deeply I had been affected, firstly by Michael's abuse to Christopher and secondly by not having my son with me. When I asked Michael to imagine how he would feel if I had treated a child of his in this manner, he became very tearful and genuinely upset, saying that he had never really thought about it in that way. He couldn't bear the thought, and he begged my forgiveness for what had happened.

Finally, I'm not sure why — Divine intervention maybe — Michael asked if I would please not tell Nicholas and Oliver what he had done to Christopher.

Oh, dear God, I felt the fear creeping through me again; should I tell Michael the truth or stay silent to keep the peace? No, I'd done that for too long; the truth must out. I told Michael that I would never have intentionally told the boys about this, but that during the terrible row at the cottage poor Christopher, in desperation, had screamed it out and therefore Nicholas was now acutely aware of what had occurred.

Before I could say another word, Michael exploded — he went ballistic. He was screaming at me in anger because Nicholas knew, and I didn't get a chance to explain that it wasn't intentional or that I had spoken to Nicholas about it. Michael was uncontrollable; he hurled the glass of red wine he was holding at our patio doors, one of which cracked under the force! I was terrified. I expected some reaction from Michael, but not to this extent. He thumped the wall and screamed at me that he would never forgive Christopher for speaking out.

Hold on a second, what did Christopher do wrong? He's the victim here, and surely is it not Christopher whom Michael should be seeking forgiveness from?

Michael stormed out of the house and slammed the front door with such force that it shook on its hinges. I dissolved into violent, uncontrollable sobs, and Dora, having heard the disturbance, came through to try and comfort me. "Why does he have to get so angry?" she asked. "I hate to see you like this."

Michael didn't return home until very late that evening, and when he did, he completely ignored me.

He continued banging and crashing around, still evidently enveloped in anger.

We had planned on the following morning to go as a family up to Kensington Palace to sign the book of remembrance for Diana. However, after the events of the day, I felt that this would go completely by the wayside. When I rose the following morning, Michael, as expected, ignored me, and I wondered how long this dark mood was going to last. After a short while, however, he completely surprised me by asking whether I was still planning to go to London. I replied that I would have liked to but didn't feel up to the drive. To my amazement, he offered to drive me, as he still wanted to go himself. The atmosphere in the car still felt very volatile as we drove to London, but I lived in hope that maybe during the day Michael would be calm enough to be able to accept what I had told him and deal with it accordingly.

We had to queue for a long while before we eventually reached the doors of the Palace. As we walked inside, a tremendous feeling of calm swept over me.

I pondered for a short while over what I should write in the 'Book of Remembrance', and then it came to me. "Dearest Diana, I have great respect for the work you did in your lifetime, and I thank you for helping me, in some way, to find the strength to heal my family."

As I walked outside, I noticed Michael looking at what I had written. This didn't concern me, so I started to stroll through the gardens and stopped at a stone archway to admire a 'hidden garden' through it. I was lost in my thoughts as I appreciated the beauty of the sight before me, when suddenly I was aware of an arm wrapping around my waist. It was Michael, and as we stood there, motionless, he whispered to me, "I am so very sorry. If I could turn the clock back and change what I have done, I would. I'm so sorry."

Wow! This knocked me for six, but in that instant, I knew that I had done the right thing. It was a great pity that for many reasons I hadn't been able to speak out or stand up to Michael before. I now believed he was some way to understanding the consequences of his actions. I could only hope and pray that this was a turning point and that changes were on the horizon; only time would tell.

Tragically, in spite of renewed hope of change, this year ended very sadly for us all. On 31st December 1999, lovely Dora died. She had been suffering from a weak heart for a while, but on New Year's Eve she lost the fight for life. We were all shaken very badly by this loss and decided that we couldn't remain in the home where Dora had been. It felt so empty without her, and so we decided to move house again.

In the meantime, changes were taking place in the boys' lives. Christopher, still living with his grandmother and caring for her with unflinching fondness, had met a young lady at work named Nina, who, although we didn't know it at the time, was to become his future wife.

Nicholas was now Captain of the school rugby team. He was playing rugby at representative level, and his skills and talent for the game had secured him a place with Premiership side London Wasps' Under-20 youth squad at sixteen years of age! He lived for it.

Oliver, having started at senior school, discovered a talent and love for music. He became — and still is — a very proficient saxophonist, while also playing the guitar. The school Oliver attended was a military music school, and we enjoyed many a Sunday morning attending the parades. Tartan-clad, kilted bands would march past, the sound of bagpipes and drums filling the air. Then the brass band would join in the proceedings, and we watched with immense pride as Oliver made music with his saxophone.

My dance school was still thriving, but it was becoming harder every day, the M.E. still haunting me and making it more difficult for me to continue playing an active role. I was beginning, albeit with great reluctance, to concede that my dancing days were well and truly numbered.

Chapter 32

While we were in the process of searching for a new home, a rather strange thing happened. I had cause one day to be in a particular area, and while there I had the urge to drive down a road which I hadn't been down before. So, listening to my intuition, I went on this small detour, and how glad was I that I did. This road was very quiet and fringed with woodland, and as I drove down it, I recall thinking what a lovely place this would be to live. No sooner had this thought come into my head than I passed a house set back from the road, nestled among the trees, that had a 'for sale' sign outside. I turned the car around and pulled up outside this property and was instantly drawn to it. A driveway from the road led down to a garage, to the left of which was a set of broad steps leading up to the front entrance of the property, consisting of two impressive wooden doors.

I was overcome with excitement; I had to see inside this house. Ridiculous as it may sound, it felt like a magnet was doing its utmost to pull me in. I went home and rushed to tell Michael about the house and that we had to go and see it. He informed me that it was on a very expensive road and most likely unaffordable for us, but I couldn't let it go. Therefore, to placate me, we went to view the property.

As we stepped inside the house, we found ourselves in a large, square hallway, with doors and stairs leading from it.

Before we ventured any further, I had fallen in love with the place. This house conveyed sadness to me; it needed nurturing, and I so wanted to do it. The property was laid out over three levels. Immediately to the right on entering the house, a small staircase led to the top level, which housed two double bedrooms overlooking the front garden, a family bathroom and a huge master bedroom, complete with dressing room, en suite bathroom and its own balcony looking over the rear garden. I was completely amazed.

Returning to the entrance hall, being the second level, directly ahead was a study, which housed a trap door leading down to a cellar. To the left of the entrance hall, a doorway led into the dining room, and continuing ahead, another door led into an enormous kitchen.

As you entered the dining room from the hallway, immediately to the right were three wide steps leading down to a beautiful lounge with glass doors looking out onto a large, decked balcony, or rather what was at one time. This area was inaccessible as most of the wooden planks were rotten and protruded out at all angles. Again, returning to the entrance hall, to the left of the upward staircase was another small flight of stairs leading down to the lower level. Here we found an internal door to the garage, a utility room and two further reception rooms, one of which contained a sauna! From this room, patio doors led out to a paved area below the decked balcony, from which one could access the swimming pool. The pool was currently full of rubbish, covered in green slime and was the residence of many toads!

Beyond the pool was a green lawn, although extremely overgrown, surrounded by trees. As we walked round, it was evident that the house required a tremendous amount of work done to it. But as I looked at kitchen cupboards coming away from the walls, the tiredness of the overall decoration, the derelict pool and decking, etc, my heart went out to this house. I wanted desperately to turn it into a home.

Michael was right, being able to buy the house was one thing, but finding the funds to renovate it was looking to be impossible. In the end, the decision was made to sell our Cornish cottage and put the proceeds towards this new home. We hadn't been able to make use of the cottage as we had hoped, and it now held only sad memories for me, so I was happy to let it go.

Fortunately, the cottage sold very quickly, our offer was accepted on 'The Lodge', and we finally became the owners of 'my dream house'.

As I walked into our new home on moving-in day, I felt as if a warm blanket was enveloping me. I felt comfortable; I felt as if I had lived here forever. For some reason, this house needed me as much as I needed it.

We set about the renovation with a vengeance. New bathrooms and kitchen were installed, the decking repaired and the swimming pool returned to its former glory. What fun it was, in the loosest sense of the word, trying to catch and dispose of an army of toads who were very reluctant to leave! When the major work was completed, Michael gave me a free rein to completely redecorate. I was in my element, having decided to theme the rooms to give them their own character.

The master bedroom became a sandy yellow and coral retreat, with vivid linen to contrast. I adorned the room with the precious Egyptian artefacts Michael and I had brought back from our trip to Egypt; which you will read about later. These colours continued through to the dressing room and en suite area of the house.

The boys decorated their own rooms to their taste and also the family bathroom, which was mainly used by them. I must confess to initially being a little wary of their choice of slate grey and pastel green, but I was completely wrong — it looked amazing! The delicate pastel peach walls of the hallway and landing housed Chinese fans, pictures and statues, while the study, which was to be my workplace, became my dance room. I filled it with statues and pictures from many years in the industry, all with their own tale to tell. The kitchen became a traditional farmhouse heart of the home. What I loved most was having the space to accommodate a rustic table, therefore enabling us to eat here when we wished, something I'd always hankered after.

The dining room became a formal, medieval space, with an old oak dining table and high-backed oak chairs. Pictures of knights, Arthur, Merlin and Guinevere adorned the walls, while statues from this age complemented the overall effect. This theme was carried through to the lounge, albeit on a more subtle level.

One thing Michael had always desired was to own a baby grand piano, and although through sad circumstances, his wish was eventually granted. An old singing teacher of his from his youth sadly passed away, but generously left Michael her baby grand. The piano took pride of place in this room, where Oliver was occasionally heard tinkling the keys.

Another field (forgive the pun!) that Oliver was making great strides in, was his rugby. On starting at senior school, Oliver was initially put into the second team, of which he was made captain. However, there was another coach at Oliver's school who had come from Australia on a year's coaching programme. On seeing Oliver play, he immediately questioned why he was playing for the Seconds, and pretty quickly Oliver was moved into the first team. How thrilled he was and how proud we as parents were.

During his time at senior school, he went away to Wales on a very successful rugby tour. Through his whole school rugby career, Oliver's team only ever lost one match — quite an incredible record by anyone's standards. This match was the semi-final of the *Daily Mail* Cup competition, which they played at Whitgift School.

Oliver's opposite number during this game was a young man named Danny Cipriani, who went on to play fly-half for England. Oliver was able to say, 'I played against one of the best, but I certainly gave him a run for his money!'

As I was writing this book, I asked Oliver, apart from the obvious enjoyment of the game, what he felt rugby had given him. His answer was — it teaches great respect for others. During a match, your team is a solid united front, and each member would literally put himself or herself on the line for a fellow team-mate.

He likened it, with immense admiration, to soldiers serving abroad, in Afghanistan for example. How these incredible young men and women take selfless risks for their comrades. He was in no way comparing a game of rugby to what our military are doing, but the emotional comparison was a good one.

No disrespect intended here to any football fans, but Oliver's final comment was, "Football is ninety minutes of pretending that you're hurt, while rugby is eighty minutes of pretending you're not!"

Although I adored our new home with its new outlook, there was still sadness about it that I couldn't understand. The only thing I was aware of, and slightly disturbed by, was that when I walked into the dressing room to access the en suite, I always felt a cool chill and uneasiness, and could find no logical explanation for this. I eventually decided to confide in my meditation teacher Ann about this, and she suggested that perhaps an unhappy event had occurred in this room in the past. The negative energy from that had been absorbed, and this may be, with my high level of spiritual sensitivity, what I was picking up on.

She suggested a small ritual I could try that might release the 'Presence'. I waited until I was alone in the house one day and set about doing what Ann had suggested. I sat down in the centre of the dressing room and lit a candle. I performed a protective process for myself and then proceeded to speak the clearing words Ann had suggested. What I experienced was quite incredible! As I sat there, it felt as if the room was rising above me. Please don't worry; I wasn't going mad, this actually happened. As I sat there, just going along with this experience, an immense feeling of calm came upon me. The room 'settled again' but had taken on an entirely different persona; the sadness had gone and in its place was calmness and contentment.

During the years spent at 'The Lodge', it became my most favourite home I had ever lived in. I felt that maybe my purpose for coming here was to release the 'stuck' entity; but whatever the reason I was drawn to this house, I was very grateful.

The one sad thing to come out of all this was that 'The Lodge' was to be our final family home together.

Chapter 33

In the summer of the year 2000, we were fortunate to experience a unique holiday. Michael arranged, being a part of the field of work he was in, a School Rugby Tour to Australasia for the senior rugby teams at Nicholas's school. Michael excelled himself. The arrangements for the tour, the organisation of all matches to be played and the social events were tuned to a fine art. I really must praise Michael very highly for the fantastic job he did.

Michael was, of course, to be going on the tour, to support Nicholas and ensure that everything ran smoothly. As some of the other team members' parents were also going along, it was decided that Oliver and I would go also. We were so excited to be going to the other side of the world, something I would previously only have dreamt of doing.

Christopher and my mother were going to stay at our house while we were away to care for Chad, our lovely collie dog. However, it didn't turn out quite as expected. After a couple of days, mother told Christopher that she had to go home as she was convinced our house was haunted! She didn't like the place, and so poor Christopher was left alone with just the dog for company!

Michael flew out with the team and their coaches, while Oliver and I followed a couple of days later. When Michael collected us from Sydney airport, he said, "I have to show you something straight away that will completely take your breath away."

I must confess to being somewhat tired after the flight, but Michael was so excited, I happily agreed to see what he had in store for us. He stopped the hire car after a short while and out we all got. Michael told me to close my eyes, and he took my hand and led me onto a platform with a guardrail around it. "Now, open your eyes," he said.

I was rendered speechless at the majestic scene unfolding before me; I was looking at the famous Blue Mountains of Australia. Mountain ranges that seem to stretch to eternity and did look blue. Creeks, waterfalls, dramatic canyons and glens resembling the densest jungles, all this extended beyond me. I stood, soaking up the sheer unbelievable beauty of this place, running my eyes over the scenic landscape. My naive impression that Australia was all barren desert — although, of course, much of it is — was completely shattered by this inspiring experience.

The Australian people are incredibly hospitable, and while we were there, they opened up their homes to us with unflinching generosity. Our sons were billeted in the homes of their opposing Australian team members, while other parents from the local schools provided accommodation for us parents. They were incredibly welcoming and arranged various social functions for us outside of the boys' rugby matches.

Our second day in Sydney took us on a Harbour Cruise, enabling us to see the famous Harbour Bridge and Sydney Opera House. That evening, Michael and Oliver climbed over the Harbour Bridge and were able to experience Sydney by night, which they enjoyed immensely.

The following day, our team had a match against Shore School, and afterwards they laid on a lovely tea for us. Apart from this, a surprise for Oliver came in the form of a birthday cake and presents from our team and the Australian boys. Apparently, word had got out that Oliver's birthday was on 11th July, and our hosts and our boys wanted to recognise this for him. Oliver was thrilled, as were we, at this incredibly generous gesture. We ended the day by watching the All Blacks (New Zealand Rugby Team) play the Australians at Stadium Australia. It was a great match, with the All Blacks winning. Not the best result for the Aussies playing at home, but nevertheless a terrific experience for us.

The following morning, we moved on to Brisbane, and on arrival took a trip around Brisbane Zoo. We saw many animals, but the most exciting were the wallabies, kangaroos and koala bears, being well-known Australian animals. The koalas certainly looked very sweet, and we had the opportunity to stroke them, although with great caution. Even though they look very innocent and cuddly, they can apparently be quite vicious.

The following day the team was playing a match against Ipswich Grammar School, and it was extra exciting because Nicholas was captaining the team. Our boys played phenomenally and won the game, after which we were all guests at a dinner hosted by the school.

During the evening, one of the Ipswich coaches approached Nicholas and made him an unbelievable offer. He had been so impressed with Nicholas's skill on the rugby pitch, both as captain and player, and the way he used his 'Rugby Brain', that he wanted to offer Nicholas a year's contract coaching rugby at Ipswich School! My son coaching the Australians — wow, what a wonderful compliment for him.

This was an incredible opportunity for Nicholas; he was thrilled by it and was immediately very keen to accept. Although this was perfect for Nicholas, I did, however, have many concerns regarding the practicalities of him remaining in Australia. I was worried at the prospect of leaving Nicholas to fend for himself on the other side of the world. He had been on school trips before, but this was a whole new ball game. After much discussion during dinner with the appropriate Ipswich staff and being assured that Nicholas would be provided with food and accommodation, that the school would take full responsibility for his welfare and that any problems or concerns Nicholas may have would be dealt with immediately, I had to concede. My son wanted this desperately, and who was I to stand in his way? I think the coach could sense the reservations of a mother, even though Nicholas was now a young adult, and he said to me later, when I was alone, "Don't worry, Jessica, I will look after your son; he is in good hands."

This personal confirmation made me feel better, but I still knew it was going to be very hard to leave Nicholas behind when we returned home.

I recall after another of the boys' matches that a barbeque had been laid on for us. I couldn't believe my eyes when, instead of the usual burgers and sausages, a large table beheld us, piled high with the most giant beefsteaks I have ever seen! Apparently, this was normal as the meat was so readily available. Good food, music, dancing and fantastic company — what a wonderful evening was had by all.

On another occasion, the boys and parents were treated to a visit to a sheep-shearing farm. The skill with which they shear the sheep is quite incredible, fast and precise. Some of our boys were then invited to have a go, and we all laughed hysterically as Nicholas and a friend of his tried to hold a sheep still while attempting to shear it, poor sheep!

The farmer then decided that Oliver should be included in the fun, and he proceeded to straddle a sheep, thus rendering it stationary, while telling Oliver to do the same. Gripping onto the sheep's wool, Oliver hung on for dear life, as once the farmer had moved away the sheep decided to give Oliver the runabout. Everyone cheered as Oliver tried to stay astride the sheep. What fun we all had that day.

The boys played a number of matches against the Australian schools; some they won, some they lost, but all came together afterwards in great harmony, and I know that the Aussie lads certainly showed our boys a good time in the evenings when they took them to their local haunts. There were most definitely more than a few sore heads when we met up with them the following mornings!

During our stay in Australia, the teams had a few match-free days, which they could use as they chose. Michael had arranged for Nicholas, Oliver, himself and me to go to visit Moreton Island, with an overnight stay. Moreton Island is one of nature's undisturbed wonders. It is naturally formed from sand and sits in the middle of the Moreton Bay Marine Park. The island measures approximately thirty-eight kilometres in length, ten kilometres wide and is about thirty-five kilometres from Brisbane. On arrival, we discovered an island paradise. The golden beach stretched as far as the eye could see, dotted with sheltering palm trees. Set back from the beach was our delightful cabin accommodation.

The crystal-clear water allows you to see a spectacular array of sea life. From Cape Moreton Lighthouse, it is possible to see turtles, whales, dolphins, manta rays and numerous species of magnificent fish, all enjoying life in the beautiful waters of this island paradise. Another interesting feature of Moreton Island is that it is home to the largest sand dune in the world, known as Mount Tempest. Apart from appreciating the sea life, while on the island there was opportunity for sunbathing and sand tobogganing. We had an incredible couple of days here, before returning to the mainland and joining the rest of our companions for a farewell meal with our Australian hosts.

The tour was due to move to New Zealand for a couple of weeks, and it was arranged that Nicholas would take up his new position when we returned to Brisbane to catch our flight home. We all moved on to Auckland, New Zealand, where again we were welcomed with open arms.

One fascinating but somewhat intimidating experience we had was that before each match the boys played, the opposing team would perform the 'Haka'. This was the ceremonial war dance that the All Blacks, the New Zealand professional rugby team, can be seen performing before their matches. They chant and stamp their feet, as they stare out their opponents and march towards them, intimidating them. This all takes the form of them issuing a challenge to the opposition. What was so incredible was that during the New Zealand matches, the entire school turned out to stand on the side-line and support their team. Not only this, but at the given cue, the whole school joined in with the 'Haka'! Our poor boys were majorly outnumbered as we, their small clan of supporters, cheered and screamed in supporting them. But they were not daunted; they stood tall, linked elbows and faced the New Zealanders squarely. At one point they even broke into song themselves, and strains of 'Land of Hope and Glory' rang out in sheer defiance!

As I watched my son confront and play these incredibly strong opponents, I was filled with such pride. I must confess to shedding tears of joy when yet again, in his classic, unstoppable way, he dived over the touchline and forced the ball to the ground to score another try. Nicholas had developed, through his training, into a very fit, muscular and determined young man, not to be argued with on a rugby pitch; and yet off the pitch he was kind, supportive and very personable, a 'Gentle Giant'. His talent was unquestionable, and apart from his hands-on skills, he had what his coach called 'a rugby brain', he could dissect and plan the game as it evolved. It seemed highly likely that a career in professional rugby was very achievable if that was a route Nicholas chose to go down.

Whether it became his future career or not, Nicholas had gained many attributes from his ongoing love and involvement in his rugby. Camaraderie and team spirit topped the list, standing by your mates through thick and thin. Many friendships were formed, friendships which are as strong in Nicholas's life today as they were in his youth. Commitment, perseverance and the drive to succeed were other life skills learnt through his sport.

Nicholas and his team-mates held their own against these players from a country that completely worshipped the game of rugby, players who would 'rip your head off in the name of the game'.

New Zealand is a beautiful country, very lush and green, and the hospitality matched in every way that which was bestowed upon us by the Australians. While in Auckland, Michael, Oliver and I stayed with a lovely couple that had a minuscule, somewhat crazy dog called Daisy, who soon made a firm friend of Oliver. One evening, I was telling Sheila, the lady of the house, about my having had a New Zealand penfriend while I was at school, who lived in Auckland. She asked me if I was going to be seeing her. I replied that sadly we lost contact many years ago now and that I didn't even know if she still lived here. Sheila was determined that I should try and find Shirley, my penfriend. She said that I couldn't travel halfway around the world to where she may be and not attempt to find her.

This incredibly generous lady handed me her telephone and instructed me to phone everyone in the phone directory with Shirley's childhood surname to see if anyone knew of her. This was a tremendous, long-shot, but this lady was so kind and insistent, I felt I had to try. There were twenty-three listings in the directory with Shirley's surname and I worked my way through the numbers, only to be told that no one knew Shirley. By number fifteen I felt like giving up, but Sheila insisted I finished the list.

I dialled number nineteen, and a man's voice answered the call. "Hello," I said, "I'm sorry to disturb you. You don't know me, but I hope you will not mind me asking you a question." I went on to explain that I was trying to find my long-lost penfriend, and when I told him her name, I almost dropped the receiver in shock.

"Yes, I know Shirley," he said, "I'm her brother John! You must be Jessica; I remember you and Shirley corresponding for quite a while." He told me that Shirley was married with two children and still lived in Auckland, although over the other side of the city. He proceeded to give me her number and suggested I call to try and arrange a meet! I was flabbergasted that Shirley had been found and immediately dialled her number, my heart pounding with excitement, while Sheila was giving me the thumbs-up. Shirley was dumbfounded to hear my voice and, assuming I was calling from England, asked how I found her number. When I told her that I had spoken to John and that I wasn't at home, but I was in Auckland, she screamed down the phone with excitement!

We arranged for our two families to meet in a restaurant in the middle of town the following evening, and as we hung up, we were both beside ourselves with excitement and anticipation. Michael, Nicholas, Oliver and I were first to arrive at the restaurant the following evening, and when Shirley and her family joined us, it was as if the last thirty-six years melted away. We recognised each other immediately, which was pretty good, as we only knew each other from childhood photos. We had the most enjoyable evening; we didn't stop talking at all, and there was so much to catch up on. We parted company very late on a high and promised to resume writing to each other, which we still do, to this day. What a wonderful bonus to an already fantastic trip.

The following day we all travelled to Gisborne, where a very exciting event awaited our team. The boys were treated to a training session with Gordon Tietjens, an ex-All Black rugby player. This was a wonderful experience for the boys, although extremely hard work, and they acquired much knowledge from Gordon.

One particular day, however, while in New Zealand, I did encounter a severe problem. When I awoke, I couldn't move my neck and had to be helped up. I was in excruciating pain from my head to my hips and I couldn't bear even to try and turn my head. My M.E. and fibromyalgia had decided to deal me this horrible blow. On this day, there wasn't a rugby match and our hosts had arranged a social function for the team and ourselves. Firstly, we were to experience 'Morning Tea'. This was an occasion where everyone, being chauffeured by their relevant hosts, gathered at one house and every mother of the New Zealand School team baked cakes. This was to be followed by a trip to a New Zealand farm, where we were to enjoy a traditional hog roast, then the boys were to take part in a clay pigeon shoot, and all this was to be rounded off by a barbeque. This sounded like a phenomenal day's entertainment, but I told Michael that, unfortunately, I would have to remain at our lodgings, as by now the pain was making it hard for me to even take a deep breath. I couldn't possibly consider walking around and didn't want to spoil everyone else's enjoyment.

However, when Annie, our chauffeur, arrived in her timeworn Land Rover to collect us for 'The Tea', she wasn't having any of it. My pleading fell on deaf ears, as she insisted I would not be left behind. Annie said that she would drop Michael and Oliver off for tea, where they would join the teams and their parents, and that she would then take me to see a friend of hers who was a holistic masseur. Annie insisted that he would 'cure' me in no time, and she wouldn't take no for an answer. I really couldn't see how this was possible, but I was in too much pain to argue.

When, after an excruciatingly painful journey, we arrived at the home where tea was being served, the welcome was fantastic and the food — well, I've never seen such an enormous selection of home-made cakes and pastries in my life, and they just kept coming!

After a bite and a cup of tea, Annie and I set off to visit her miracle man. I apologised to Annie for this inconvenience and spoiling her day, but she replied in genuine amazement, "That's what you do for your friends, isn't it? If someone is in need, you step up to the mark." This took me aback; in her eyes, Annie wasn't doing me a favour, she was just doing what is normal — helping out. I told Annie that back home this wasn't necessarily normal, but I was nevertheless extremely grateful to her. She told me that her friend was just round the corner and was expecting us. Forty-five minutes later, crying with the pain of being bumped about, we arrived. "There," said Annie, "told you it wasn't far!"

She helped me to the front door and introduced me to her friend, who I can only describe as an Adonis! He was very tall and muscular, with white, blond hair, jet-blue eyes and a smile that would make any woman weak at the knees. "See you in a couple of hours," he said to Annie.

"Okay, I'll wait in the motor," she replied. Before I could object that she couldn't possibly sit and wait outside for this length of time, I was ushered into a room with a massage couch and was introduced to the man's wife, who worked as a masseuse also. Between them, they somehow managed to get me lying on the couch.

I was by now involuntarily crying with pain, and Marcus the Masseur consoled me by saying that in a couple of hours I would be a different person and not to be afraid to let my emotions out. When Marcus first touched my neck, it was excruciating, but as time progressed, the pain began to decrease, and I was able to start to relax. The most interesting thing was that Marcus's treatment was very gentle but at the same time firm, which is very hard to describe or understand.

Gradually, the blood started to flow through my muscles; they began to give under his direction, as he gently kneaded my neck until it could no longer resist and had to move as he desired.

At the end of my treatment, Marcus asked me to stand up. I very slowly started to do so and gasped in amazement. What miracle had this man performed on me? I could move my neck without any discomfort, and my entire body was pain-free, something I hadn't experienced since the road accident. I felt as if I was floating on air; a miracle indeed had occurred. I couldn't believe the result and profusely thanked Marcus and his wife as they escorted me to the front door. "All in a day's work; glad to have been able to help," came the reply.

As Annie came to the door to collect me, she said, "Oh, wow, girl, you look a lot better; told you he was good."

"Good?" I exclaimed. "Unreal! I haven't felt this good for years!"

"Right," Annie said, "don't know about you, but I could eat a pig. Come on, let's join the others."

As we made our way to the farm, I felt marvellous. How long it would last? I didn't know, but I was determined to savour every moment of having a pain-free body while it did. Unfortunately — but, of course, understandably — Marcus and his wife rejected my suggestion that they move to England to be my personal masseurs!

Still, the generosity of these people was quite incredible. Marcus refused to accept any payment for my treatment as he flashed me that amazing smile, and when I dared to suggest to Annie that I give her money for fuel for driving me, I got my head bitten off in no uncertain terms!

As we walked into the barn to join the hog roast, a loud cheer broke out; no one could believe the difference in me, least of all Michael. We partook of the hog roast, which was delicious, and the remainder of the day was great — clay pigeon shooting and ending with a barbeque. I fell asleep that night still pain-free.

Sadly, though, by the time we returned to England, my pain was as severe as ever. Unfortunately, I have never been able to find anyone like Marcus, or any treatment to match the incredible relief his therapy gave me.

The boys in the team were very fond of Oliver and would often throw a ball around with him after a match. Oliver was in his element when they did this. He thoroughly enjoyed training with Nicholas's team, and it gave him an opportunity to show and develop his skills.

On one such day, they were doing just this. Oliver was having a great time when suddenly, trying to catch a ball, he slipped and broke his wrist! Thus followed a trip to a medical centre, which was quite an enlightening experience in itself. At the centre, a nurse assessed Oliver's injury immediately. He then saw a doctor, who sent us into an adjoining room for an x-ray. We quickly returned to the doctor, who, on confirming that Oliver had broken his wrist, sent us to another room, where Oliver's wrist was placed in a green plaster cast (his choice of colour!). We then paid the receptionist a minimal charge for the service and went on our way. All this happened under one roof, in an incredibly short space of time.

We then all moved on to Rotorua, where all of the boys and some parents went white-water rafting, which they all enjoyed immensely. While in Rotorua, we visited the Maori arts centre and bathed in warm spa pools after visiting the Whakarewarewa Geysers, all great experiences.

One evening we went to The Tamaki Maori Village for a concert and Hangi. A Hangi is a traditional Maori feast consisting of succulent meats which have been steaming for hours on hot rocks under the earth, fresh vegetables, Maori bread and salads, seafood and desserts; all in all, truly delectable.

On arriving at the village, no one is allowed to enter until the Powhiri, the formal welcome ceremony, has been performed, during which challenges are conducted by the village warriors, each one more intimidating than the last!

A peace offering (Teka) is then laid at the feet of your appointed chief, and visitors must signal their peaceful intent on entering the village. The spine-tingling Karanga, or welcome calls, echo through the forest, as the women sing to announce your arrival. This feels unnerving and yet exciting and thrilling at the same time. You are then no longer considered a guest, but one of the Maori people or Tangata Whenua, and as you enter the village you receive the traditional Maori kiss, the touching of noses!

Then follows a walk through the village as it comes to life. As you step into a different world, you encounter the small dwellings, hear fires crackling, songs being sung, observe women crouched around the fires, weaving and making Maori crafts. There are 'warriors' training for war with traditional weapons, while villagers tell stories of their ancestry and much more. It is like something out of a school geography book that has just come to life.

All of this is followed by a colourful concert of song and dance, and the evening ends with the traditional Hangi Feast. As we made our way to the building where food was to be served, the most wonderful aromas filled the air. The combined smells of earth, smoke and cooking meat wafted into our nostrils, taste buds started flowing, and we couldn't wait to savour the culinary delights that were on offer. We were not disappointed; the meat simply dissolved in our mouths — there was no need to chew. Tasty vegetables and salads we had not seen before were served with succulent fish and Maori bread. This was a never to be forgotten experience.

Near the end of the tour, all of the boys and some parents went skiing for a couple of days. While they were away, I did some sightseeing around Christchurch, enjoying strolling around the Cathedral and Craft Centres. Everyone returned from skiing with a glow in their cheeks; one of Nicholas's friends also returned with thirty stitches in his head, after having an argument with a rock. OUCH!

After two wonderful weeks in New Zealand, it was time to return to Brisbane and face the journey back home, a journey without Nicholas. Before leaving Nicholas, we saw him settled into his accommodation, and Michael found him a small jeep so that he could drive himself around.

Leaving Nicholas was excruciating. The furthest he'd been before was on a short school trip to Russia, and now he was going to be here for a year. The thought was unbearable. But he was so happy and so wanted to do this that I fought hard to hold back the tears.

"Please don't cry, mum," he said. "I'll be okay, and I'll keep in touch."

As we drove away and I looked back at Nicholas waving to us, my resolve failed, and I cried uncontrollably, my arm around Oliver, who was also very upset at having to leave his brother.

I may sound feeble, but this was a big deal. Nicholas had never had to fend for himself with complete independence until now. How was he going to cope? My tears didn't stop until we were up in the air and well on our way, when I eventually slept through sheer exhaustion.

While we waited to board at the airport, I begged Michael to go and fetch Nicholas and tell him that he couldn't stay after all. But, of course, he didn't; I was just selfish. To Nicholas, this was an adventure, the next chapter in his life, and I couldn't stand in his way. Being a parent is a source of great joy, but at times can be extremely painful, as I'm sure many of you know.

As it turned out, Nicholas was excellent. He loved his job; his e-mails conveyed a euphoric young man having a great experience, and I was always thrilled to receive them. I missed him terribly, but missing a child was not a new experience for me, and I just had to deal with it as I had before.

Halfway through the year, however, Michael arranged for me, on my own, to go and visit Nicholas. I was so thrilled and overflowing with excitement, as I couldn't wait to hug Nicholas again.

On arriving at the airport, he wasn't there to meet me as planned, and although I was a little concerned, I told myself to remain calm, and he would be here soon. Suddenly, the airport doors swung open, and Nicholas and a friend came charging towards me. "Mum!" he screamed and flung his arms around me. "So sorry we're late, mum; we went to the wrong airport!"

Nicholas was on two weeks' holiday and had arranged a wonderful itinerary for us both. During our time together, two events stand out for me the most.

Firstly, we had gone sand dune riding in a little jeep and were enjoying ourselves so much, driving over the sand dunes and laughing hysterically, that we forgot the time. We had to get to the end of an extremely long beach to catch the last ferry back to the mainland. However, this wasn't our only problem. The tide was coming in rapidly, and Nicholas was concerned that we might start the drive along the beach and not make it before high tide. However, there wasn't an alternative; we had to go for it. "Hang on to your hat, mum, you're in for a thrill!" said Nicholas. I hate to think what speed we travelled at, as we raced along the sands with the tide lapping around our wheels. We, fortunately, arrived in one piece by the skin of our teeth, and as I saw the ferry ahead of us, I was very relieved. Nevertheless, I must confess to finding our race against the tide incredibly exhilarating. It was probably as near to 'living on the edge' in an extreme activity as I have ever been, but it was thrilling, and I live to tell the tale!

The second and most incredible top-of-the-list activity Nicholas had arranged was scuba diving. While in Australia he had been taking a number of exams in this activity and was now at divemaster level, whereas I had never dived in my life. We flew on a minute airplane to Lady Elliot Island, a very small island entirely dedicated to this sport. Nicholas had arranged a crash course for me in the basics of diving, and then we were taken out to sea in a small boat. Three people were assigned to an instructor, and when our turn came, we lowered ourselves down into the ocean by holding onto a rope dangling over the side of the boat. This process took a little while as it takes time for the pressure in your ears to adjust.

As I reached the ocean bed and released the rope, the sight beholding me was incomparable in its beauty to anything else I had previously experienced. As our instructor kept his eye on our gauges, he pointed out parts of this hidden world to us.

The ocean bed was completely covered with sand, and the sun was so strong above that it illuminated everything this far below. This was a silent world of exquisite magnificence, presenting corals and fish of numerous shapes, sizes and colour brilliance. We were very fortunate on our dive, and the envy of some of the others, as we saw some amazing marine creatures not often seen on a first dive.

Our instructor pointed to a particular point on the ocean bed, and initially we weren't quite sure what we were looking at. Suddenly, an enormous Jenkins Ray rose from the sand right in front of us — absolutely breath taking! During our dive, we also saw a turtle, which swam very close to us, and a tiger shark! I would have to say that this was one of the most incredible experiences of my life.

When it came to returning home after my holiday with Nicholas, I felt extremely happy and content. Not only had I spent the most wonderful time with him, but seeing him look so well and happy, my concerns for him were put into perspective, and I knew he would be fine.

While he was away, Nicholas had the opportunity to play with a professional Australian rugby team. "They are phenomenal, mum," he wrote, "like rhinos when you make contact, but their skill is amazing, and I've learnt so much from them and acquired a fair number of souvenir bruises!"

Nicholas returned from his time away not a schoolboy, but a confident young man. He had matured and gained independence, which filled me with great pride.

Chapter 34

While Nicholas and Oliver were growing up, I remember that when they were at home, they would both spend a lot of time in their bedrooms, either together in one room or alone in their own. At the time I just thought they were being teenagers, wanting their space, and perhaps they were. Now, with hindsight, I wonder, with deep regret, whether they shut themselves away to avoid witnessing Michael's outbursts.

Sadly, however, this was not always possible to do. I recall one particular occasion when Nicholas had brought a friend home after school one day to stay the night.

Unfortunately, Michael became outraged with his computer, which wasn't responding to him quickly enough, and he soon became very audible. Nicholas, wanting to diffuse this situation to avoid embarrassment in front of his friend, went to ask Michael what the problem was and if he could help, and to ask his father if he could calm down as he had a friend here.

Meanwhile, Dominic, Nicholas's friend, had followed Nicholas down to Michael's office and heard Michael in full flow as he told Nicholas in no uncertain terms to mind his own business, not tell his father what to do and to go away. Michael then lifted his computer in the air and threatened to throw it through the window!

Nicholas, with Dominic in tow, ran up to his room and slammed the door shut. I can still feel today, with anguish, my poor son's emotional pain and humiliation at the way his father had behaved in front of his guest. I went straight down to confront Michael over this and received the same response from him that Nicholas had. Realising I was wasting my breath, I then went up to Nicholas's room to try and console him in some way. I knocked on his door and on receiving no response, knocked a second time. Still no acknowledgement came, so I opened Nicholas's door and entered his room. I was shocked to see that neither he nor Dominic were there — they must have left the house while I was down speaking with Michael. Feeling very upset and concerned, I went to tell Michael what had happened, but he wasn't interested; he said the boys would be back when they were hungry! He was still so angry with his computer that there was no reasoning with him.

I tried to remain calm and started to prepare dinner. After about forty-five minutes, my concern for Nicholas and Dominic was beginning to increase. Nicholas wasn't answering his phone, and I was becoming anxious, not only for him but also for Dominic, who was my responsibility for the night. Suddenly, the house phone rang and I leapt to pick it up, hoping it would be Nicholas. It was my mother's voice I heard on the other end of the line. She told me that Nicholas and Dominic had just arrived at her home in a highly distressed state, told her what had happened and asked if she could feed them and give them a bed for the night, which, of course, she agreed to do.

Mother told me that Nicholas was extremely upset, and while he was in her bathroom, Dominic had told her that Michael had been so angry and rude to Nicholas. He felt so sorry for him; he was his friend, and he didn't like to see him hurt like this.

Unfortunately, this was all too regular an occurrence for poor Nicholas. Unlike other children, he never brought friends over to play or stay often, and always stayed at friends' houses because he was so embarrassed by his father.

I thanked my mother and put the receiver down, feeling humiliated, upset for poor Nicholas and very cross with Michael. The following morning, Dominic's father collected him and Nicholas from my mother's and brought Nicholas back home. He was incredibly charming and made no reference to why the boys had stayed at my mother's house, and Dominic behaved as if nothing untoward had occurred, which I respected them both for immensely. Michael, having got over his 'tantrum', said nothing to Nicholas about the previous evening and carried on as if nothing had occurred!

How very sad, to think our sons lived their lives in such a situation, one that, as I keep saying, could have been resolved if their father had accepted his anger problem and sought help to address it.

Chapter 35

By 2001, Christopher and Nina had grown very close, and Nina moved into my mother's cottage to live with her and Christopher. Christopher had taken on the job of maintaining the cottage for his grandmother and had done a fantastic job carrying out any repairs and decorating for her, while also continuing to care lovingly for his grandmother on a daily basis.

On returning from his year in Australia, Nicholas had gone to university to read Geography, and while there he worked as hard and diligently as ever, eventually graduating and obtaining his degree with flying colours.

Oliver, meanwhile, was doing very well at school, still thriving with his music and rugby. It appeared on the surface that all was going well for him. However, this wasn't altogether the case.

Oliver was a very private young man and didn't choose readily to confide any problems he may have had.

On discussing this with Oliver during the writing of my book, I learnt, to my intense dismay, that Oliver did indeed have his fair share of problems while growing up but chose not to make me aware of them. He didn't want to burden me, which, although admirable, made me wish vehemently that he had. I would have wanted to help him in any way I could and support him through his problems.

I think, on reflection, Oliver also wishes that he had been more forthcoming.

There is one incident that stands out in my mind that occurred shortly after Nicholas returned from Australia. By now a clear picture of Nicholas as a protective brother to Oliver should be apparent. This was proven once again one evening. It had come to light that Oliver was being bullied at school, and this had been going on for some months. During this time, Nicholas was obviously in Australia. The sad part is that I was not aware of this and, even worse, was not aware of the cause. Some horrible children at Oliver's school were tormenting him because of his father. They were aware of how volatile, violent and angry Michael was, and took it upon themselves to remind Oliver of this on a daily basis. Being told your father was an insane person must have been terrible for Oliver. To this day I can't forgive myself for not reading the signs and protecting my son.

Nicholas immediately noticed something was wrong and, due to their unyielding bond, Oliver confided in Nicholas. The response from Nicholas was as you would expect from any brother wanting to protect his siblings. However, upon request from

Oliver, Nicholas agreed not to go down to the school and confront these boys. Then something happened!

One evening, while Michael was away, two cars drove past our house. The occupants threw empty beer bottles out of the window at the house wall and then shouted obscenities towards Oliver. This happened three or four times before Nicholas or I realised. Once Nicholas heard them shouting about Michael from the road and seeing Oliver in tears on his bed, he snapped.

I only discovered, on near completion of my book, when Oliver opened up to me, just how long he had been contending with these bullies. However, in his words, he was 'dealing with it'. He wasn't prepared to be a 'victim'; he was standing up for himself and confronting the problem head on.

On the evening in question, though, when the bullies decided to pay us a house call, neither Nicholas nor I were aware that Oliver had the problem under control. Therefore, Nicholas's immediate reaction was to help his brother because he thought that was what was needed.

Nicholas grabbed the first thing he could find, which happened to be a wooden baseball bat. He stormed out of the house after the cars. The cars sped off, but Nicholas was not done. He jumped into his car and followed them. The two cars had pulled over further down the road. The five kids inside, not realising they were being followed, decided to stop and congratulate themselves for the hurt they had just inflicted. To this day I am sure they wish they had not stopped!

Nicholas drove round the corner and saw the boys in the two cars. He drove past, turned his car around and drove it right into the first car parked on the side of the road. It was not fast, but it got the attention of the boys. Nicholas jumped out of his car, thankfully leaving the bat inside, and ran to the driver's window. At this point, I will state that I never condone violence or completely agree with his actions, but I thank him for it and understand completely why it happened. I believe Nicholas not only wanted to protect his brother, but also had to vent so much pent-up anger caused by his father. He could relate to what Oliver felt as he had gone through so much of it during his childhood.

Nicholas punched his fist straight through the driver's window of the car, shattering it into pieces. The boys inside had by this point stopped laughing and had turned a bright white colour. Fear had very quickly replaced their sense of satisfaction and achievement.

Nicholas grabbed the 'leader of the group' by his shirt collar, whose name I will not mention, and pulled him through the window. He then proceeded to scream at him that if he ever so much as looked at Oliver again, then he (Nicholas) would ensure he did not see the following day. This seventeen-year-old boy, who was the big kid around the school and liked to pick on many children, proceeded to wet himself in fear!

With that, Nicholas left and returned home to comfort Oliver. The result of this incident was that word very quickly spread around the school, and the boy no longer tormented anyone, especially Oliver! Once the other children heard about his toilet trouble, he received a taste of his own medicine. Nobody wanted to mess with Oliver any longer for fear of upsetting his big brother! Take from this what you will, but it is hard to imagine many people not wanting to protect their family. My heart goes out to Nicholas, who over the years, in many different ways, did protect his younger brother, who to this day is thankfully unaware of many of the circumstances.

Although Nicholas was there and stepped in to support Oliver that evening, I now believe that Oliver would have eventually brought these scumbags to task. I feel very proud to see the strength and endurance Oliver showed, and as he grew older, these qualities developed further.

It has transpired that Oliver was far more aware of happenings at home than I was led to believe. He became Nicholas's support when he was having problems, particularly with his father. Nicholas would confide in Oliver, and the brothers supported each other through thick and thin. I am so pleased that, along with Christopher, this incredible closeness continues.

During his time at senior school, Oliver's musical skills developed and he built a terrific relationship with his saxophone teacher, and Michael and I became good friends with Robert. Each Christmas, a wonderful event took place involving Oliver, Robert and some of Oliver's fellow music students. Robert, his students, parents and friends would meet one Sunday lunchtime in December, at a local pub, where Robert would then lead his mini school band as they played a selection of Christmas music and carols. During the performances, the landlord generously fed us mince pies and we all sipped a drink or two!

After a short while we all moved onto a second pub, then a third, then a fourth, and I think you are probably getting a general idea! One of the highlights of this event was the transportation provided to take us on our 'musical pub crawl'. The local brewery, in the form of two carts, provided the transport for the band and parents, each pulled by two beautiful shire horses. Local farmers turned out with tractors and trailers to provide transport for anyone else who needed it.

By early evening, we ended back at our first pub, very merry and rosy-cheeked, to be greeted by a spread laid on by the landlord. This we gratefully devoured, as Robert and some of his musician friends provided an evening of entertainment. This yearly event was held to raise funds for charity, and on our journey, we would proffer buckets to passers-by. The whole event was for a great cause and was a fabulous occasion.

Following school, Oliver moved on to technical college and excelled in design and technology. During his time there, he very proudly represented the college by entering into the Audi All England Design Competition a beautiful, modern-design coffee table that he had made; how thrilled and proud we were when he made it through to the finals!

On not such a positive note, while at college Oliver, who rode a motorbike, was the innocent victim of an accident when a careless driver knocked him off his bike. This resulted in Oliver suffering a shoulder injury which prevented him playing rugby to the extent he would have wished.

I was so angry that my son had been deprived of doing something he enjoyed because of the stupidity and negligence of another road user. I knew only too well how Oliver felt, from my experience of losing dance after my accident.

As for Michael and me, we continued life in the same vein. When times were good, I was so happy and couldn't give up on him. However, when things were bad, a part of me wanted to get as far away as I could, but I just couldn't leave; in spite of everything that was wrong in our tumultuous relationship, I still loved this man and couldn't give up on him and walk away.

Chapter 36

By 2003, my struggle with ME and fibromyalgia, had become increasingly more challenging. I had lost many battles with this debilitating condition, as it fought determinedly to prevent me from leading a normal life. I was often unable to summon the energy required to perform many a simple or everyday task. Tragically, in the spring of this year, I lost the war.

I had to concede that I could no longer continue teaching dance and was forced to retire. I was devastated beyond words; I was crying inside, as the pain of loss was so intense. My life's vocation was being snatched from me far too soon.

I began to interview young teachers who expressed an interest in taking over KAPA from me. After much consideration, I decided to put my life's work in the hands of a young lady who had achieved her teaching qualifications at The Royal Ballet School and had a fair amount of teaching experience under her belt.

With the official business concluded, we decided to hold a farewell get-together at KAPA, where Valerie would have the opportunity to meet parents and pupils before she took over the reins at the beginning of the new school year in September.

On 3rd July 2003, Julie and I, our parents, families and friends, our current pupils and their family members and friends and a number of ex-pupils who had responded to an invitation to my farewell, all gathered at KAPA Everyone sat at small tables on which snacks were laid out and chatted and reminisced happily, while Christopher, Nicholas and Oliver acted as barmen, serving wine and soft drinks to everyone.

A large screen was erected at one end of the dance hall on which a video show ran continually, showing pictures of KAPA events over the past thirty years. Julie and I moved around the tables, speaking with everyone, while also introducing them to Valerie. Michael strolled around the hall with his video camera and filmed the students as they vocalised their best wishes and thanks for me. This was a wonderful memento, and I enjoy watching it still.

During the evening, some of my pupils performed a small dance entertainment, which was received enthusiastically by all. There was so much love and camaraderie at the school that evening that I was bursting with joy.

Eventually, the inevitable moment came when I had to publicly step down and hand KAPA to Valerie. All of the students, Julie and I gathered onto the stage and sang a song of farewell together, which I had written. Everyone in the hall then stood and sang together our adopted 'School Song', 'Thank You for the Music' by ABBA. As we sang and everyone waved their arms above their heads, I was also thanking God for the wonderful thirty years I had enjoyed here and the hundreds of children I had had the pleasure to teach.

At the end of the song, I invited Valerie onto the stage and, with an enormous lump in my throat said, "Valerie, I give you KAPA" I then left the stage quickly, followed by Julie, and we dissolved into each other's arms as we tried to keep control of our emotions. I hugged the children as they left that evening, some of them in tears, and promised that this was most certainly not the last they would see of me. I was very pleased that all parents without exception had decided to give Valerie a chance to prove herself and keep their children at the school.

KAPA is still thriving today, and over recent years I have thoroughly enjoyed attending some of their dance shows and taking a trip down memory lane. However, as I stood alone in the centre of the hall that evening, after everyone except Michael, Julie and I had left, I was bereft. How was I ever going to get over losing what I loved doing so much? The tears flowed uncontrollably as Julie escorted me outside.

Both she and Michael told me that I would find something new to take the place of dance in my life, but I never have. There is still a deep, dark void inside me that I don't think will ever be filled. Nothing can replace this loss.

The KAPA motto was 'To Dance is to Live'; how, therefore, was I supposed to live without it?

Chapter 37

2004 was a very eventful year for us all. It started with Nicholas moving to Thailand! He had landed himself a job as an instructor at a dive school there, and while teaching he was to further his qualifications and become an underwater videographer. Nicholas's passion for this field of work had never waned, and he was never happier than when he was beneath the ocean, discovering and filming amazing underwater creatures.

While he was away, he would send me superb photos of his work, and on more than one occasion he sent close-up photos of sharks! As I looked at those enormous teeth, I was naturally very concerned, but on questioning Nicholas, was told that, yes, he was that close to them, but no, if you knew how to behave, they wouldn't attack you! I don't recall this putting my mind at rest. However, I did learn that there are only a few dangerous sharks and that shark attacks are statistically rare. In fact, you have more chance of being run over by a bus than being attacked by a shark! Actually, on a yearly basis, vending machines kill more people than sharks. My son has spent a long time, convincing others and myself that sharks are the single most misinterpreted species on the planet.

Nicholas loved everything about Thailand — his work, the beauty of the country and the Thai people, who were incredibly friendly — and it was here that he was to meet the love of his life, Tamara, who was from Austria. He spent many a happy evening sitting on the beach as the sun set, sharing a beer and conversation with friends of many nationalities.

During this year, I was able to realise a lifelong dream. Ever since I was a young child, I have had an obsession with Egypt and was determined that one day I had to visit the Pyramids at Giza. Well, that day arrived when Michael told me that he had to go to Egypt on a business trip, and I could accompany him. This was amazing, and when he produced the itinerary that his Egyptian colleagues had put together for us, I was completely flabbergasted. Not only was I going to see the Pyramids, but much, much more.

As we stepped off the plane at Cairo Airport, the heat hit me like a wave; I expected it to be hot, but this intensity was unimaginable. A very smartly dressed and polite Egyptian gentleman greeted us at the airport and showed us to a car where a driver was waiting.

What happened next was quite amusing. As the driver went to open the front door for Michael, his boss, while gesturing to the back door of the car, spoke to him quietly, but still audibly enough for me to hear, "The lady, we must look after the lady."

The driver then proceeded to open the car door for me, and the smart gentleman retrieved a beautiful bouquet of flowers from the car, which he handed to me as he assisted me into my seat.

What makes this amusing is that, in their part of the world, these gentlemen would not show their women this type of respect; their culture dictates that men are superior, and women are treated in an inferior way. This meant that if they were to impress Michael, with a view to him sending business their way, and being aware that in our culture women are treated as equals, they had to go completely against their beliefs and treat me with the utmost respect. They knew that is what Michael would have expected. I must admit I felt a little sorry for them, but that feeling didn't last long as I felt even more sorrow for their womenfolk!

The following day we had a very early start and set off immediately after breakfast to begin a day packed with sightseeing. Our first scheduled stop was The Pyramids and Sphinx, and I was like a child on Christmas Eve, unable to conceal my excitement at the prospect of actually seeing these great monuments. I couldn't believe I was here! My first reaction on arriving at the site was one of shock. We drove down a road in Cairo and at the end of this road palm trees ran across it. We disembarked and walked through these trees, to come face to face with The Pyramids! I, rather naively, had imagined the Pyramids to be situated in the middle of the desert, with nothing else for miles around; and yet here they were, on the outskirts of the town. Moreover, I was incensed by the amount of litter which was lying on the ground around these fantastic works of art; I couldn't understand the apparent lack of respect for this historic site.

However, as I walked towards The Great Pyramid, jaw dropping in complete amazement, all of this paled into insignificance. The sheer magnificence and monumentality of the structure before me was completely beyond belief. Amazing, awesome, incredulous, all words which would describe this feat of ancient Egyptian engineering. As we strolled around the pyramid site, gazing in wonder at the three different-sized monuments, our guide, who had been provided for us, willingly imparted his knowledge.

The Great Pyramid, being the largest, was built for the pharaoh Khufu (also known as Cheops). As I stood next to it, each large block being at waist level, I couldn't help but wonder in awe and appreciation how they managed to build it without the cranes, diggers and elaborate tools which the construction industry has at its disposal today. Many people believe that slaves built Khufu's Pyramid, but research shows that this is not true. For three months of the year, the River Nile's annual flood occurred, making it impossible to farm the land, the occupation that provided employment for most of the population. Therefore, approximately one hundred thousand people, while not farming, worked on the pyramid for three months each year and were apparently treated well, being supplied with proper food and clothing.

The second largest pyramid was built for Khufu's son Khafra (also known as Chephren), and finally, the third largest pyramid was built for the pharaoh Menkaure (also known as Mycerinus).

As I stood and soaked up the energy of this magical place, it was easy to understand why The Pyramids at Giza have been named as one of the Wonders of the Ancient World. Equally inspiring is the colossal Great Sphinx, a large lion with the head of a human, carved from natural rock, which proudly guards the front of Khafra's pyramid. King Tuthmosis IV, who lived around 1400 BC, erected a granite stela, rising to about twelve feet, between the paws of the Sphinx.

The beginning of a story is written on the stela about the young Prince Tuthmosis, who, while on a hunting trip, rested and fell asleep under the Sphinx. While he slept, he dreamed that the Sphinx promised him the throne of Egypt if he cleared away the windswept sand that had covered the Sphinx up to his neck. This Tuthmosis did, but unfortunately, the rest of the story has now gone, so the ending is left to the individual's imagination.

Before leaving the pyramids, Michael and I went on a camel ride, which took us a short distance out into the surrounding desert. This was the most fantastic, albeit very smelly, experience! As we moved out into the wilderness, with Cairo behind us, all we could see was sand. The sheer barrenness of the land stretched as far as the eye could see and was incredibly surreal. The hardest part was trying to look dignified and maintain your balance, as the camel dropped onto its front legs in preparation for you to dismount, hopefully without landing flat on your face!

That afternoon, our guide escorted us around the Museum of Cairo, a fascinating building housing the largest collection of Pharaonic antiquities, as well as many treasures of King Tutankhamun. Although we saw many beautiful and exciting objects, those of Tutankhamun were for me the most fascinating. Howard Carter discovered his tomb in The Valley of The Kings in 1922. Although in ancient times the tomb had been partially robbed and then resealed, the coffins and sarcophagi were found in excellent condition. Other items were also found, such as alabaster vases, a decorated chest, which may have been used as a type of closet, weapons and instruments which were used by the king and jewellery, amongst which were found ivory and gold-decorated necklaces and bracelets. In all, over three thousand artefacts were found in the tomb, but the best known is the famous Gold Mask, which was placed over the bandages that were wrapped around the King's face. This exquisite Mask of King Tutankhamun, composed of eleven kilograms of solid gold, has now come to rest at The Egyptian Museum, proudly displayed for all to gaze upon and admire.

After leaving the Museum, our final stop of the day was the Khan El Khalili Bazaars. I can honestly say, this was the most exhilarating and mind-blowing experience ever! The narrow streets of Cairo are dirty, noisy, crowded and somewhat unnerving, as it feels as if eyes are piercing into you from all directions — and they probably are! At the same time, these streets are colourful, vibrant, full of life and exciting. They are lined on either side by small shops selling anything and everything — clothes, leather goods, jewellery, souvenirs, artefacts, papyruses and much more. Outside of each shop, the owner also displays his goods on a stall, and then there is the owner himself. He and his colleagues do everything in their power to drag you over to peruse their wares and force you to buy. As the passage between the stalls is practically non-existent, it is tough to escape. On more than one occasion, Michael had to rescue me from the clutches of a very determined Egyptian!

We arrived back at our hotel that night exhausted but on a high, unable to believe the extent of what we had experienced in just one day. It would be impossible for me to describe our entire Egyptian trip without writing another book, so I will just expand on a couple of my favourite events.

During the remainder of our trip, a second guide, called Ahmed, who was an extremely personable and polite young man and spoke impeccable English, escorted Michael and me.

On our second day, we embarked upon a Nile Cruise, relaxing on board by the pool and then stopping at certain points of the river for sightseeing. We visited a number of temples — Luxor, Karnak, Edfu and Philae, to name a few, all fascinating experiences. We gazed at the colourful wall paintings and hieroglyphics and soaked up the majesty of the enormous pillars and statues, and, of course, the baking sun!

A favourite experience was leaving our cruise boat at a stopping point on the Nile and sailing in a felucca, a traditional Egyptian sailing vessel, to a point on the far side of the river. From here we were escorted to a traditional, ancient African village. As we entered the small dirt-covered square, it was like stepping back in time. This area was surrounded on all sides by very small stone huts, each containing just one room. Inside each room could be found a few old cooking pots and utensils, a couple of blankets and little else, except bird excrement, which seemed to cover everything! It was very humbling and quite distressing to see that people lived like this.

Suddenly, we were brought back into the twenty-first century as one of the village ladies appeared, offering us a can of fizzy drink and a henna tattoo! We gratefully accepted the drinks, and as it was obviously a form of income for these people, I decided to have a tattoo done. I sat patiently while the 'Eye of Osiris' slowly appeared on my upper arm, and the result was beautiful. I loved it and vowed I would wash around it to keep it pristine as long as possible!

As we left the village to return to our cruise boat, I was very humbled and lost in thought, feeling extreme gratitude for our modern amenities and the clean and healthy way we were able to live our lives.

The final place I would like to mention is St. Sargius Church, the oldest church in Egypt. St. Mark the Evangelist came to Alexandria around the year 61 AD, and in spite of the persecutions of the harsh Roman Emperors, Egyptians were converted to Christianity and by the end of the fourth century, Christianity had become the official religion of Egypt. In the early fifth century, the building of churches began, and St. Sargius Church was built by St. Sargius and St. Bacchus.

I am not going to delve into Egyptian religion but would like to say why I loved this place so much. The church is entered from the street by descending a few stone steps and passing through a door at the bottom. Until you are inside, you wouldn't even know this was a church. The church itself is very small, and the nave is divided into three parts, each being separated by twelve pillars, on each of which there is an icon which represents one of the Apostles. One of the pillars, however, has no cross; it is made as a sign to Judas Iscariot, who betrayed Jesus. A screen of immense beauty contains panels inlaid with ivory dating from the eleventh century. In the church can also be seen Byzantine paintings and carved wooden images, my favourites being one which represents the miracle of the loaves and fishes and another representing Bethlehem. The altar takes the form of a wooden table, above which is a wooden canopy, and inside this is painted an image of Jesus surrounded by angels.

For me, the most fascinating part of this magnificent building was the crypt, which, according to tradition, was built on the spot where the Holy Family stayed during their flight to Egypt.

To see and to be in such proximity to a place where Jesus, Mary and Joseph were filled me with complete fascination and wonderment.

My visit to Egypt was amazing; it was everything I had expected and much more, and the best thing of all was that Michael and I had a wonderful time together. He remained calm and attentive, and I will always remember this time with great affection.

The year 2004 ended with a real bang; a fantastic event took place — the wedding of Christopher and Nina. On 3rd December, family and friends descended upon a beautiful hotel in Arundel, where there was to be the civil service, sit-down meal and an evening buffet and disco.

The atmosphere was buzzing as the guests filed into the Wedding Room, and as I took my seat in the front row and watched my handsome young son, immaculately attired in his wedding suit, I glowed with pride and affection for him. To think of what he had endured in his young life and yet was now able to stand here, as an independent man, in control of his life and totally in love with a young lady who completely loved him in return, was incredible. It filled me with immense happiness to see what he had achieved.

Nicholas and Oliver, having both finished their work contracts and being back home again, performed their duties as ushers impeccably, and when, as a witness, I signed the register at the end of the ceremony, I must confess to having tears of joy in my eyes.

After a delicious meal, we all laughed hysterically at my brother Dennis's witty best man speech, while Michael filmed the occasion. He had taken on the task of doing the wedding video and certainly did an exceptional job. During the evening everyone let their hair down and took to the dance floor as the disco began, and I took this opportunity to move around the room and socialise with everyone.

All of my sons led me in a dance around the dance floor (not all at the same time!), and they made me feel like Royalty. However, the time came when we 'oldies', feeling exhausted after a long but beautiful day, needed to retire to our rooms and leave the youngsters to it.

I rose early the next morning to wave Christopher and Nina off on their honeymoon. They were going on a Caribbean cruise, a fantastic start to their life together.

As I watched them drive away, I offered up a silent prayer for them, wishing them health, happiness and all the luck in the world. They certainly deserved it.

Chapter 38

Nicholas and Oliver had always expressed an interest in property development, and this was the path they now took. Nicholas managed to purchase a small, derelict Victorian cottage, which he planned to renovate and resell, and Oliver was going to help with the design and work on site for Nicholas. Nicholas found himself a superb workforce and project managed the development, while also working hands-on himself, thus improving his skills.

Oliver, meantime, used his excellent design skills and did a superb job installing the new kitchen and staircase. I saw the property when Nicholas first purchased it, and I must admit I couldn't see how on earth this could be brought back to its former glory. However, I understood that Nicholas had a vision, rather like the way I could see a full musical stage production in my head, months before it came to fruition. He was able to see beyond the dereliction and focus on the result. I, therefore, believed that if anyone could do this, he could.

The finished result was stunning; a pile of rubble had been converted into a beautiful property, with a new extension on the back. This meant the cottage now offered two double bedrooms, a family bathroom, two reception rooms and a spacious kitchen. What also made the cottage so appealing was that the renovation had, after much searching around, been done using bricks to match the original building, so you were unaware that the original building had, in fact, been extended — except for Michael, of course, who insisted he could tell the difference! I was extremely proud of this achievement, and it turned out to be the first of three properties that Nicholas purchased and, with Oliver's help, redeveloped.

Things at home had taken a turn for the worse, and an incident that occurred while the work was going on at the cottage caused me great concern and made me take serious action. Nicholas went out one day to purchase some wooden flooring for the cottage, and Michael went along with him. There had been a promotional offer on this flooring a few days previously, but, unfortunately, on the day Nicholas went to buy it, the promotion had ended and therefore he had to pay the full price. Nicholas accepted this and was prepared to do so, but Michael, on the other hand, was not prepared to step back and allow Nicholas to do this. He told the shop assistant that with such a large purchase they should still allow the discount, but, of course, the assistant wasn't able to do this.

I was at home when the telephone rang, and it was Nicholas on the other end of the line. He sounded very distressed and was crying as he spoke to me, and I knew therefore that if my strong, rugby-playing son had been reduced to tears, something quite major must have happened. He asked me to go to the wood shop straight away as his father had 'gone completely mad'. I had to get Michael help because he had 'completely lost it'. Michael had gone into one of his rages and yelled at the shop assistant so abusively that she had dissolved into tears, and poor Nicholas didn't know what to do to resolve the situation.

I jumped into my car and drove to the shop as quickly as possible, where I found Nicholas outside waiting for me. He told me he had to leave the store because he was so embarrassed and humiliated.

No sooner had I arrived than Michael came out to join us, enquiring what I was doing there. When I told him that Nicholas was upset about the way he behaved, Michael, reacting as I would have expected, stated that Nicholas shouldn't let people walk all over him. It was a matter of principle, and he was quite within his rights. He then got into his car and returned home as if nothing untoward had occurred.

I escorted Nicholas back into the shop, as he wanted to apologise on Michael's behalf for what had happened. The manager and the shop assistant, who had now calmed down, were very accommodating, ensuring Nicholas that what had happened was in no way his fault. His custom would still be welcomed and appreciated, although probably better in future to visit without Michael's support!

Tragically, Nicholas often became involved in or was witness to Michael's anger. Being that much older, he was more aware of what was going on than young Oliver was. He was also very protective of Oliver and did everything he could to protect his younger brother from what was happening at home, regularly putting himself in the firing line to protect Oliver.

However, years later, Oliver has brought it to my attention that he was far more aware of the negative side of home life than I thought he was. He, in fact, remembers the incident regarding the flooring very clearly and stepped up to support Nicholas.

One of the very worst incidences involving Michael and Nicholas which sticks in my mind happened one day when Michael was working in his office at home, and I was ironing in the adjacent utility room. Nicholas came down to his father's office and they began a conversation. I don't recall what it was about, but I do remember that at one point Nicholas said something and Michael told him he was wrong. Nicholas attempted, very calmly, to tell his father that he was, in fact, definitely right in what he was saying, and I knew without question, as I couldn't help but overhear their conversation, that Nicholas was most definitely right.

Michael would not budge. As I've said before, he would never be wrong. He continued arguing with Nicholas, his voice becoming louder and his anger rising as he did so. As the atmosphere became more volatile, Nicholas did as I usually did and fell silent. I could see tears welling in his eyes and his fists, hanging against his thighs, were clenched in suppressed frustration.

Nicholas would not stand up to Michael in a disagreement because, firstly, and it saddens me to say it, Nicholas, like me, was afraid of his father. Secondly, he once admitted to me that if he once let his true feelings out and confronted his father, he wasn't sure he would be able to keep control. The result could prove irreversible. So, on this occasion, Nicholas gave in and stopped trying to make his point to Michael, and as Nicholas looked at me in total despair, Michael stood up, came towards his son and yelled at him. What he said was completely unforgivable. "DON'T YOU ARGUE WITH ME, YOU UNGRATEFUL YOUNG BASTARD. CLEAR OFF. I WISH YOU'D NEVER BEEN BORN!"

To this day I have never seen my son like I did that day. As a result of years of living in fear of his father, Nicholas avoided confrontation at all costs. It is important to make clear that Nicholas was and is a very strong young man both physically and mentally. However, because of his relationship with his father, during his young adult life he was regularly walked over by people as he tried to avoid standing up for himself. It has taken Nicholas many years to become strong, and today he is a just, yet firm man. He will always treat people with the respect they deserve, but God help them if they cross him.

On this particular day, something changed in my son. I saw him grow from a boy to a man in a matter of seconds. I could see, upon hearing what his father said to him, his muscles flex and go hard. His fists tightened so hard they went purple, and the look in his eyes was one of pure hatred. Hatred for everything he had put up with over the years. The abuse, the embarrassment and the need to protect both his younger brother and me. I do not know how, but he restrained himself. I could see he was ready to unleash on his father, and if there hadn't been a desk between them, it would have happened. They squared up to each other, and I was afraid of what was about to occur.

Although Michael was a strong and powerfully built, fully grown man, I knew that my son could and would have done serious damage to him on that day. He had too much inside him, and I will always admire him for finding the control he always did with his father.

Nicholas fled, tears of anger streaming down his face, and he ran out of the house. I immediately screamed at Michael, fear surging through me, "How dare you speak to him like that? You'll never undo the damage you've done now!"

Michael's reply was that Nicholas should learn respect for his father.

I retaliated that, "Respect is a two-way street, and you certainly didn't show your son any! He was right in what he said, but you just won't ever be wrong, will you?"

With that, I turned my back on Michael. I couldn't bear to be anywhere near him, and I left the house. I found Nicholas in the woods, opposite, sobbing uncontrollably. This kind-hearted, generous, lovely young man had had his heart broken by his own father, and as I folded my arms around him to try and comfort him, I knew that too much damage had now been done.

Like his elder brother Christopher before him, Nicholas had now been through too much misery at the hands of his father. Their relationship was now damaged beyond repair. To this day my son has never forgiven his father, and in his words, "will tolerate him for the sake of everyone".

As was the usual pattern, Michael never mentioned, least of all apologised to Nicholas about that morning's confrontation. Nicholas took on the role of protector; he became a rock, not only for Oliver, as Oliver became for him over time, but also for me. He had changed inside; fear had given way to hatred, and he threw himself in the firing line at every opportunity to divert Michael's rage away from Oliver and me. When I look back now, though, it is with much appreciation but also with deep regret that I realise he took far too much onto his young shoulders, and I still feel guilty that I didn't realise this at the time.

The incident at the wood shop and the fact that things were going from bad to worse, on a daily basis, made me decide to speak to Michael about how bad things were. I felt we should try counselling together as a starting point in attempting to deal with his anger and get things back onto a better footing. Initially, Michael was completely against this idea, stating that he didn't trust counsellors and that we should sort out our problems ourselves. I wasn't prepared to accept this; our problems had been going on for far too long without being sorted and of late were getting much worse, so Michael, realising I wasn't prepared to take no for an answer, reluctantly agreed to try it out.

We arrived at our first session to be greeted by a very pleasant lady, who turned out to be completely neutral, non-judgmental and listened to what we both had to say in an impartial way. During these sessions, I was able to speak to Michael in a way I was afraid to do at home. I told him how his anger made the boys and me feel, and initially he didn't appreciate that the way he reacted was in any way abnormal. When given some examples of Michael's outbursts, Linda, the counsellor, informed Michael that she also would have been scared, and this genuinely surprised Michael.

Linda told me that as I had never seriously confronted Michael and told him how he made me feel, then how was he supposed to know that his behaviour was unacceptable to me?

When I told her that I was too scared to do this, she understood and said that we were now in a vicious circle that had to be broken if we were to move forward. She explained that relating to anger, Michael and I were at totally opposing ends of the scale. Michael's anger was out of control and right at the top of the scale, whereas, as a result of my terrifying experience with John, I couldn't 'do' anger and was therefore at the bottom of the scale. For any improvement to take place, Michael and I had to be able to meet in the middle. We were encouraged to open up and express our emotions freely, and Linda gave her opinion as to when she felt I was in the wrong and also when Michael was in the wrong.

The most emotional reaction from Michael came when I told him that I was afraid of him. He had tears in his eyes while telling me he had no idea this was the case and that he would never hurt me. The problem was, as Linda explained to Michael, because my mindset, partly due to my past experiences and quite involuntary, was that anger leads to devastation, and as I was unable to think outside of that box and was so frightened when Michael became angry, I was unable to believe anything to the contrary. I feared what consequence Michael's anger would result in, unable to do anything other than expect the worst.

We attended a few sessions, and I was glad that we were both freely able to say what we wanted and then 'leave it in the counsellor's room'. However, nothing changed at home and Michael eventually, feeling that they weren't proving beneficial, decided to discontinue our sessions.

Things came to a head one day and changed my life forever, when a strange thing happened to me, out of the blue. We were having a new basin fitted in our en suite bathroom, and Michael, his intention being to help the plumber, removed the old basin and then proceeded to put the new one in place, in preparation for the plumber just to plumb it in. However, as Michael was doing this, the new basin fell onto the floor and unfortunately cracked. I heard the noise as the basin made contact, followed immediately by Michael's explosive vocal.

What happened next was unbelievable; Michael threw the pedestal of the basin into the bedroom, and it landed at my feet! A couple of seconds later, he threw the basin itself out, which hit the pedestal and smashed into fragments around me.

Usually, I would have walked away, shaking, to get away from Michael's anger. Today I didn't; I stayed rooted to the spot. I then heard a voice in my head, which said, "Enough is enough, now is the time." I didn't initially understand this, but as I stood motionless, looking at the debris at my feet, the voice came again, repeating itself, "Enough is enough, now is the time."

Where or how it came, I don't know, but my voice then projected itself very loudly from my mouth, saying, "What the hell do you think you're doing? That was an incredibly stupid thing to do — you could have injured me!"

Michael's response was, "Well, it made me feel better."

I replied, "Well, it doesn't make me feel better, and you can clear up the mess!" I couldn't believe I had spoken to Michael in this way, and I then walked out of the bedroom and left him to it. I still couldn't believe what I had just done; had I stood up to Michael at last?

Michael cleared up the mess, made a cup of tea and then went out to buy another basin, while I sat at home thinking over what had happened. I realised what 'The Voice' had meant.

I had tried for twenty-four years to turn our relationship around and change the good-to-bad ratio but had failed. I wasn't blameless and played my part in our problems, but Michael just wouldn't address his anger, and this was the major stumbling block. For the first time in my years of marriage to Michael, my eyes were fully open, and I saw so clearly what I hadn't seen or hadn't wanted to see before. Of course, there had been high points and enjoyable interludes during our time together, but there had always been an underlying conflict between us. Michael blames much of this on my mother, not wanting to let Christopher go when Michael and I first married. He felt that she interfered in decisions regarding Christopher and that I always sided with her.

What Michael failed to understand was that not only had my parents saved mine and Christopher's lives, which in itself created an extraordinary bond between my parents and me, but also the intense need to protect this child from any further harm. I wasn't putting my mother's feelings before Michael; I simply understood the pain she was experiencing after caring for and protecting Christopher for four years. I am convinced that had he been put in this situation, Michael couldn't have just let a child of his go so easily.

As I sat and thought over our many years together, it became apparent I had spent most of this time walking on eggshells, waking each morning and praying the day would pass without becoming volatile, which, sadly, it inevitably did.

I had lost my true identity and over the years had become an entirely different person. I had become a sponge, soaking up everything that was thrown at me, while hoping it would change. My self-confidence had been shot to smithereens, and I had become a sad, pathetic shell of my former self.

It was quite incredible that a flying basin could make me realise the truth of the situation I was in, but I had been given a new inner strength to do what had to be done.

In that split second when the basin landed at my feet, the feelings inside me I had had for Michael, which had kept me with him for so long, vanished. I felt nothing, no emotion at all, just emptiness. I no longer loved Michael, and there was, therefore, nothing to keep me with him. I didn't need to subject myself to this misery any more. If things changed, would my feelings? I didn't know, but unless things did change, I would walk away, for the sake of my sanity and my sons. I had no choice.

A couple of days later, I spoke to Michael and told him how I felt; my newfound courage was amazing me. I, albeit reluctantly, accepted he wouldn't seek further counselling, and therefore I purchased and read a book on self-help for anger management. I offered this to Michael, explaining that I had already read it and thought the advice and exercises in it could prove very helpful. Michael's response was that he didn't want to read it, he didn't need help from anyone, he could change himself. If that was the case, then why hadn't he done it before?

It was apparent to me that after all this time he couldn't. I gave Michael an ultimatum, he used the book or sought alternative help for his anger, or I would walk away. He still insisted he could do this alone and therefore I gave Michael the news that I couldn't be in this volatile relationship any more, and as I didn't seem important enough for him to do as I asked, I had made the decision to leave him and end our relationship.

Chapter 39

Initially, Michael's reaction to my decision to leave him was one of anger, which then turned to indifference. "If that's what you want to do, then you can just go and do it!"

The hardest thing was having to break the news to Nicholas and Oliver, and I specifically requested of Michael that we sit down together and break the news as gently as was possible. As it turned out, Michael couldn't even do this for me.

The following morning, he went out with Nicholas, and when they returned, the look of sheer confusion on Nicholas's face told me immediately that Michael had told him of my decision. I was furious; how dare he do this to my boy? I apologised to Nicholas, telling him his father should not have broken the news in this way, but yes, what he said was true. I turned to Michael, asking him how he could be so insensitive. His reply was, "Well, he had to know some time." Yes, he did, but not like this!

The boys should have been told together in a calm environment and at the most suitable time possible under the circumstances. We were forced into a position where Oliver had to be told the news now. I asked

Oliver to come downstairs as we wanted to talk to him, and his initial reaction, poor boy, was, what had he done wrong? As Oliver entered the lounge and before we even had a chance to sit down, Michael, as if he hadn't already done enough damage, blurted out to Oliver, "There's no easy way to tell you this, your mother's leaving me." Dear God, the total look of shock and disbelief that came over Oliver's face was dreadful.

"For goodness' sake, Michael!" I said. "Have you no compassion?"

"You're joking," Oliver said. "Is this a wind-up?"

"No, son," I replied. "I'm so sorry it isn't, and you and Nicholas should never have been told in this totally insensitive way."

Oliver sank to the floor in sheer disbelief, and Nicholas sat and put his arm around his brother's shoulder. Two young men sitting in silence, looking as if they had been knocked over by a tornado. My heart went out to them; there was nothing I could do at this moment to ease their pain. They were hurt, upset, confused, and I felt utterly helpless.

A couple of minutes later, Oliver leapt up and ran out of the house, and Nicholas immediately followed him. I wanted to go after them but took a step back and decided to leave them together to absorb what was happening. At this moment, they certainly wouldn't want me stepping into their space.

After many, many years, I was now experiencing an, until now, hidden emotion… ANGER! I was furious with Michael and told him so. He retaliated that it was my fault, and I would have to live with the consequences. My fault? How was this my fault?

He had driven me to the end of my tether after rejecting many opportunities to change our situation; how dare he say that this was my entire fault! This was never going to be easy, telling your children that their lives were about to be turned upside down, but it couldn't have been handled more poorly.

A while later, Nicholas returned home alone. "Where's Oliver?" I asked in desperation. Nicholas was now very calm and told me that Oliver was in shock and just had to get away. Nicholas had taken him to Sally's, his current girlfriend, house. He didn't want to come home at the moment, and he needed some space. I was desperate to go to Oliver, but Nicholas's wisdom won through.

"Leave him be, mum, he'll be okay; he needs time to evaluate what is going on. I'm going to take him some clothes over, and I'll ask him to speak to you soon."

In spite of what he was dealing with himself, Nicholas was taking control and putting his younger brother's needs before his own. How my heart went out to him.

Later that afternoon, Oliver did telephone me. Oh, the sheer joy and relief to hear his voice. "I'm okay, mum, it was just too much to take in. Please don't cry," which I was by now doing. "It will be okay, but I want to stay here at Sally's for a few days, if that's all right."

"Of course, it is" I replied, knowing full well that what I wanted, was to have my youngest son home with his brother and me, but my desires were of no importance at this time, and if this was what Oliver needed, then that is what he should have.

"Look after yourself, son. Please let Nicholas or me know if you need anything, and when you're ready to come home, we'll sit together and talk things through properly. Remember, I love you and your brothers so much and will always be here for you, no matter what."

"Love you, too, mum," came the reply. With that, he hung up and, unable to control my emotions, I went out of the house into the woods opposite and sat on a fallen tree trunk. I cried uncontrollably, as if I had a river inside me, fighting to come out.

Chapter 40

During the next couple of months, my decision became an acceptance, and the practicalities had to be dealt with. 'The Lodge' was put on the market to be sold, with a view to Michael and I finding separate homes. It sold very quickly, and I remember with fondness the look on the face of the lady who purchased it with her husband on the first viewing. She looked just how I felt the first time I saw this house. "I just have to have it," she said. "I can't explain, but I need to live here."

I told her that I had felt the same way and was so pleased for her when the sale was successfully completed. Resulting from such a quick sale, neither Michael nor I had anywhere to move on to, so Nicholas very generously offered us short-term accommodation in his cottage, even though he had an offer on it, which he turned down for us. This ended up costing my son a great deal of money. When he eventually did sell the house, it was for far less than he was initially offered. He never once complained or blamed us for this, and for a long time he was struggling to make up the money he lost on the sale of his house.

Part of the problem was that we had planned to rent somewhere together after leaving The Lodge, to give us time to find alternative accommodation. However, as we had our lovely rough collie dog to consider — he was eventually going to go with Michael — finding rented accommodation with a pet was proving tough.

The day we moved out of The Lodge was a complete and utter disaster. Beginning about a month before, I had packed the entire contents of the house, leaving the boys to do the same with their belongings, and had left Michael the contents of his office and the garage to pack. In spite of continued pleading, Michael had made little attempt to begin this task, and on moving day itself, Michael was still packing up his office, while the garage remained untouched. In desperation, the boys went round the garage themselves, throwing everything — old paint pots, tools and much junk — into black sacks.

Michael decided we would do the move ourselves, which meant a hired van and our cars were to be used to move our belongings. Fortunately, most of our furniture had been sold with the house, to the new owners, but we still had a tremendous amount to be moved.

The new owners were waiting outside to take possession of The Lodge, while Michael was still packing his office. This resulted in Nicholas and Oliver moving our belongings to the pavement at the top of our long, steep driveway, and when Michael had eventually finished in his office, he and Oliver began transporting these to our new temporary home, while Nicholas continued moving our possessions out of the house. At one point, as he was trying to drag a large, full filing cabinet of Michael's up the driveway, the very patient new owner sympathetically stepped in to help Nicholas. As I have said before, Nicholas was an active, well-built young man, but that task was just absurd and could have resulted in serious injury. Regardless, he took it upon himself to try, as Michael was of no help and the situation had become embarrassing.

I appreciated that Michael wanted to cut costs by not hiring a removal company, but it was too ridiculous for words to expect the boys to undertake this enormous task. The boys did not stop that day, even for a minute, despite being yelled at repeatedly by Michael for one reason or another.

As we were moving from a fourteen-room house into a two-bedroom cottage, I had suggested that while packing, a brutal sort out and disposal of unwanted items was carried out. Michael, however, had a different opinion, and everything of his was stuffed in anywhere, to be sorted at a later date. The result of this was that, much later that evening, when the move was eventually complete, the cottage was so stacked to bursting that we could hardly move from one room to another. This situation could most certainly have been avoided with better planning. Michael feels that I blame him for this dreadful move, but it's nothing to do with blame. He had said that he would make arrangements to put into storage some of our things that weren't needed while we were at Nicholas's cottage; my complaint was that he hadn't done this before we moved.

Over the next couple of days, we unpacked what we needed and the boys moved as many boxes as possible into the garage and garden shed. Michael set up an office in the dining room, and some form of orderliness began to take shape.

In spite of the pain and turmoil that we were going through at this time, an incredibly joyful event took place on 19th November 2005. Nina gave birth to a beautiful baby girl, named Victoria. Christopher and Nina were now parents, and I was a grandmother; very hard to believe, but nevertheless truly wonderful.

As I walked into the hospital room that evening and saw Christopher sitting in a chair, cradling his little daughter in his arms, a look of pure wonder and joy on his face, my thoughts flashed back. Back to his birth, the same joy his father and I had experienced that he and Nina were going through at this moment. All that had happened in my son's life and now, here he was, a young, well-adjusted young man, with a family of his own, in control of his life. I felt very grateful and proud as I hugged Nina and Christopher and the precious bundle that was my grand-daughter as she was placed in my arms. I knew for certain at that moment that Victoria was indeed a God-given gift and that somewhere, somehow, John was looking down at his son and glowing with the same pride that I was.

Meanwhile, Nicholas was planning to move into a flat with a friend, and Oliver had decided to live with me when the time came.

Oliver and I found a pleasant two-bedroom flat to rent, which we moved into early in 2006. Oliver's strength and maturity were becoming very apparent as he unflinchingly helped me in the task of choosing and setting up a new home. Michael remained in Nicholas's cottage until later that year, when he moved down to the West Country, and dear Nicholas was eventually able to sell his property. I was so grateful to him; without his generosity, we would have been homeless.

However, the evening before Oliver and I were due to move into our new home, Michael and I had the most dreadful row, as a result of something I had done during the past week. To pay the deposit on my flat I had needed to withdraw from our joint bank account some of my share of the equity from the sale of The Lodge. Without giving it much thought, I decided that while drawing some of my money, I might just as well transfer all of it into my account. I saw nothing wrong with this, as I wasn't taking anything that wasn't rightfully mine.

Michael, however, took a totally different view, and on discovering what I had done, told me I was dishonest and had behaved in an underhand way.

I had been out that afternoon and on returning had discovered that I had lost my mobile phone. I asked Michael if he had seen it, which he denied. Oliver helped me search the cottage and then we went into the front garden with torches to see if I had dropped it there. After allowing us to do this, Michael then decided to confess that he had taken my phone as he had discovered that day, on checking our bank account, that I had taken my money. I don't see the relevance of taking my phone!

A huge argument then developed, and Oliver, who was in his bedroom with Sally, came downstairs at one point and said, "Could you keep it down, guys, it's rather embarrassing with Sally here, having to hear this."

I apologised to Oliver, but Michael told him to mind his own business and go back to his room. Oliver, however, wasn't having any of it and informed his father that it was indeed his business if a guest of his was being made to feel awkward. Michael insisted that this was nothing to do with Oliver, and if he didn't like it, then too bad.

What happened next was astonishing. Young Oliver, who was usually of a calm and placid nature, turned tail, heading back upstairs, and in sheer frustration, he punched the wall, which, being plasterboard, was left with a small dent in it. Michael leapt out of his chair and flew upstairs after Oliver, yelling, "Two can play that game," and he then also punched the wall, making the dent into a large hole!

By now, being in a real rage, Michael rushed into Oliver's room, and I followed, arriving just in time to see Sally step in between them, halting Michael, arm raised, in his tracks. I feel it may have come to blows if she hadn't done so, but nevertheless, it was an incredibly brave thing to do.

Oliver and Sally then rushed out of the house, returning later and going straight up to Oliver's room without saying a word.

Yet again a major upset caused because Michael couldn't or wouldn't control his anger. He had now alienated Oliver.

I had previously asked Michael if he would go out on the morning Oliver and I were due to move, as I felt it would make things a little easier all round. The following morning, he did this, but just for a short while, and when he returned, Nicholas and Oliver were still loading our hired van. Michael offered his help, but Nicholas declined, while Oliver ignored his father and never spoke to him again that day, nor looked back as we drove away. Michael did write to Oliver, apologising for what had happened that evening, and eventually they were able to put it behind them; but again, if Michael had learnt to control his anger, this very ugly incident could have been avoided, as could having to repair the hole in Nicholas's wall!

As we unpacked in our new home that evening, Oliver seemed much happier, as he and Sally pulled his new room into shape. As we sat on the lounge floor that night — we didn't yet have a sofa or chairs — tucking into a takeaway meal, we started making plans to turn our flat into a comfortable home. This was, although a very painful journey, the beginning of a new chapter of the rest of my life.

Chapter 41

Over the next few weeks and months, both Michael and I experienced many emotions — sadness, doubt, frustration and anger, to name a few. I'm sure, though, that any of you who have suffered a relationship breakdown, let alone one after being together for so many years, will appreciate the many difficulties to overcome. Michael and I were determined that our separation should be as amicable as possible, and eventually we sorted our affairs out together and were able to achieve a mutually acceptable conclusion.

We weren't without hiccups along the way, one of which I remember most vividly, as it hurt me very deeply. During our chaotic temporary move into Nicholas's cottage, Michael's mother's engagement ring had very sadly been lost. Michael had put the contents of a drawer of his, which included Dora's ring, into a plastic crate, the sides of which had holes in them. It is most likely that, unfortunately, the ring slipped through one of these during transportation.

Nonetheless, on one particular day, I met Michael as arranged in a local car park to sign some of our agreement papers. On arrival, I climbed out of my car, went over to where Michael was waiting and let myself into the passenger seat of his vehicle. It was immediately obvious that Michael's mood was very negative, as he thrust the papers into my hand without even so much as a hello. Okay, I thought, sign the papers, which I did, and leave here as quickly as possible. However, as I went to get out of Michael's car, he said to me, "How much did you get for it, then?"

"Pardon? What are you talking about?" I replied.

Michael's next words hit me like a slap round the face. "My mother's ring — how much did you get for it, after you sold it?"

I couldn't believe what I was hearing; Michael was accusing me of stealing and selling his mother's ring. How could he do this? Surely, he knew me well enough to know I would never dream of doing such a despicable thing. I was so stunned; I slammed the car door on him and fled back to my car. I wanted to put as much distance between Michael, with his appalling accusation, and myself. I was devastated and incredibly hurt by what Michael had said. I had loved Dora very much and understood how much her ring meant to Michael; and besides, I certainly wasn't a thief!

A couple of days later I received a letter of apology from Michael for the accusation, but I'm sorry to say, it didn't help; the damage had been done. What Michael had done was extremely cruel and the hurt it caused me still cuts like a knife today.

Chapter 42

As 2006 progressed, life began to take on some semblance of normality. Nicholas had purchased his second property for redevelopment and Oliver was again working for him.

I had taken on some freelance work, health permitting, as I needed to generate income, and on one Saturday morning in May, I had been doing some exam coaching for a local dance school. As I left at the end of the morning, little did I know that the next major trauma of my life was waiting around the corner.

What started out as a lovely sunny day had changed during the morning, and as I left the dance school, torrential rain was falling tumultuously. I was driving with caution along my usual route home, a road with many bends in it. As I went round a double hairpin bend, a terrifying thing happened — my car took off! The wheels left the road and what followed took a matter of seconds but felt like a lifetime. As the wheels made contact again with the road, I couldn't control the car; it was like being on an ice rink. My car shot towards the verge on the side of the road, and then bounced along and hit three or four trees. All the time this was happening, I remember saying over and over again,

"Help me, God; help me, God!" In that instant, I was convinced I was going to die. Suddenly, as my car bounced off the last tree, it felt as if I was flying, completely out of control, spinning through the air, and then... nothing.

When I regained consciousness, my first thought was that I was dead; my second thought was that I wasn't, as the searing pain all down the right side of my body confirmed. I couldn't breathe without it feeling as if a thousand knives were stabbing me, and yet at the same time, the relief on realising I was breathing was phenomenal. I was disorientated; I didn't recognise where I was, and then slowly and gradually realisation dawned. I was lying on the inside of my car roof, in the back of the car!

As my car hit the last tree, it had flipped over and was now lying upside down in a ditch. Terror flooded over me; I was trapped. Nobody knew I was here, and there was a horrible smell of car fumes wafting over me. I had to get out, but how?

As I looked around me, the horrific reality of my situation set in. The driver's side of my car was completely crushed, the roof embedded into the driver's seat. I was lying on the passenger side, in the back. How on earth had this happened? I was wearing my seatbelt, so how could I have been thrown into the back of the car? But if I hadn't been, I would have been crushed to death. At that point, I was physically sick. My head was spinning as I drifted in and out of consciousness with the unbearable pain.

Okay, I thought, there is only one answer, my time isn't yet up. My survival was down to Angel intervention; for me there was no other answer. They had helped me this far, so I asked them to complete the task and get me out.

The rear window was far too small to get through, so the only possible exit from my destroyed vehicle was through the front passenger window, which was still intact. How was I to break this window? If I tried to move even an inch, I screamed out loud in agony and floated off into semi-consciousness.

I was aware of cars driving past on the road, but their occupants couldn't see me. All that was visible was my car in a ditch, and nobody could have known there was anyone in it. How many times have you driven past a wrecked car in a ditch, without so much as a second glance, assuming the driver and passengers had been attended to? I certainly have, but since this accident, if I see a car on the side of the road, I always have to stop and check.

"Please, Angels, help me!" I screamed in pure desperation and pain. Then, before my eyes, a miracle occurred. There was a loud splintering sound, and as I gazed in awestruck wonder, the passenger window shattered before my eyes and the glass fell out!

"Thank you, thank you," I sobbed. Here was an opening to the outside world and rescue. If I could just get a foot through the opening, it would be visible from the road, and someone may see and stop. Summoning all my courage and strength, I shifted my body towards the open space and, screaming in agony, pushed my feet through.

Suddenly, from where they came, I don't know, but three young men were standing by my car. I can only describe them as beautiful. Their eyes were all bright blue and piercing into me with overwhelming compassion, and I felt drawn to these young men like a magnet. One of them seemed to take charge and spoke to me in a very gentle and caressing voice, "We can't wait for the emergency services; we have to move you away from the car, as we fear it may blow up."

As I felt three pairs of strong arms reaching underneath my body, there was a brief surge of excruciating pain as they pulled me from my car. However, as they lifted me and carried me down the road to a safe distance, my pain completely vanished, and I felt as if I was floating on a cloud.

"Aaaaaaaaargh!" The pain hit me again like a lightning bolt as I was lowered to the ground and again blacked out. When I opened my eyes, I was aware of my three rescuers beside me. One was cushioning my head with his arm, looking at me with such care, with those ocean deep eyes, while the second was so gently laying my jacket over me, which he must have retrieved from my car. He then took my hand, which was so comforting. The third was standing at my feet, looking at me, with his hands clasped in front of him; it looked as if he was praying!

I was aware of a car pulling up to the side of the road and a man getting out. He came to me and immediately dialled a number on his mobile phone. I thought it rather strange that no conversation or acknowledgement passed between my three heroes and this gentleman, who, for clarity, I will call the 'Telephone Man'.

After a short while, I heard a loud bell ringing and saw the Telephone Man waving at the ambulance as it came around the bend.

"Wake up, can you hear me, tell me your name." As I came round again, there were two paramedics kneeling beside me. My three young rescuers were all now standing at my feet and, for some reason, the Telephone Man was looking very perplexed. I later realised why.

"My name's Jessica" I gasped, and, looking towards them, said, "These wonderful men... pulled me out." The paramedic said nothing as he glanced at the Telephone Man.

As I smiled so gratefully at the three young men who had saved me that day, their faces lit up like sunshine as they smiled back... and then they disappeared!

"Where have they gone?" I gasped. "I haven't thanked them properly."

"She's very confused," said the paramedic, as a collar was placed around my neck and I was painfully lifted onto a board.

"Right, come on, let's go."

With that, I was carried into the ambulance and rushed off to the hospital. I lost consciousness twice more in the ambulance and as I came to, in response to the paramedic calling my name, I recall asking if I was going to die. Also, where were my rescuers? They couldn't just disappear.

His response was, "No you're not going to die; well, not today anyway!" — but he said nothing about those three young men. Why would no one speak about them?

As we arrived at the hospital and the ambulance doors were thrown open, I seemed to be surrounded by doctors and nurses, all giving or receiving instructions. "She's tachycardic, pupils are dilated, get a line in, please, and arrange a trauma CT." Thinking back, it was just like *Casualty* on television!

My clothes were cut from me, as I was examined thoroughly and then given morphine to ease my pain… Oh, what bliss. It turned out that, miraculously, I had been very lucky, that the injuries I had sustained were not a lot worse. I had broken my shoulder, resulting in severe nerve damage and my ribs and had to have surgery on my shoulder, but the doctor in the accident and emergency department told me that he didn't know how I had survived such a crash at all. It was a miracle.

A while later, when I saw my car, I had to agree that there was no way I should have come out of it alive. I was certainly being looked after that day. The police later informed me that during the investigation they had found grease on the road where I had skidded, which had probably been discharged by a passing lorry. I was just the unlucky victim, entirely blameless; and if it hadn't been me, it would have been some other unfortunate driver in trouble.

As I lay in bed that evening thinking over the dreadful events of the day, I realised that the reason nobody had spoken about my three rescuers was because they hadn't seen them!

The only car parked at the accident scene was the one belonging to the Telephone Man, who arrived after I had been pulled from the car.

These three young men didn't get out of a car, and the way they just appeared and disappeared, coupled with the wonderful loving connection I felt towards them and received from them, brought me to the conclusion that they were indeed Angels. They had answered my prayer, broken the car window and rescued me, to live another day.

Some of you may think that as I was slipping in and out of consciousness, I may have been confused and imagined them, but I know differently. I saw them, I felt them, without a shadow of doubt, and will always remember the feeling of complete and utter love which radiated from them.

This wasn't to be the end of my interaction with the Divine that day. During the evening, when the pain became unbearable, I called the nurse for some more pain medication. As she left my room to fetch this for me, I was suddenly overcome with an immense feeling of calm. As I looked towards the foot of my bed, I was aware of a circle of very bright light. As I looked at this light, squinting with its brightness, a figure emerged from the light, and I was able to open my eyes fully. At that exact point, my body became completely pain-free. As I gazed in wonder at this figure, I noticed that he was dressed in attire resembling that of a Roman soldier, but his clothes were all golden in colour. He had large wings, a golden halo around his head and he brandished a sword. I stretched my hand towards this figure; I had no idea who he was, but I so desperately wanted to make contact with him. Suddenly, the nurse came back into my room and the figure instantly disappeared. As it did so, my pain came flooding back.

Later, when I was back at home, I spoke to my meditation teacher, Ann, about my experiences the day of the accident. She agreed without a doubt that I had indeed been the blessed receiver of an Angel rescue; and concerning the figure that appeared to me in the hospital, she felt it was the Archangel St. Michael. She believed he had appeared to me as a sign to let me know that I wasn't alone and that I would eventually come through this traumatic experience, just as I always had before.

Ann later sent me a picture of St. Michael, and I was amazed to see that the figure in this picture was exactly the figure that had appeared before me!

After I was discharged from hospital, I was instructed not to be alone for a few days, and so I accepted Michael's offer to go and stay with him. While I was there, Michael cared for me unflinchingly, catering for all my needs, even providing a cup of tea and painkillers when I woke up crying in pain in the middle of the night. I had to sleep sitting up, as trying to lie down was excruciating.

I was grateful to Michael for his generosity, but after a few days I just wanted to be back home inside my four walls. Michael, responding to my request, took me home, where my boys and the rest of the family took over my care until I was fully recovered.

After a second operation, it took eighteen months of physiotherapy to begin to regain any feeling in my right shoulder, and although I still suffer pain there now, it is a small price to pay to be alive. When I get a twinge, I think of my Angels and offer up a silent prayer of thanks.

Chapter 43

Following my accident, apart from recovering physically, I struggled emotionally. I had agreed to help look after Victoria for Christopher and Nina during the day while they were both at work. Because of my injuries, I was unable to do this and felt dreadful that I was letting them down. The fact that it wasn't my fault didn't help at all; I felt wretched. The outcome was that Nina continued working full-time, while Christopher stayed at home to care for Victoria and thus became a househusband.

Now, seven years on, I am filled with admiration and pride for Christopher, who is still running the home and caring for Victoria, for the fantastic job he has done and is still doing.

The house is immaculate, washing and ironing always done, dinner ready for Nina when she gets home from work, and Victoria is a credit to them. Since she was of a very young age, Christopher has spent much time with his daughter, reading, writing, playing anything from dressing dolls, being princesses, to having tea parties and doing craft work and hands-on play with her. His devotion to Victoria has paid off. She is excelling at school, and the most incredible bond exists between her and her father, one that will never be broken.

Meanwhile, following my accident, Nicholas and Oliver were continuing work refurbishing their latest property, and by early 2007 the house was complete, and another beautiful result was achieved. This property also sold quickly, enabling Nicholas to purchase and embark upon renovating his third and final property.

During this time, Nicholas and Oliver were living together in a flat in London. While there, an old school friend of Nicholas's invited him and Oliver to play in a sevens rugby match for the Law Society. Oliver decided his shoulder could stand up to this, so both boys readily agreed to play. It was a particularly great opportunity, because it was the only time Nicholas and Oliver ever played rugby together.

At one stage during the match, a rather amusing incident happened, a real example of brotherly love. Oliver had possession of the ball and knocked down one of the opposing team. He then charged at a second, but, unfortunately, this guy brought Oliver down and took possession of the ball. Within a minute, Nicholas had flattened this guy and repossessed the ball. The message was quite clear, you do that to my brother, and you get what you deserve!

During the summer of 2007, Oliver went to Greece for a couple of weeks to visit a good friend of his who was teaching water sports at a resort there. Oliver also got to know a young lady named Katherine, who was also instructing at the resort. On returning from Greece, Oliver decided that he so loved being on the water that he would like to consider training to become a water sports instructor himself. Michael was very supportive of Oliver's ambition and generously financed him to attend a number of courses at a venue on the Isle of Wight. By the spring of 2008, Oliver was a fully qualified sailing and water sports instructor. He then secured a summer coaching position at the same resort he had visited in Greece the previous year. The work was very challenging, but Oliver rose to the challenge.

He also became the victim of hero worship, when a young seven-year-old girl whose parents had booked a sailing lesson for her with Oliver, decided to ask her parents if she could spend her holiday having sailing lessons, but it had to be with Oliver. During his time off, when Oliver was around the resort, if he bumped into this young lady, she would always stop and wave or say hello, and Oliver, of course, responded. I imagine he quite enjoyed the admiration, albeit from a young child!

Two weeks after Oliver had started working in Greece, who should arrive to also take up a summer coaching position? Katherine! By now, Oliver and Katherine had finally got the message and soon became a couple and remain so very happily to this day. Coincidence or not, being a true romantic, I like to think that they were destined to be together!

Back home, Nicholas had completed his final renovation, but decided not to sell the beautiful house which materialised as a result of his and his brother's many skills, but to keep it as a possible home for himself at a later date. In the meantime, he planned to maintain the property as an investment and offer it up for let.

Christopher continued to do an amazing job working at home and caring for Victoria. On many an occasion, I would go to visit and find them both kneeling on the floor, shoulder to shoulder, engrossed in colouring pictures, playing a game, or sticking various objects, such as sequins, pipe cleaners and coloured cotton wool balls, onto a card to make imaginative and colourful creations!

We have now come to the point where my story began. You will recall me telling you about my recurring nightmares, which started in 2007. How I worked with Sarah, my counsellor, to confront and deal with the many terrors and traumas which I had experienced. The experiences I have now shared with you.

Sarah was fantastic through the time I worked with her; she was so supportive and understanding, both during and, if I needed it, outside of office hours. By the time my sessions with Sarah had come to an end, I was an entirely different person. I felt my old confidence and independence returning, my nightmares and panic attacks disappeared, and I was armed with the 'tools and techniques' to deal with them, should they choose to rear their ugly head once again.

The final piece of advice Sarah gave me when I felt ready to do so was to write a book about my life story, thus putting all the bad parts, along with the good, on paper. This would act as a cathartic exercise, to release all the demons from my life; not, though, to be forgotten, as that would never be possible. Rather, they would be put into a place where I would be able to stop them from continually haunting me. At the same time, it would also release from my body the long-term build-up of debilitating emotional stress that had manifested itself as physical illness. In doing this, I would still remember the happy times in life because I wanted to do so and be able to focus on those instead of the bad.

So, here I am, doing just as instructed, sitting here and nearing the end of writing my book. It has been a very difficult, painful and yet rewarding task. At the end of each day, I acknowledge and deal with the variety of emotions that my day's work has generated, and as I approach the end of my book, I am feeling freer, and in more control emotionally, than I have felt for a very long time.

I would hope that nobody reading my story will have suffered as much as I have. However, many of you will have experienced similarly painful and challenging times. From experience, I would say on a practical level, never be afraid to seek help. Without Sarah, I would not be able to function as I can today. If professional help is available, accept it.

I have also learnt that however much you hope bad situations will change, it doesn't happen by itself. It took me a long time to realise this. To find the courage to act and change mine and my sons' lives for the better.

At your lowest ebb, draw on that incredible inner strength that we all possess. Find your purpose in life and use that purpose to give you the strength you need to do whatever it takes to bring about the change you need.

In my case, it was always my beautiful sons. Without them, I would never have survived. They were my driving force. I always have and always will live for them and their happiness. They ARE my life.

Whatever or whoever your purpose is in life, remain focused on that, even when you feel you are at the end of your tether.

Be strong, be patient, and, above all, believe in your own abilities. You can and will succeed.

Chapter 44

My story hasn't quite reached its conclusion. 2009 saw Nicholas and Oliver travelling to far-away destinations and much hotter climates. Nicholas returned to Thailand to immerse himself once again in his passion for diving. While he was away, Nicholas and Tamara became very close, and eventually they moved into a little hillside apartment together on their Dream Island. I would like to add here that 'they lived happily ever after', but sadly, this wasn't to be exactly the case.

Meanwhile, Katherine's law studies were taking her on a student exchange scheme with a university in Sydney, Australia, for a year. I knew what Oliver was going to say to me before he even had a chance to open his mouth! He, of course, wanted to accompany Katherine — there was no way he would be apart from her for that length of time. Also, what better place to use his instructor skills than Australia? Oliver had always wanted to work in that part of the world, but circumstances had never before made it possible, so I was thrilled for him to have this opportunity.

On arrival, they settled into their temporary accommodation, while seeking something more permanent, and Katherine continued her studies at the university. Oliver, meanwhile, secured a teaching position at a sailing and water sports school in Sydney Harbour. He loved the work, and during his time there showed he had great potential and organisational skills, thus earning his employers' trust and resulting in a promotion. At one point, Oliver even trained one of the Women's Junior Olympic Squads!

I missed the boys dreadfully while they were away, but knowing they were happy and following their dreams made me happy, and therefore the distance between us more bearable.

Oliver and Katherine almost made it through their year away without mishap, but not quite! When it was time to return home, they decided to divert en route and stop off for a couple of weeks to visit Nicholas and Tamara in Thailand.

Nicholas's best friend Andrew, who knew and also got on very well with Oliver, joined them on arrival. I thought this was a lovely idea, giving the boys an opportunity to catch up with each other after being apart for a long while. They had a very good time, with Oliver, Katherine and Andrew making the most of the diving facilities while they were there, always under the watchful eye of Nicholas. By this stage, Nicholas had become one of the most senior Master Instructors in the region. He was able to show the others some beautiful sights under the water and take them to places very few tourists ever visited.

Unfortunately, it all went pear-shaped when Oliver was involved in a nasty accident. One particular morning, Oliver and Andrew were on a moped-type bike, as this was the most popular form of travel on the island, heading down to the Dive School to prepare for a day's diving. Nicholas and Katherine were following behind on a second bike.

As Oliver approached a junction, having the right of way, a young Thai boy, aged about fourteen, also on a bike, headed straight across the junction without stopping. Consequently, this caused Oliver to try to swerve to avoid a collision. Oliver and Andrew were knocked to the ground as their bike skidded along the dirt track which served as a road.

Andrew and the Thai boy were okay, but Oliver was seriously injured. His leg had been trapped beneath the bike as they skidded along the ground and resulted in a large gash in his leg, from his hip to his foot!

Nicholas and Katherine arrived on the scene, and Nicholas immediately took control of the situation. Oliver was in agony and his leg was in a very bad way, so he was rushed to the hospital. Not, as one would imagine, in an ambulance, but instead he was bundled into the back of a pick-up truck driven by two locals!

Meanwhile, the local police arrived and took the young Thai boy away. Nicholas had to follow later to make a statement to the police, and what he saw when he arrived, he was incensed and angered by. The young boy, in custody, was receiving a horrendous beating from the officers for being so careless and causing injury to a foreign visitor. Nicholas — being Nicholas — stepped straight in and insisted they stop immediately, which, although reluctantly, the police did.

Nicholas made it quite clear that he was furious that his brother had been injured through this young boy's carelessness. But that's what it was, a careless accident, which didn't justify what was being done to this young boy. It wasn't going to change the situation. Nicholas insisted he was released. One thing I will say about Nicholas is that he never takes any crap from anyone and will always stand up for people. This is an incredibly endearing characteristic and was formed, I believe, as a result of his childhood experiences with Michael. The Thai police could have easily thrown him in a cell for arguing with them, but that did not stop him from protecting that young boy.

Once at the hospital, poor Oliver went through hell, but hell that, it turned out, saved his leg! Oliver's wound was very long and deep and full of grit and gravel from the track. Therefore, a cleansing system was used which makes me cringe even to write about it. Nicholas likened the cleaning swab to a Brillo pad, and he, Andrew and Katherine had to forcefully hold Oliver down while he screamed in agony as his wound was scrubbed!

Oh, my poor boy, I can't bear to imagine the pain and distress he went through. The most awful thing was that this process had to be repeated consistently for a few times, so Oliver knew what was coming when the nurse approached. When they were satisfied that the wound was dirt- and infection-free, it was then stitched. Oliver ended up with over forty of them!

I wasn't told the severity of Oliver's injury until he and Katherine returned home, when, on meeting them at the airport, I was confronted by Oliver on crutches and his entire leg bandaged from top to bottom!

"We didn't want you to worry, mum, so I just told a little white lie." The little white lie I was told was that Oliver had a little accident and came away with a few cuts and bruises! If ever the boys now accuse me of not telling them if I am unwell, I tactfully remind them of their little white lie!

What followed for Oliver was weeks of attending our local surgery to have his leg examined and dressings changed regularly. On speaking to the practice nurses about Oliver's Thai treatment, they informed us that without this deep cleansing, although excruciating at the time, Oliver may very well have lost his leg, as serious infection would have inevitably set in, with severe consequences.

It was a long job, but Oliver's leg eventually healed, although his foot, where the wound had been especially deep, took a while longer. I will always be eternally grateful to the Thai hospital staff — not, of course, for the pain it was necessary to inflict upon

Oliver; I understand this was a means to an end, but for saving my son's leg.

Katherine returned home to Glasgow to continue her studies at university there, and when Oliver was recovered, he and Katherine decided that their long-distance relationship was proving too difficult for them, and this resulted in them deciding to set up home together in Glasgow, where they very happily remain still.

Chapter 45

2010 saw Oliver and Katherine building a new life together. Katherine's law studies were continuing and Oliver, being unable to teach water sports in the centre of Glasgow, took the necessary exams to qualify as a Chartered Financial Adviser. A complete change of direction for him, but he now has a very good position working for a company in the city. Nicholas and Tamara were still happy living and working in Thailand, and Christopher and his little family were working hard and coping with daily life.

Victoria was now in school full-time and loving it. She seemed to have a thirst to learn which, although at times could prove difficult to quench, we were of course, very pleased that she was and still is so keen to learn.

As for me, well, another blow hit home. I had been suffering for a while from abdominal pain, and eventually my doctor referred me to the hospital for further investigation. During an ultrasound, a very vigilant radiologist spotted some 'unidentifiable objects' on my liver. A number of various scans later, I found myself sitting in a hospital waiting room, nervously awaiting the result of their findings. My brother Dennis was with me. I had confided in him as I needed support but didn't want to worry my sons perhaps unnecessarily.

As we sat before the surgeon and awaited the news, I felt myself begin to shake. I was terrified of what he was going to say. I'm sure many of you have been in a similar situation and know exactly what I was going through.

When the surgeon told me what they suspected, I recall my immediate response was, "Is it life-threatening?" When he replied that potentially it was, I was struck silent. The surgeon then very tactfully made an excuse to leave the room and left me alone with Dennis. As Dennis put his arm around me, I broke down in tears. I wasn't ready to die, and it couldn't all come to an end now. I was so scared, but as Dennis comforted me, and told me that whatever lay ahead, we would face it together, I began to calm down, and my pragmatic nature kicked in. I would fight this, no matter what; I wasn't ready to throw in the towel yet.

Arrangements were then made for my surgery, and before we left the hospital, Dennis sat me down in the cafe and put a scone and a cup of coffee in front of me. He then very cleverly lifted the mood by saying to me, "This will keep you going until you get home, and then you need to fix yourself a large vodka and tonic!"

On questioning Dennis as to whether, under the circumstances, that was really wise, he replied, "I wouldn't worry about it; the damage is already done!"

Some of you may think this sounds callous, but it wasn't, it was just his way of throwing some light on a very difficult situation, and it worked. For a few seconds, I actually laughed.

A short while later, I underwent major surgery, and thankfully, Saint Michael was watching over me again, and because of him and the incredible skills of the surgeons, I am still here and fighting today.

Chapter 46

In 2011, tragedy, unfortunately, hit Nicholas and Tamara, and their idyllic lifestyle came to an end. Following the dreadful aftermath of a tsunami, their island was subjected to terrible storms and flooding, resulting in there being no power on the island and virtually no fresh food or water. They lived for a number of weeks eating mainly tinned food, drinking bottled water and coping with a flooded apartment!

The island and the dive school were eventually reduced to mud and rubble, and Nicholas and Tamara were left with no alternative but to return to England. Even this was initially tough, as there was no way off the island. Eventually, the Thai Navy was able to begin lifting people off by Chinook helicopter, but Nicholas and Tamara, like everyone else, had to wait their turn.

Eventually, they arrived at Heathrow Airport with the clothes they stood up in and a few personal belongings, looking utterly desolate and exhausted. Most of their possessions had been destroyed, and larger items such as furniture they had to leave behind. The most important thing was that they were safe and back home, and things could only get better.

As Nicholas had tenants in his house, I offered them the opportunity to move in with me until they got back on their feet. They were initially taken aback by my suggestion and declined, saying it was far too much to ask. Of course, it wasn't; they were currently homeless, and when your children need help, you try to provide it.

Over the next year, Nicholas and Tamara made themselves comfortable in my flat, and I decided to spend quite a lot of time with my mum, who was living on the south coast, near her sister and her husband. Firstly, I wanted to give the youngsters some space to get their lives back on track, and secondly, the sea air was excellent for me, and I welcomed the opportunity to spend quality time with my mother.

Meanwhile, Oliver and Katherine were doing very well in Scotland and were devoting much of their free time in pursuing cycling and walking. It is a regular weekend activity for them to cycle one hundred miles in a day! It makes me tired just thinking about it!

Oliver says that it is a very challenging sport, but also a very social one. When confronting a tough hill, it becomes an individual battle. Each cyclist goes into their little world, in which their focus is on nothing else except reaching the top. On achieving this, everyone relaxes, and the group intermingles socially.

One thrilling incident happened a while ago, which terrified me when Oliver told me about it. He and Katherine and a couple of their friends had cycled over

Crow Road, which leads to a hill overlooking the north of Glasgow. The most exciting and exhilarating part of this ride was the descent down the side of the mountain.

As Oliver started his descent, he clocked up a speed of forty-eight miles per hour, and then, with complete abandon, increased his speed to fifty-two miles per hour! This was the fastest he had ever gone, and at the point when Oliver was considering applying his brakes, what should happen? Katherine passed him! I daren't think what speed she was doing, or what this did for Oliver's ego!

Oliver and Katherine also cycle for charity, and I feel very proud of what they achieve. Two examples of the charities they are involved in are the RS50 cycle charity event, which is a fifty-mile ride taking place in August, and a two-day cycling event in aid of Maggie's Cancer Charity. This is a hundred and sixty-five-mile ride from Inverness to Aberdeen!

Oliver likes to embark on personal challenges and finds it very satisfying to realise what you can do under your own power. The human body is indeed an incredible machine.

One such challenge was walking the West Highland Way. This is a ninety-five-mile walk from Milndaurie (North of Glasgow) to Fort William on Scotland's West Coast.

I have great admiration for both Oliver and Katherine for the work they do for others, but also because they are determined to stay fit and healthy while doing so.

At the end of 2011, a very thrilling event took place. Although Nicholas and Tamara were working and making plans for their future together, they nevertheless were desperately missing their diving.

Tamara's parents very generously gave her and Nicholas a wonderful Christmas, and as they were both thirty that December, a joint birthday present. They had arranged for them to go on a two-week diving holiday to the Maldives. How phenomenal was that!

They both had the most incredible time, and while they were away a very exciting thing happened — Nicholas proposed to Tamara, and she accepted! What made this even more special was the way in which he went about the proposal.

You may or may not know that to communicate underwater as an alternative to hand signals, divers use something called whiteboards. These are a small version of the standard school blackboard, on which the diver can write messages with a waterproof pencil while underwater.

One day, while he and Tamara were on a dive, Nicholas secretly hid a costume ring (obviously not the real thing!) in some coral. He then produced his whiteboard on which he had written 'WILL YOU MARRY ME?' and held it up to Tamara. He then produced a second board which had the word YES on one side and NO on the other. He offered this to Tamara, and she showed him the word YES!

Nicholas then retrieved the ring from the coral and placed it on Tamara's finger.

On later hearing their fantastic news, I told Nicholas that it was the most romantic proposal I had ever heard of, and it would certainly take a lot to top it! They returned home a very happy couple, with many plans for their future under their hats.

Chapter 47

Nicholas and Tamara, after much discussion, had decided to start their future life together in Austria, Tamara's home country, where her parents and family were still living. Tamara's father had an apartment in Graz, which he generously offered to Nicholas and Tamara. They would have to take on a complete refurbishment of the property, but they were more than happy to do this, and Nicholas would be able to put his design and building skills to good use. So, off they went, to start a new life together in the beautiful town of Graz in Austria.

The boys were getting on with their lives and trying to make a success of such with their lovely ladies, and this, as with any parent, brought me great pleasure and relief.

At home, Victoria had discovered her performing skills, which my mother insists she inherited from my sister and me. She's possibly right. Victoria started to attend a weekly club which offered an hour session of acting, singing and dancing. She took to it like a fish to water, and the club remains the highlight of her week. At the end of each term, the children are in a short presentation, and every ten weeks, I have the task of producing the required costume for her part in this. It gives me great pleasure, and when I watch the performance, with Nina and Christopher, I glow with pride at this adorable (most of the time!) and confident young girl who has blessed all our lives.

Unfortunately, during this year I had to have more major surgery, but again I came through successfully and was well enough in September to join the rest of the family at a celebration dinner for Christopher's fortieth birthday. What a truly fantastic evening this was, and as I looked at my eldest son, I was overflowing with pride to see what that young boy — who had suffered beyond belief during his young life — had become. An independent, competent, and loving young man, who was glowing with happiness as he savoured his family around him and realised how important he was to them and how loved he was by them.

2012 ended on a rather sad note with the passing of David, John's stepfather. Over the years I had maintained contact with him and John's sister Hannah, and I was saddened by this news. Unfortunately, however, following John's death, Pamela had completely cut me out of her life. She blamed me for her son's death and, tragically, she refused to have anything to do with me or accept any support I wished to offer.

The only communication I ever had from Pamela came via Hannah in 2002. Pamela had apparently returned to her native Northumberland and wanted to have John's body exhumed and taken with her. Although I felt and understood Pamela's pain, there was no way I agreed to this. As I was married to John at the time of his death and therefore his next of kin, I was entitled to make the decision. My dear John's body was staying where it was.

As I attended David's funeral with Hannah, I stood at the graveside in the pouring rain, and my life flashed before me; so much had happened in one lifetime and I was still here to tell the tale.

Before leaving the cemetery, I went across to John's grave and planted a fingertip kiss on the cameo photo on his headstone. I quietly whispered to John that I forgave him for the misery his actions had caused, that I still loved him to this day, and, as for his son, John should be glowing with pride for the wonderful young man he had turned out to be.

Chapter 48

I am almost at the end of my story, and I feel it is a time for reflection. I certainly have many traumatic and unhappy events to reflect on, but now it is far more important to think of the good things that have blessed my life.

My three sons have grown into generous, supportive, loving, happy and well-balanced young men. What more could any mother wish for? I think they are right when they say that their pasts have made them into the people they are today. However, although we are all looking to the future, I will never be able to forget the terrible times my sons went through and how amazing it is that they are where they are today.

With hindsight, I should have made the decision to leave Michael much sooner than I did. I'm not sure about Oliver, but Nicholas, I know, believes he would have had a much happier childhood away from his father. In his words, "I wouldn't have lived in fear of my father and had to walk on eggshells all of the time."

I will never know how Nicholas honestly feels, and there is no point talking about 'what if?'. I do, however, get the impression from many of our discussions that he believes a life without a father would have been better than the life he had with his father.

Growing up, Christopher could never really understand why, although he was very happy with his grandparents, I chose to send him to live with them. He accepted my fears for his safety, but, like Nicholas, questioned why I just didn't walk away from Michael. I hope that now, through having a child of his own, Christopher will find some understanding of my actions. He has never wished to discuss my book in any way, although he entirely supports the cathartic value of writing it. He will never read this book, as he remembers the pain and misery he endured in his past, too vividly. He has no desire to relive it. I wish that I could discuss Christopher's childhood with him, in the hope that it may give him some peace and understanding. However, he doesn't want to do this, and hard though it is, I must respect his wishes and allow him to deal with his past in his way.

Until an individual is in this situation, you can never really know what to do or what is right. My children always were and always will be my top priority and reason for living. Perhaps Nicholas has a point, or perhaps he does not. I will leave you to close your eyes, imagine you have lived my life, and then formulate your views on this.

I won't ever be able to dispel the guilt I feel for the wrong decisions I made, but they were always made out of love and the belief that at the time I was doing the best thing.

I can't turn back the clock and change my sons' childhoods, but if I could I most certainly would. All I can do is offer Christopher, Nicholas and Oliver my sincere apologies for all they have endured and hope that one day they may be able to find some understanding and eventual forgiveness.

As far as Oliver is concerned, on reading my book, he chose to discuss his feelings with me. Oliver feels that there were certainly times when his father, due to his behaviour, was the last person he wanted to be around. However, he also feels there were times in his life when Michael was the only person that he wanted by his side, supporting him.

Oliver, like Nicholas, found my book very distressing to read. They learnt things about my life which they didn't know before. Oliver says that although he certainly doesn't condone his father's bad behaviour, because he wasn't personally involved in much of it, he couldn't judge Michael on his conduct towards others, but only towards Oliver himself. Again, I must respect the way he feels. He doesn't wish to dwell on the past but is now at a stage in his life when he wants to focus entirely on the future and enjoy every day to the full.

As for me, I have succeeded in what I set out to do. Write about my life, in the hope that in doing so, and reliving my past, I could lay it to rest. I won't ever forget what I've been through, but I now feel able to push it away, tell myself I don't need it any more, and start on the next phase of my life. I also hope that by reading my story, any of you in similar situations may be able to find help and solace. Whether you agree or disagree with my past actions is your prerogative, but it may help you to make your choices more wisely. Also, I hope you can see that we all have something in life worth fighting for, something to hold on to in times of adversity. Whether that is your faith, your family or simply yourself, never give up.

My advice is, don't let other people run your life; I learnt the hard way. Be true to yourself and, above all, listen to your intuition and be kind to yourself. Love others the way you want to be loved.

Love is what saved me. My love for my wonderful and precious sons.